Dedicated to the memory of my father Eugene German,
whose generosity simply knew no limits.

Your Storytelling Potential

YOUR STORYTELLING POTENTIAL

The Underground Guide to Finally Writing a Great Screenplay or Novel

MITCHELL GERMAN
WITH RUSSELL PHILLIPS

NEW YORK

LONDON • NASHVILLE • MELBOURNE • VANCOUVER

YOUR STORYTELLING POTENTIAL

The Underground Guide to Finally Writing a Great Screenplay or Novel

Published in New York, New York, by Morgan James Publishing. Morgan James is a trademark of Morgan James, LLC. www.MorganJamesPublishing.com

Proudly distributed by Ingram Publisher Services.

ISBN 9781636980348 paperback
ISBN 9781636980355 ebook
Library of Congress Control Number:
2022944306

Cover and Interior Design by:
Chris Treccani
www.3dogcreative.net

Morgan James is a proud partner of Habitat for Humanity Peninsula and Greater Williamsburg. Partners in building since 2006.

Get involved today! Visit: www.morgan-james-publishing.com/giving-back

TABLE OF CONTENTS

ACKNOWLEDGMENTS

October 2021 I began to promote my new course called *Your Storytelling Potential.* It had taken me over a decade to put together and evolve my storytelling ideas that I planned to share during the 10 week online course. Shortly after I began promoting the course, I received an email from an existing student of mine named Russell Phillips. Russell had already taken my original screenwriting course, *The Screenwriting Mega Course,* years earlier. He explained how that original course had changed his entire way of thinking about stories and writing. Having signed up for my new course, Russell offered to help me in any way possible. I suggested he could take the transcripts from the live sessions, clean them up, and add in all the relevant images. He readily accepted that task.

It turns out Russell had a different vision than I did. He didn't just clean up the transcripts, instead he took the material, rewrote it, clarified it, and expanded on it when needed. This book is the result of that simple assignment. Therefore, I'd like to extend a huge thank you to Russell Phillips for helping to make this book a reality.

After Russell completed his initial draft of the book, I reviewed and edited it, and then I excitedly distributed the first draft to my existing students. That same day one of the participants in the course named Laurence Starn reached out to me asking for an unlocked version so he could make some notes and corrections to the text. It turns out, not unlike Russell, Laurence had his own vision for the book, and over the next many months Laurence would spend countless hours reviewing and editing the text and material of the book as it evolved into its final version. Therefore,

I'd like to extend a huge thank you to Laurence Starn for helping to make this book a reality.

And to all my students, clients and customers over the years. I remember when I first started selling my original online course, *The Screenwriting Mega Course,* and then my software, *Plot Control 1.0*, I knew in the beginning the names of every single person who signed up. Before long, that list of names became too long and too many. And that list of names grew and grew, first into the hundreds, then thousands, and then tens of thousands. To each and every one of you, I thank you for your support and small help in making this book a reality.

And to so many others who supported me and my efforts to make my software Plot Control, Chapter Control and Episode Control the most powerful and useful tools for creating stories for movies, novels and TV Shows.

Finally, I'd like to mention some not so unimportant people, namely my wife, children, mom, and extended family who continue to support me and my efforts to share this incredible story information and transform as many writers as possible.

A NOTE FROM THE AUTHOR

Over the past decade, I've been fortunate to work with so many amazing writers, from household names to first time writers. I'm continually amazed at how few writers truly understand stories, and what makes a story really special.

Unfortunately, not only do most aspiring (and professional) writers not understand what makes for a great story, but they also don't have a process to work through the complex layers and Thematic Connections that are **absolutely required** for any compelling novel or screenplay.

Most writers who come to me have shallow and disconnected story ideas based on the prevailing "single storyline" concept, which inevitably results in stories with no depth, no Thematic Layers, and nothing to carry their stories through a second act to a meaningful **CLIMAX** and **RESOLUTION**.

To make the situation worse, nearly every writer I have worked with has invested enormous amounts of time, energy, and in most cases, money (sometimes A LOT of money) reading books, watching videos, attending seminars, and even working with high-priced consultants who don't know what they're talking about.

I'm excited to bring my knowledge of storytelling to those who want to learn what actually makes certain stories great, and who want to have a step-by-step system they can use to create stories with their **Own Extraordinary Writing Potential**.

Mitchell German
Creator of Your Storytelling Potential

P.S. One important note for the reader: In developing my approach of storytelling, I have developed many terms that are unique to this system. Some of these terms may seem familiar but are in fact used in a nuanced and unique way. To help you with this, we have included a comprehensive glossary of the terms used throughout this book, and any time a glossary term is mentioned for the first time it appears in all **CAPS & BOLD**, subsequent uses of the term are Capitalized.

P.S.S. Before you get started, I recommend you download the worksheets that go along with this book. You can download your free worksheets here:

https://www.yourstorytellingpotential.com/worksheets

(These worksheets are fully editable and can be opened in the free Adobe PDF Reader or nearly any web browser, such as Google Chrome or Microsoft Edge. The PDF format allows you to fill out the forms and save your ongoing work.)

CHAPTER 1:

Hidden, Revealed and Unknown

Welcome to *Your Storytelling Potential*. Prepare to enter a new world. With the right mindset, the principles presented here hold the power to become a tremendously transformative catalyst for your personal evolution and adventure as a storyteller.

It may not be evident now, but what you just read in that brief opening paragraph contains the lifeblood essence of many of the core concepts that shape the Your Storytelling Potential Method—the key to this unique system for constructing deeply-layered, three-dimensional stories. And this system applies to the broad spectrum of storytelling applications. Whether it's for the screen, the stage, the campfire, or the page, if you want to tell a story there are some universal truths for telling an effective one.

Here is the first universal storytelling truth: Great stories are *not* random events.

Your Story

Before you decided to dive into the Your Storytelling Potential Method, you had a backstory as a storyteller. Whatever walk of life, since the day you were born, you have been growing through your experiences, your education, your lineage, and your unique personality. There are more influences on the way you think and process your world than we can name. All of that history and your inherent traits shape who you are as a storyteller. Your story is important to you, and you wish to tell your story in a way that captures and holds the attention of your audience from the very **BEGINNING** and all the way through to the end.

It is very likely if you have aspirations as a professional storyteller—someone who brings your work to the market to find an audience—that you have studied storytelling in some fashion. You have taken courses. You have read countless how-to books. You have participated in workshops. You have joined live or online communities to discuss and learn from peers.

Or maybe not.

Perhaps you are just starting out in your storytelling journey. (Don't worry if you are an absolute beginner! This book will explain clearly everything you need to know.)

The point here is, as with every experience within the bounds of *your life story* and, specifically, your story as a storyteller, the Your Storytelling Potential Method represents an *intersection* between you/your story *and* a potentially **TRANSFORMATIVE EVENT**.

Prior to this, you did not know this information about storytelling told precisely the way it is presented here in this book. *Now* you are beginning to be exposed to the Your Storytelling Potential Method. At some point in the near future, you will have completed this material. And then you will resume your life as a storyteller, hopefully *transformed* by what you have learned.

Does it make sense so far? It doesn't matter; let's get started…

The First Takeaway

Throughout *Your Storytelling Potential*, we will explain all of the concepts in the system using lots of examples so that everything will be clear.

The first concept is **CONVERGENCE**. Start thinking about stories as the intersection among three major **ELEMENTS**, or *BRANCHES*: a **MAIN CHARACTER**, and *two* major stories (the **A-STORY** and the **B-STORY**). Visually, a complete well-told story looks like this:

Figure 1: A Complete, Well-Told Story

Don't get overwhelmed by this Venn diagram. By the time you complete Your Storytelling Potential, all of this will be explained and demystified.

This is just the first of many images we will be looking at throughout *Your Storytelling Potential* that illustrates the concepts making up this system. Some will be more complex. Some will be very different in design. Some, which we will get to shortly, will be simpler derivations from this starting point that actually deepen your understanding and introduce further concepts you cannot quite see here.

But this initial image offers an essential 30,000-foot view of the Your Storytelling Potential approach. And it highlights the emphasis we are placing on *Convergence*—on thinking about stories as the intersection among these three central Elements. *Every* well-told story can be thought of as the product of the interaction among a Main Character, the A-Story (which is the new **SITUATION** that the Main Character now faces as a result of a **PROBLEM** or **OPPORTUNITY**), and the larger B-Story (which is the Main Character's life experience that provides the forward **MOMENTUM** for the narrative).

There are other components present in the story diagram above. And bear in mind that, by the time we're through, you will see that there are *many* more components to consider. These will be visualized in many ways. We will take each in turn as we build the explanation of this system. For now, just focus on that essential three-element relationship.

The A-Story Element in the Your Storytelling Potential Method

By now you may have caught on that we are using this introduction as a metaphor for introducing the basic concepts of the Your Storytelling Potential Method.

You, naturally, are the *Main Character* of a story about a person who desires to tell stories and seeks out educational tools to improve their skills and abilities.

Your life, specifically your education and experiences that shape the storyteller you are before, during, and after this encounter with Your Storytelling Potential is the B-Story. (Hey, don't get insulted! We haven't discussed B-Stories yet, but you're about to learn that B-Stories are generally *much* more important than A-Stories in the grand scheme.)

This book is the A-Story. It's the potentially Transformative Event that represents an *Opportunity* that has appeared in your present life as a storyteller. And to fully understand this element, you should know a little bit about this A-Story's history.

Much like most of you, we here at *Your Storytelling Potential* have spent many years in formal and self-directed education on storytelling, trying to get that leg up on our writing aspirations. Film school, books, seminars, you name it, we've tried it.

The problem we had, which is likely the same problem you've had and continue to have, in fact, is the same problem most writers have. You've followed all the "rules" and studied all the "experts," yet your screenplays, novels, and stories lack the potency you desire. Something is still missing in your understanding of the way stories operate. Something is still missing in the expression of your Characters and **PLOTS**. Something is still needed to elevate your stories into the stratosphere so that you can join the ranks of the professional-level elite storytellers.

That's all in the past. You're here now, and everything is about to change. And it all begins from a very unexpected place: The 1997 Jim Carrey movie *Liar Liar*.

This is *not* to say that *Liar Liar* is an extraordinary work of narrative genius. It's an entertaining film. It has been generally well-received by audiences and critics alike. But so far as what it means for *Your Storytelling Potential*, it merely happens to be the movie that unlocked an "a-ha!" moment of epic proportions. Expect to see many of the concepts illustrated with examples from *Liar Liar* as we move forward.

What *Your Storytelling Potential* is NOT (And a bit about what it is...)

Often, introductions for books like this contain a section outlining "Who this book is for?"

Let's be clear: This book is for you.

You picked this book up. Maybe you're taking the Your Storytelling Potential course as well (and we highly recommend you do). That very action says you are someone with an interest in telling stories. As a matter of fact, when you consider how much of the business world is driven by marketing or, deeper still, how much of life is a process of persuasion and negotiation—for which the ability to weave a spellbinding tale is indispensable—our sincere belief is this information can benefit virtually everyone. Definitely everyone seeking a career as a professional storyteller.

So rather than talk about the intended audience for this book, let's focus first on what this book is not about.

The Your Storytelling Potential Method does not teach you how to write. You will not find anything related to grammar and composition.

This is not a book about creative writing. This is not a book about novel-writing. Bear in mind the storytelling principles you will learn apply as much to speakers giving oral presentations as they do to the written word.

This is not a screenwriting book. You will find no information in these pages about formatting screenplays, for example. We do not discuss industry requirements for submissions of manuscripts. We are not concerned with strategies for locating and landing representation.

It is true that *Your Storytelling Potential* has its roots in ideas that were first developed for screenwriters by a script expert. The essential storytelling philosophy we espouse was first presented in the Screenwriting Mega Course and then adapted for the Plot Control software.

You might notice that a lion's share of the examples we draw upon are from major motion pictures. Again, we emphasize this is not a screenwriting-only system. While we strive to present as many relevant examples as possible covering the major forms of storytelling expression, the simple fact is that major motion pictures are the most ubiquitous, and they are quickly and easily digested. They are the most widely known and therefore easiest to relate to. The same reasoning applies to the choices in the book series mentioned throughout. These references reflect the standing of these various properties in the public consciousness. These works have all struck chords with wide audiences, so it makes sense to refer to them for common understanding and relatability.

One further thing this method is not: A step-by-step guide or formula. Many methods of story creation instruction teach a rigid structure born of a formulaic application of preset "beats" and/or a checklist of the necessary **ARCHETYPES** to include. "Place Mentor A into Threshold Crossing B, secure with Plot Turning Points D, G, and H, and you will have a properly structured plot."

Don't get us wrong. This is not challenging the need for solid structure. But we aren't assembling IKEA furniture here. This system is predicated on the idea that all Elements operating within a well-told story—structure included—mesh together organically when the author has a proper understanding of how they interrelate. Formulas don't lend insight to why things happen and what makes every part of the story Relevant.

RELEVANCE is key. This goes back to the first takeaway we discussed: Convergence.

Another way to think of this is chemistry.

Everyone knows H_2O, the chemical formula for the water molecule. Without going too deep into the science, all you need to understand is that to create a molecule of water, you must have two hydrogen (H) atoms bonded with one oxygen (O) atom.

Stories are much like molecules or any other chemical formula. We could supply you with a particular formula to follow. But does it not make better sense to master the underlying chemistry for yourself? So you understand why elemental atoms bond to one another? And then empower you with the ability to manipulate the atoms to create various stable substances (stories) of your own?

You can be the mad scientist in your story-building lab! Once you have a firm grasp of the chemistry that supports the process, then you can employ your own madness (read: creative instinct) to give your narrative brainchildren life!

That is very much part of our goal: to offer an analysis of the mechanism that makes almost all of the very best stories work. Commit to implementing the concepts shared in this book, and you are going to learn what makes great, engaging stories that connect with your audience and leave them fulfilled by the experience. You will be armed with a process for creating your own well-rounded, rich, thematically relevant, potent stories that accomplish those things.

Once you have a fundamental understanding of great storytelling, then you will have the potential to write great screenplays, novels, and anything else.

So don't think of this as just another how to write a story book. Truly, this is a how to think about crafting a story book.

Three Branches

We just ended the last section stating that our focus is *how to think about* crafting stories. The place to begin with that is reframing how *you* think about stories. With a new frame, we can then work to fill in the complete picture.

Let's take another look at the Venn diagram from the earlier section on Convergence. This one is even a shade simpler. Notice we have removed the arrows leading inward toward the Climax. We will get to that shortly. For now, just take note of the three major Branches and how they relate and overlap.

Figure 2: A Complete Well-Told Story Simplified

As we mentioned earlier, every storyteller should be aware that a well-told story has these three Elements, which we are calling the *Branches*. A Main Character, an A-Story, and a B-Story.

The Main Character is probably self-evident and easy to understand. The *who* the story is about. In a well-told story, the Main Character should be *indispensable*. The story should not be the same if it were to be about anyone else. It has to be *this* specific Main Character, at *this* specific time.

The A-Story is fairly easy to grasp. It's the current *what is happening* in your Main Character's life. It essentially defines where the story *you tell* begins and ends. The A-Story contains a Situation that presents itself as a Problem or an Opportunity. The Resolution of the Problem or Opportunity presented by the A-Story Situation defines the Climax. The A-Story is usually the reason your audience buys the ticket.

Terrorists have seized a building.

The Main Character has just met the person of their dreams.

A regular kid learns he is a wizard and has the Opportunity to go to wizard school.

A nobody farm boy on a desert planet discovers he has special skills and information needed to destroy the powerful weapon devised by an evil galactic empire.

How about the B-Story? This one might be a bit more challenging to comprehend right off the bat.

Here is an important idea to note: The B-Story does *not* mean *subplot*!

The question that might spring to mind is, "Does this mean that *every* story is actually *two* stories?"

Answer: *yes!*

So let's be clear about B-Story versus Subplot(s). There may be many **SUBPLOTS**. There is only ONE B-Story. The B-Story may be revealed by way of the Subplots. Subplots most often serve to express **THEME**, therefore they usually are pulling a sort of double duty. But these two terms are not interchangeable.

So what is the B-Story?

In short, the B-Story is essentially the Main Character's *personal life*. The life they have been living before they encounter the Problem or Opportunity in the A-Story. And the B-Story is that part of your overall story that goes on *after* the Resolution of the A-Story ends.

If the philosopher in you starts to exclaim "How do I distinguish a **CHARACTER** from the life they lead?"—just relax a bit. This isn't a treatise on existentialism. We're speaking on a simple, practical level.

An easy way to draw the distinction is to imagine if we took you, the Main Character of your story, and drop you on a desert island, or send you into witness protection, or ship you to an alien world. The Main Character is the essential person; it's still you. Your inner thoughts, your personality, the choices you make are based on your innate spirit and the

VALUES you adopted throughout your personal history. The B-Story, on the other hand, is the life you have left behind. You can't speak with your friends and family. The concerns you had about your job and paying the rent or mortgage for your housing, etc.—that stuff exists independently from you. And it persists for the most part. It just goes on without you. And as you adapt to your new environment and make new relationships, you are fashioning a new B-Story there.

In a well-told story, the B-Story *also* presents the Main Character with a *Problem or Opportunity*. If your Main Character is a law officer and the A-Story is about the *Opportunity* to advance their career by solving some Big Case, then the crafty storyteller likely gives the officer a *Problem* on the home front, such as a spouse who feels abandoned and threatens to leave if they don't stop working so much. If the A-Story is about a Problem, the B-Story might offer an Opportunity to the Main Character. And vice-versa. Of course, there are always exceptions to any rule, and you can find stories that are Problem-Problem or Opportunity-Opportunity (it may be the dilemma of two conflicting opportunities that *creates* a Problem, for example).

This kind of dynamic, where the A and B Stories push-and-pull on the Main Character, adds a **LAYER** of dimension, creates tension, and makes the story more compelling.

There is *so* much more to say about all of these concepts, which we will discuss later in greater detail. But this use of "B-Story" is unique and fundamental to the Your Storytelling Potential Method, so we want to begin by clarifying the element a bit before we dive into the whole.

Hidden, Revealed and Unknown Outer and Inner Worlds

The next significant thing to note about the Venn diagram we have been looking at is that it represents *more* than the story you tell.

The portion of the story that is *expressed*—written, filmed, told—is the center part of the previous image (see above). The areas where the three Branches overlap form something that looks like the blades of a propeller:

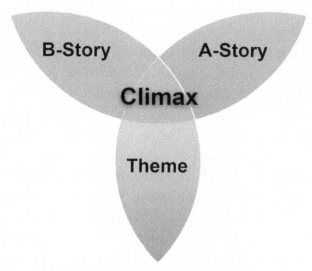

Figure 3: The Revealed Story/Inner World

Notice we refer to the Expressed Story as the **REVEALED STORY** or the **INNER WORLD**. And now it becomes clear that, in the context of that story *you tell*, you must keep in mind these three blades of the "propeller."

The Main Character is, of course, involved in both the A-Story and the B-Story, as the Main Character is the one for whom the events of the story are playing out. The Main Character is either reacting to events unfolding or driving things forward through their choices and attempts to resolve the various Opportunities and/or Problems they encounter. (In that way, it *is* appropriate to think of the Main Character as inseparable from the story. Be aware, though, that the Main Character is *revealed* through the story, and not defined by it. This revelation makes your Main Character three-dimensional and whole, not just simply a 2-D cartoon sum of their functional parts within the context of the needs of the story.)

The third "blade" of the Revealed Story propeller is something we have not yet discussed: Theme.

Theme can be a difficult concept to define and master. It's one of those things like irony that seems to elude some people (just ask Alanis Morissette). Even literary scholars don't always seem to operate from the same definition of Theme.

A lot of storytelling instruction mistakes *subject matter* for the Theme. But the Theme of movies about soldiers in battle is *not* "war." Nor is "sports" or "the spirit of competition" the Theme of most any sports story. Same with police procedurals or courtroom dramas and "justice."

Oftentimes people think of Theme as being the *message* of the story. But a story is not a soapbox lecture for the audience. The author/storyteller is not a preacher in a pulpit. This kind of thinking leads to some very on-the-nose interpretations about Theme. The pro-environmentalist writer who is writing a story with an "earth first" Theme makes their Main Character a Greenpeace Hero, overtly battling some demon polluting corporation, a white knight triumphant in winning a big case in court. That is an extreme example, but it makes the point, even if we soften how this version of Theme was executed, it remains off-base to the true concept of Theme.

We are increasingly living in a social responsibility-oriented world, and there may be causes that are near and dear to your heart. But this type of overt message weaving into your stories is not likely to persuade. Subtlety has a proven record of being the more productive path. The best stories may look to contribute to the public conversation by simply casting the spotlight on a topic. A skilled storyteller does well to learn to argue both sides of any issue and find the humanity in all of their characters.

For the Your Storytelling Potential Method, Theme is a *unifying idea*. It is the glue that binds the A and B Stories. Generally speaking, it is *not* a message for the audience but rather an *argument* for the Main Character. We will see that much of what transpires in the A-Story and the B-Story focuses on the Main Character wrestling with the disparity between a Theme *and* its **OPPOSING IDEA**.

The Revealed Story (the expressed story being told) is about the Main Character dealing with the interplay of the A-Story (a new Situation they are working through) and the B-story (the ongoing, larger story of the Main Character's world) on a battlefield of opposing thematic ideas until the Plot events reach a final Climax and Resolution.

And the next thing to know about this conceptual model is that this Revealed Story takes place in the **NOW**.

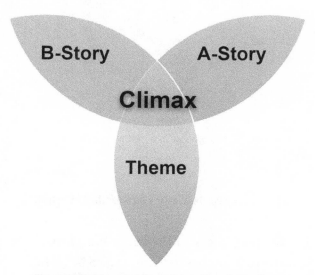

Figure 4: The Revealed Story Takes Place in the Now.

This concept may seem self-evident at first read. On one level, it sounds rather obvious. Trust for the moment that this concept of stories taking place in the Now is a major key. We will explain as we go on why this is a deep concept in this method and a very important consideration for you in the story-building process.

While we are on the topic of *time*, notice the spiraling arrow we've added to the center of the "propeller" in the next diagram. The spiral depicts our story's timeline conceptually. Relative to this propeller image of A-Story, B-Story, and Theme "blades," the spiral illustrates the Main Character's **JOURNEY** moving through each of the Branches repetitively as the Revealed Story progresses, until it all comes together in a Climax. This means the most satisfying, complete Climaxes are those that incorporate all three Branch Elements.

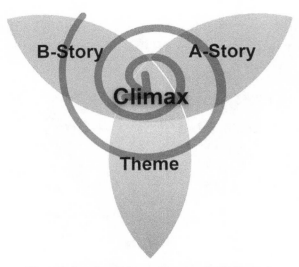

Figure 5: Complete Climaxes Incorporate All Elements

If there is a Revealed Story of the Inner World that takes place in the Now, then logically that implies there must also be a Hidden Story within an **OUTER WORLD** that *does not* take place in the Now. As we return to our Venn diagram and remove the Now of the Revealed Story, we see this idea illustrated:

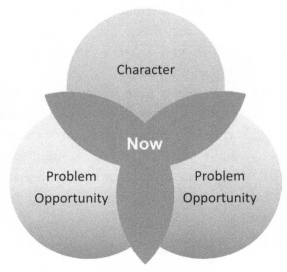

Figure 6: The Hidden Story of the Outer World

The larger point of this image is that the **AUTHOR-STORYTELLER** must be aware of the untold Hidden Story of the Outer World. Having this consciousness creates the possibility of depth and resonance with the audience. It keeps the storyteller mindful of dimensions that *can be* explored and drawn upon as the story develops. The Outer World is conceptual *potential* for the Inner World of the story expressed in the Now.

Another aspect of Hidden Story to be mindful of deals with time. Your Revealed Story takes place in the Now, but it's just as important to know the **HIDDEN PAST** and the **UNKNOWN FUTURE**. This is particularly relevant for the B-Story, though all Branches have a past and future to be mindful of. The Hidden Past is foundational for the events transpiring in the Now. But it's just as significant to understand where the Main Character's life is headed into the future once the credits roll or the reader reaches "The End." In a small way, your Revealed Story will hint at the future in its final moments; this we call the **REVEALED POTENTIAL**. Most good stories wrap things up either positively (and they lived happily ever after) or else tragically (as in the case of a dark, cautionary tale). We will discuss much more about what transpires in the Now of your Revealed Story, but in the broadest sense, you should recognize that the point of any story is to chronicle a Transformative Event, as the Problem or Opportunity presented by the A-Story intersects with the ongoing life of the Main Character in the B-Story. With that recognition, you can appreciate the Unknown Future as the target.

Ultimately, of course, the Outer World is only conceptual. The storyteller won't have (nor need) all the details about the Hidden Story/Outer World as they will about the Revealed Story. But that is to say, those details of the story you end up telling emerged from the fertile ground of the Outer World, which you explored until the Revealed Story was finalized. It's about selecting and incorporating appropriate details from the Outer World to make your Revealed Story vibrant and convincing.

Another way to think about this is to see your Revealed Story as the first of a potential franchise, even if you have no such designs.

Unless you just arrived on this planet last week, you know that George Lucas created *Star Wars*, the epitome of movie franchises. The first movie was released in 1977, with sequels that completed a trilogy by 1983. Of course in the decades since, the *Star Wars* universe has grown to include two more sets of trilogies, countless novels, comics, video games, and an ever-expanding roster of TV show spin-offs.

Interestingly, those first three movies were subtitled Episodes IV, V, and VI. Clearly from its inception, *Star Wars* was intended to become a sprawling saga. The first film tells a complete story about a young farm boy who accidentally receives crucial data loaded into a pair of robotic droids, becomes involved with the spiritual warrior-master the message was intended for, and embarks on an adventure to rescue the princess leading a rebellion against the evil space empire that has built a devastating weapon, before using that data to destroy the empire's weapon. Lucas had built that entire expanded world—that B-Story for his hero, Luke Skywalker—and had a tremendous sense of the Hidden Outer World of his story. Both the rich Hidden Past history and the potential of the Unknown Future.

Three Branches, Part II:
Introduction to the CORE ELEMENTS

Students of the Screenwriting Mega Course and users of Plot Control software are familiar with this method's Core Elements. As we detail this method, it should become increasingly clear that stories have an *internal logical* **STRUCTURE** of conceptual Elements in balance with one another. This Structure is every bit as important, really more so, than the commonly described Structure of three (or more) *acts* and the *beats* within them plotted on a linear (and usually peaked or arched) timeline. This balanced internal logical Structure of concepts relies on *Relevance*, as we have already discussed.

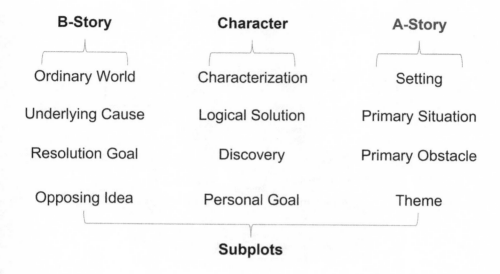

Figure 7: The Twelve Core Elements

A full discussion of the Core Elements is coming in future chapters. Each of the Elements is vital and requires a thorough discussion. There are Twelve Core Elements in the Your Storytelling Potential Method. We will say more about why there are twelve and how they work to achieve that Relevance and internal Structure when understood and applied. But it is appropriate to discuss three of them in this introduction because, as you might guess, they are directly related to our Three Branches.

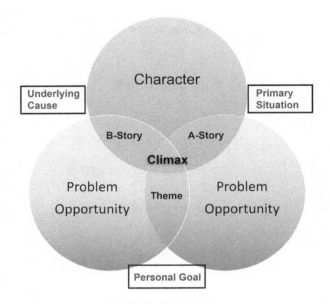

Figure 8: The Entire Story Expressed

Notice there are some important added descriptors associated with the three Branches: **PERSONAL GOAL**, **PRIMARY SITUATION**, and **UNDERLYING CAUSE**. These are three of the Core Elements of any complete story.

Let's first focus on the Personal Goal.

When we think about the internal landscape of your Main Character that is reflected in their words and actions, this is a crucial element that drives the story forward. Something ethereal in your Main Character's Mind and soul, something intrinsic to their make-up and the way they process their world gives rise to a Goal. This is something they **DESIRE**. The goal may be tangible. It may not be. The goal is often something conceptual, reflective of their Desire to see a deeply held Value manifest in their world in some way. But whatever that is, the Personal Goal continually informs how your Main Character interacts with the Problems or Opportunities in the story. It affects the Main Character's choices in dealing with the Problems or Opportunities they encounter, the words they choose, and how they relate to all of the other Characters.

The A-Story has a Momentum created by the main Problem or Opportunity, often (not always) fueled by the direct actions of an **ANTAGONIST** and their agents (more on this later). The B-Story, as we have discussed, is generally the larger story of the Main Character's life, and gains its Momentum from various Subplots where there is an attempt to aid the Main Character or present a **COMPLICATION** for the Main Character as they deal with the A-Story Situation. And now we understand that the Main Character Branch also exerts a Momentum force acting on the story's flow that stems from the Main Character's Personal Goal, like an X-Factor.

Also, note how the Personal Goal impacts the Theme blade of the Revealed Story propeller. This placement will become critical in understanding and applying the Your Storytelling Potential Method because the Personal Goal functions as the deepest expression of the Main Character, the deepest expression of the rich Thematic Ideas at play in a story, and most importantly, the *link* between the A and B Stories.

Yes, the Main Character supplies the Personal Goal as something intrinsic to their makeup, but the way the Personal Goal is *expressed* in the Revealed Story is through Theme. That interplay between a unifying idea and its opposite. Theme comes out in this overlap where the A and B Stories overlap. (We know this may sound overwhelming right now, don't worry, we're going to provide concrete examples of all of this in the coming chapters.)

The other two Core Elements we need to look at here—the Primary Situation and the Underlying Cause—are to be understood as synonyms for the A and B Stories. These Elements get to the heart of the function of these storylines.

The Problem or Opportunity arising in the Now of the Main Character's life presented by the A-Story is the Primary Situation.

The Primary Situation is a NEW Problem or Opportunity that arises in the course of the Revealed Story. This new Situation in the Main Character's life becomes the focus of their attention in the Now and drags them out of their **ORDINARY WORLD** of the B-Story, and into the world of the A-Story.

It's important to understand that the A-Story doesn't exist in a vacuum, it has its own Hidden Past. The Situation that's about to hit the Main Character is like a tsunami racing towards the shore. That tsunami has its own starting point, its own cause, which took place prior to its intersection with the Main Character. And there is always one major relevant Character associated with that cause.

We call these the **PROXIMATE CAUSE** and the **PROXIMATE CAUSE CHARACTER**. These are essential Elements that we will explore in-depth in later chapters. Suffice for now, there is always one significant Character, apart from the Main Character, who has a major vested interest in the outcome of the A-Story. Oftentimes this is an Antagonist, but *not* always (more on this later).

All of these Elements are related to and seen from the perspective of your Main Character. Although all **3 BRANCHES** have a Hidden Past, the B-Story is the B-Story *because* it is your Main Character's personal life and history. So, yes, while the A-Story has a Hidden Past of its own, it is only relevant to the Revealed Story and is thought of as the Situation your Main Character *now* faces because it has *emerged in* or *converged with* your Main Character's world and life.

As it stands, the Author-Storyteller chooses the perspective of the story. Most often we tell stories about Main Characters we identify with or want to root for. Most often those Main Characters tend to be essentially moral (however we define it), though flawed.

So the point here is the Primary Situation often has the appearance of being an Opportunity or Problem that suddenly came out of nowhere to confront your Main Character. And from your Main Character's *perspective,* it may seem that way. But if your Main Character is a world-class superspy and the Primary Situation is a terrorist organization that has stolen nuclear weapons and is blackmailing the world for a big payday, those criminal masterminds have been plotting that for some time. Or if your story is about astronauts having to plant bombs on a runaway asteroid before it destroys Earth, that asteroid has been hurtling through the universe for eons.

Primary Situations have an emergent quality *relative to* your Main Character and the B-Story. But they have a full "life of their own," so to speak, their own Hidden Past.

The last of the three Core Elements related to our three main Branches and another way to think about the B-Story is the Underlying Cause.

Hopefully, by now, the notion of B-Story is growing clearer. As we move forward, we will dig even deeper into just what makes it so important to be able to identify and differentiate the A-Story/Primary Situation Branch from the B-Story/Underlying Cause Branch, because traditionally storytelling has not been taught with this approach. We usually hear about a **PLOTLINE** that concerns itself with moving a main story (in our lingo, the A-Story) forward, and the Author-Storyteller has the job of filling in a Main Character's backstory and developing several Subplots to enrich that single storyline.

Meanwhile, we are emphasizing that a *well-told story* is truly developed through the interplay between two equally important but not intrinsically related main stories *linked by* the involvement of the Main Character.

Underlying here does *not* imply *subordinate*. It is much more meaningful to call it *foundational*. The A-Story/Primary Situation *plays out in the context of* that larger B-Story/Underlying Cause from the perspective of the Main Character.

And as we have already outlined, the Main Character is heavily invested in the Underlying Cause (after all, it's essentially their personal life—at least as it is *relevant* to your Revealed Story). There is a recognition that resolving the Primary Situation Problem or Opportunity has ramifications for the Main Character's B-Story world. And, reciprocally, what is happening in their Underlying B-Story should affect (likely complicate, sometimes aid or attempt to aid) the Main Character's ability to deal with the Primary Situation.

Recall that the best stories also have an Opportunity or Problem coming from the Underlying Cause. Most of the time, the broadest challenge the Main Character faces is this very two-front *war* of dealing with the Problem or Opportunity stemming from the Primary Situation *and* the Opportunity/Problem of the Underlying Cause *at the same time*.

The Your Storytelling Potential Story Model Illustrated
Case Study: *Liar Liar*

[SPOILER ALERT! Be forewarned that exploring these ideas with case study examples from movies and books in the public eye means we will be discussing these stories thoroughly. We urge you to get familiar with the examples used, although it is not necessary. If you are not, however, you will learn key Plot details.]

Assuming you are familiar with the movie *Liar Liar*, if someone were to ask you what is the Primary Situation (namely the A-Story) of the film, how would you answer? We do not assume everyone reading this book has studied storytelling in depth. But it remains very likely that the majority of you have a long-term interest in becoming better story builders, and this is not your first exposure. With that in mind, forgive us if part of the effort involves working to unteach some ideas people have likely learned, counterprogramming to popularly held concepts.

When people think about the core of a story, the tendency is to deliver what is commonly called a *logline*. If you don't know what a "logline" is, it's a short, one or two sentence summary of a story—generally 25 to 50 words—that authors use to market or "pitch" their work to potentially interested industry professionals. Think about the short summaries of movies offered on a streaming service page or in a program guide.

Here is a logline for *Liar Liar*: "A compulsively lying lawyer gets the biggest case of his career, but when his son's birthday wish comes true, preventing him from lying, it puts the case in jeopardy."

Another possible response might actually say less, and simply offer the movie's *high concept.* A high concept is a summary that immediately conveys a story (with a great deal of conflict) in fewer words than it takes to write a logline. In the case of *Liar Liar*, that high concept would be "a lawyer who can't tell a lie."

But when we ask about the Primary Situation (remember: the A-story), if your response includes anything about magical wishes or not being able to tell lies, would you be surprised if we told you it's incorrect? It is difficult to imagine talking about this movie without discussing the Main Character's inability to lie (after all, *Liar* is right in the title. *Twice!*) But the truth is, the A-Story's Primary Situation has nothing *directly* to do with the magical wish coming true.

The logline above does a great job of touching on all three Branches of the story. The movie's high concept mentions *nothing* about the Opportunity or Problem that stems from the A-Story.

In the case of *Liar Liar*, the hook—the sizzle that sells the steak and captures imaginations—comes from the B-Story. It's in the Underlying Cause. As we have been talking about, the Underlying Cause/B-Story is the Main Character's ongoing personal life. It's the aspect of the story that was going on *before* the Now of the Revealed Story the audience experiences and goes on *after* the Transformative Event(s) have concluded.

The current Problem or Opportunity that the Main Character, Fletcher (played by Jim Carrey), *now* faces is an Opportunity to advance his career and make partner if he wins a big-money law case for his firm. That's it. The *law case* is the thing happening Now, and there is nothing inherent in the law case that forbids him from telling lies.

For example, if the story were about an up-and-coming lawyer who wins his cases because he is unethical and tells lies, and the Opportunity was he has to win a case being argued in front of a judge who has special lie-detecting powers, *then* we could say the Problem or Opportunity in the A-Story has something to do with magical forces preventing him from telling lies to win a case. In that story, the special-powers judge would **not** be part of the Main Character's ongoing life, his B-Story Underlying Cause. (And maybe it would be a far less engaging story.)

Instead, the magical force in *Liar Liar* that removes Fletcher's ability to lie comes from a simple wish made by his son. Quite coincidentally and totally separate from Fletcher's job or the courts or any aspect of the case itself. His son has been disappointed by his father's deceptions. Fletcher misses his son's birthday party, because of the court case, and cooks up an excuse for doing so, so his son makes the wish. That Problem becomes Fletcher's major obstacle.

Now we have identified the A-Story, or Primary Situation, and the B-Story, or Underlying Cause, of *Liar Liar*:

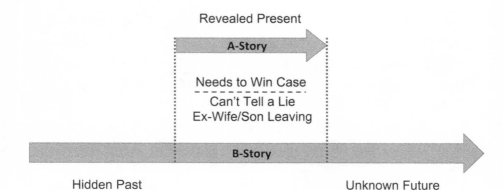

Figure 9: The Primary Situation & Underlying Cause of Liar Liar

The Theme Branch of the movie, ironically, is easier to identify. In our deeper discussions on Theme to come, we will see that for the vast majority of stories, Theme can be fairly complex and not at all what we expect. Themes aren't always incredibly deep ideas, though they can be. Often, though, Theme is expressed as a conflict between an idea (such as honesty) and its opposite (dishonesty) which are at war for the Main Character's soul. With *Liar Liar*, its Theme is expressed in the title: honesty.

In Jim Carrey's Fletcher, we meet a man whose core central trait, being a pathological liar, makes him exceptionally successful in his vocation as a lawyer but terrible in his relationships as husband and father. Deeper expressions of the central Theme in the story might show *justifications for telling lies* or *ends justifying deceptive means*. In his heart of hearts, Fletcher ultimately wants to better himself. We see that he's a pretty good Dad *when he's present* for his son. We get the sense that there is a lot his now ex-wife still loves about him. But in his mind, getting to the top of his profession makes him a better man and puts him in a better position to fulfill his role within the family. Clearly, he's lost sight of his priorities.

Liar Liar, like any compelling, well-told story, centers on a *specific* Character in these *specific* circumstances. Notice the principle of *Convergence* in this story. Fletcher's important court case is being heard *on a specific day* (Primary Situation), which coincides with his son's making a wish that his father cannot tell a lie for just one day *on that very same day* (Underlying Cause). There's not much of a story if Fletcher doesn't rely on telling lies to be successful in his job, and must be dishonest to win the specific case in question. There are many pathological liars employed in every field under the sun. It also wouldn't be a compelling story if the day on which his son makes his wish, Fletcher was merely preparing for a court case for the next week, or spending his day drafting motions he intends to file the next day. Or if the wish time period fell over the weekend. Similarly, the Revealed Story is just as dependent on the Complication that comes from the Underlying Cause. If there's no wish at all, it's an unfunny short story about an easy day winning a trial in court for Fletcher. Otherwise, maybe the Author-Storyteller finds a different Problem or Opportunity arising from the Underlying Cause, such as his son burning Fletcher's case files instead of making the wish. Finally, Fletcher must have the *Values* he does, which drives his Personal Goal. None of this makes much of a difference if Fletcher doesn't *really care* about making partner in his firm or being involved with his family. In any case, without the two main stories unfolding the way they do, for this specific Main Character, we don't have *this* story.

Embrace the Method!

You now have a pretty complete, high-level picture of the model for how stories work in the Your Storytelling Potential Method.

The Entire Story Expressed

Figure 10: The Entire Story Expressed

Admittedly, what we have shared in this first chapter, in both concepts and diagrams to illustrate them, is not entirely *actionable* without showing how these concepts work on a practical level. This is just the first chapter. Obviously, there is a *lot* more to come!

What we wish to emphasize, especially for those with a history of storytelling methodology study under their belts, is you are going to get the most out of the Your Storytelling Potential Method if you *set other systems aside*. Just for now.

Understand that the Your Storytelling Potential Method employs its own vocabulary. Terms used by other systems very likely *do not mean precisely the same thing* in this system. For example, many systems talk about an *Ordinary World* of the **PROTAGONIST**. In those models, the *Ordinary World* is a place and/or set of circumstances that the Protagonist *leaves* to enter some "new world" of the story. At the conclusion, the Protagonist then leaves that "new world" and *returns to* the Ordinary World, *bringing back* some lesson or conceptual *elixir* gained over the course of the story. You will find that *Ordinary World* in this method is not used in the same way. Most of the terminology in the following pages will be unique to this method.

We do not think the Your Storytelling Potential Method is the *only* way to tell a story.

In its simplest form, any series of events that involve a Character or are related in a sequence somehow can be considered a "story." And there is no denying that there are great pearls of wisdom to be had by learning from the recognized masters who have discussed the subject throughout history. At the same time, we assert that there are many popular instruction systems on storytelling that just get it wrong. Some explanations are murky and impenetrable. Others regurgitate concepts that have come to be accepted as authoritative but, in our view, don't stand up to scrutiny.

Finally, always does not always mean *always*. Like any philosophy based on observation and analysis, the concepts presented should be understood to be *statistically true*. True most of the time. There are always exceptions to every "rule."

When we look at the complete published and produced creative works of mankind, there will be many examples of stories that do not behave as we describe. Oftentimes, this is because works are bought and distributed by people following their understanding of popular appeal, chasing a buck by producing subpar work with some kind of gimmick—a bankable star, a sequel to something big, or work based on a true story but executed poorly. Just because things make it to market does not make them examples of great storytelling. But other such cases are certainly the products of unique genius, and usually, they do things *so* uniquely that they are impractical or impossible to replicate. *Lightning in a bottle*, as they say.

Our focus here is not merely to teach a blueprint for constructing any story. But on sharing how *well-told* stories operate. We want to open your mind to "a-ha!" moments to unlock *your* storytelling potential.

In the next chapter, we will continue to demonstrate that these concepts are the driving force behind virtually all engaging stories by exploring numerous examples of classic IPs.

Some of you just read that and are now asking, "What's an IP?"

In case you don't know, **IP** stands for **INTELLECTUAL PROPERTY**. It refers to the extended world of any story, across all formats in which that world is presented. *Star Wars* is a fantastic example of an IP. It began life as a single movie. Now it exists as a series of movies, television shows, animated cartoons, comic books, novels, video games, assorted merchandise, and amusement park theme rides. Additionally, there is an inspired, devout fanbase of creators supplementing the reach of George Lucas's seminal IP with fan fiction productions of all varieties. The extent of it is immeasurable.

J.K. Rowling has built a similar conceptual empire with the wizarding world of Harry Potter.

This is the strength of the B-Story and the recognition of building a robust Outer World. We enthusiastically invite you to think of your story ideas as the seeds for *your* IPs!

CHAPTER 2:

The Beginning Is Not the Beginning

In the first chapter, we laid out the foundational concepts for how stories operate within the Your Storytelling Potential Method. That introduction to this system presented several variations of a basic Venn diagram image to demonstrate a central principle of Convergence. As we have stated from the beginning, well-told stories are *not* a series of random events. Nor are they a series of conceptually unrelated events. We lean heavily on the idea that every strand and element of a story should work in a harmony born of Relevance. Relevance is the result of conscious choices made by the Author-Storyteller to link each part through *thematic ideas*. The result is an illusion of naturally unfolding life events that take on significance for an audience as they sense the complexity and depth in a Well-Layered, three-dimensional tale.

In this chapter, we continue the exploration of fundamental concepts. But we are going to begin the process of delving deeper towards a practical level.

With that end goal in mind, here is the second universal storytelling truth: Great stories don't start at the Beginning.

Time Traveling Transition

Just as we began our discussion about the underlying ideas in Chapter One with a foundational image, let's take a look at the first master diagram for the way we will approach the concepts in this chapter:

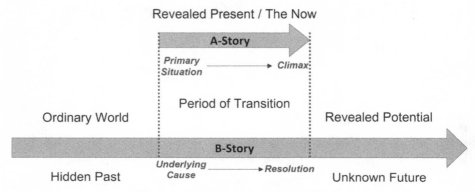

Figure 11: The Entire Story Revealed in Time

This image transforms the Chapter One Venn diagram into a linear form. It encapsulates a *lot* (and we haven't added everything yet!)

The Chapter One Venn diagram, and the propeller image derived from it, help to visualize the theoretical way stories operate. But we cannot ignore that stories unfold in time from past-to-present.

Now you may be thinking about the many stories you have read or movies you have watched where things are presented in a non-chronological fashion (looking at you, Quentin Tarantino fans!) Just be aware this is one difference between *story construction* and *story presentation*. And we are obliged to consider all of this from the foundation-up before thinking about unconventional variations.

The story you tell is a slice of the life of your Main Character. It is told from the perspective of your Main Character—even if you tell it through a third-person narrator.

For example, most of the Sherlock Holmes adventures written by Sir Arthur Conan Doyle are "told by" Holmes's fictional investigative partner and biographer, Dr. Watson. Doyle uses Watson to offer commentary and even skew perspective on the talented detective. But Watson's narration is a device that allows Doyle to keep Holmes an enigma and to keep a separation between the reader and the inner workings of his brilliant mind. (Notice the contrast between the usual depiction of Holmes this way and the cinematic version starring Robert Downey, Jr., wherein the medium allows us insight into Holmes's mental processes through bullet-time vignettes.) Nevertheless, a Sherlock Holmes story is always focused on Holmes and his life at 221B Baker Street. Each case comes along as a new A-Story Primary Situation. Holmes resolves the Problem. End of story. Next case, please.

Traditionally, Characters like Sherlock Holmes or James Bond, these uber-capable heroic figures whose adventures we follow through story after story, are what we think of as **STEADFAST CHARACTERS**. The next story in the series begins, and these people are essentially the same. Each new Primary Situation is a riddle to be solved. A mere exercise of their talents. But the adventure only serves to reaffirm their core Values and beliefs which come from their B-Story. In these stories, it's generally the case that *someone else* has their inner Values and beliefs challenged and they are the ones who change, rather than the Main Character. But this is not typical.

For the vast majority of stories, it is going to be the Main Character who undergoes a **TRANSITION**. The general goal of every well-told narrative is to chronicle a Transformative Event.

In the grand scheme, your audience becomes engaged because of the Main Character's B-Story. That is what people relate to. What the master diagram shows is that the A-Story introduces a Problem or Opportunity that represents a significant event that affects the course of the B-Story, in that the A-Story *intersects* with the ongoing life of the Main Character. Everything that is happening, in both the A and B Stories, are from the perspective of the Main Character, namely their ongoing B-Story.

What is unique and new in the life of the Main Character is the A-Story. The Main Character only deals with the Situation of the A-Story for the duration of the **REVEALED PRESENT**, the Now of the story you tell. In that cauldron of action confronting the Primary Situation, your

Main Character (or a closely related subordinate of a Steadfast Character) undergoes change.

While we do *not* want you to think about your stories as a single, main A-Story with a lot of subordinate window dressing hoping to make it feel fleshed out, there is nonetheless a sense that the *story you tell* is indeed *the A-Story*. But it is essential to understand that the A-Story, from your Main Character's perspective, *is a part of the overall B-Story.* It is what is *new* and *Now.* It is a window that lets us see the B-Story. And just like windows in a department store, the grand display of the juicy A-Story Situation is there to get you inside. How long you stay in the store (how much your audience ultimately cares) is a function of a great interior, the B-Story.

What we are getting at and continually emphasizing is that your story *needs* your conscious attention on *two* main stories. The B-Story is every bit as important as the A-Story. And if we have gone too far to build up the importance of the B-Story, understand we are in no way minimizing the importance of the A-Story. They both have equal, critical functions to play in order to tell a compelling narrative.

Traditional storytelling instruction focuses on a plot-*line,* as in just one. If you have ever taken a literature or creative writing course covering story construction, chances are there was an emphasis on *practical* Structure. These are the beats of a *first act.* This is what is accomplished in the *second act.* Somewhere there was a graph showing some *rising action* that builds until a *Climax* where it all peaks, and then the *line* descends towards some form of denouement. Sound familiar?

Here is a popular version of the above-described graph of a Plotline:

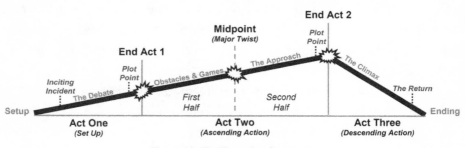

Figure 12: The Three-Act Structure

The problem with graphs that look like this is that a well-told story does *not* look anything like it. This type of *Structure* describes one common course of the A-Story, and nothing else.

It says *nothing* about a B-Story. There's not even an acknowledgment of the existence of a B-Story. Very likely what you now understand about B-Story is handled as throwaway supporting activities. *"You want to spend time writing a backstory for your Characters. You want Subplots that flesh things out so the audience sees your Protagonist as a fully formed Character with a life outside what's going on in the story."* Very secondary. All afterthought. In that view, the *important* thing is a compelling *plot*, and then you work to add the window dressing to make it seem more filled out.

There's also the prevailing concept that the Protagonist *leaves* an *Ordinary World* to enter a "new world" of the story, and then returns to their Ordinary World at the end. This is a very key difference from the Your Storytelling Potential Method. Your Main Character's B-Story, their ongoing life, their Underlying Cause, is the foundation for the story and *not* something they leave behind. Your Main Character does *not* take a vacation from their life to go off and have an adventure in some other world (even if they literally do take a vacation or go visit another world). Everything in the current A-Story Situation is playing out *in the context of* the Main Character's larger ongoing B-Story life.

This is *not* what happens in *Liar Liar*, for example:

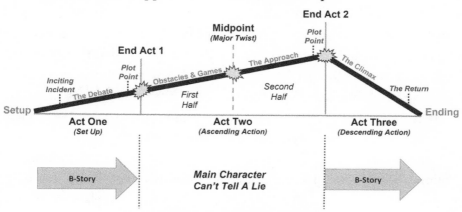

Figure 13: Great Stories Don't Look Like This

To be clear, this system uses the term *Ordinary World* in a way that breaks from its typical definition and usage. And the distinction between our use of the term *Ordinary World* and the way other writing systems and experts use this term is quite important.

In the Your Storytelling Potential Method, the Ordinary World is *not* a place (even a conceptual one) that the Protagonist *leaves*, goes off on an adventure, and then returns to. The Ordinary World describes all aspects of the B-Story *before* the Transformative Event of the Main Character confronting the Primary Situation. And that B-Story world *must change* in some fundamental ways as an expression of the **TRANSFORMATION** that takes place in the Main Character. And once the world reflects that change, it's no longer the Ordinary World, it becomes your Main Character's Revealed Potential.

To fully understand this, let's talk about *Momentum* as another important reason to adjust your thinking on stories. Take another look at that traditional model Plotline. Notice how the line begins with something labeled *Beginning*? Playing devil's advocate for defenders of such systems, the Revealed Story you tell *does* have a literal beginning. It's not that the label *Beginning* is wrong, per se. But it is misleading. And it's no place to begin thinking about your story. If anything, a better term is **INTRO-DUCTION**, because you are introducing your readers and audience to the already existing Characters and Situations.

Your Main Character needs a rich B-Story history. Most of the crucial Elements of the Revealed Story that your Main Character will be accounting for during their confrontation with the Primary Situation *already exist* before the Revealed Story begins. With very few exceptions, your Main Character isn't born on page one (or, if they are, then almost certainly there is something relative to their lineage and inheritance prior to birth that makes their infancy relevant to the tale).

This brings us to another key foundational concept: **PREMISE**. Premise is another slippery narrative term, much like Theme. Do a little quick internet search for definitions of Premise as it relates to stories, and you will discover quite a range of supposed meanings from reputable authorities on the subject.

We are going to understand a Premise as a **FOUNDATIONAL IDEA**.

What's essential to understand is that a great Premise comes from the B-Story, *not* the A-Story!

In *Liar Liar*, Fletcher was a pathological liar *before* the movie begins. He has strained the relationship with his family and is divorced from his ex-wife *before* the movie begins. He has made a reputation with his firm as an unethical lawyer *before* the movie begins. And perhaps most important to the story that is told, he is a major disappointment to his own son, who is ready to make the wish that his father would only be able to tell the truth for 24 hours *before* the movie begins.

In *Die Hard*, John McClane has a rocky marriage with his wife *before* the movie begins. They have separated, and she has taken up residence in LA under her maiden name *before* the movie begins.

In *Star Wars* (Episode IV), Luke Skywalker was hidden from his father and the emperor and lives as a lowly farm boy *before* the movie begins. Obi-Wan Kenobi is hiding out on Luke's home planet so he can watch over Luke and be available to guide him if and when it becomes necessary *before* the movie begins.

In the Harry Potter books, Harry's parents were killed by Voldemort, and Harry was sent to live with his neglectful aunt and uncle *before* the first book begins. Harry survived Voldemort's attack, bonding them inexorably to one another and making Harry a legend in wizarding circles as "the boy who lived" *before* the first book begins.

We can go on and on. The point is truly strong: a *relevant* Hidden Past from the B-Story, before the Beginning of the Revealed Story in the Now, is *much more* than nice details to make your Main Character seem more like a real person. It is providing so much fuel to the story. It is not the case that your Main Character was living a nothing hum-drum life when—*WHAMMO*—some A-Story Plotline bomb dropped into their lap. And, thus, a "story" begins.

This pressure that comes to a head in the Revealed Story's Climax has been building for some time. The A-Story Primary Situation is a *catalyst* for a change that has been a long time coming.

The Revealed Story may be the most arresting, interesting episode in your Main Character's life, which is why you choose to tell that part of the story. But the function of the Revealed Story is to link the Hidden Past of your Main Character's Ordinary World to the **UNREALIZED POTENTIAL** of an Unknown Future:

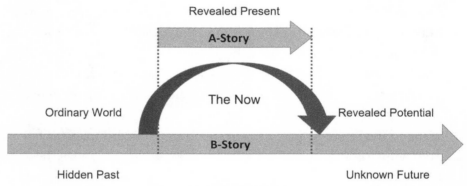

Figure 14: The Revealed Story

(NOTE: We refer to this Potential as either *Unrealized Potential* or *Revealed Potential* depending on our point of view relative to the timeline of the Revealed Story. In the Hidden Past, at the Beginning of the Revealed Story, and during the confrontation with the Primary Situation, think of this as the *Unrealized Potential*, because it is unfulfilled. Once the Main Character has undergone a Transition/Transformation through the events of the A-Story, then it becomes a *Revealed Potential* Just understand we are referring to the *same thing*!)

Let's take a look at several intellectual properties (IPs) and see how much of the story does *not* come from the Primary Situation in the Now. That means we are talking about the B-Story Underlying Cause. We just stated that these masterfully told stories have *Momentum*—this building pressure in the Main Character's life—from *before* the Revealed Story begins. There is an already existing bubble of narrative energy ready to burst. A *powder keg* ready to explode. We are focusing here on the ideas of the *Hidden Past* and that a truly great Premise comes from the B-Story.

Of course, we will begin that discussion in the place of this method's inception: insights from *Liar Liar*.

Powder Kegs and Premise Case Study I: *Liar Liar*

Liar Liar does *not* begin with Jim Carrey's Fletcher Reede deciding to attend law school. We do *not* meet him as a stable family man with an adoring wife and a son in whose eyes he can do no wrong. It is *not* the case that Fletcher from the Beginning of the movie wins a Humanitarian of the Year award or ministers to youth in his church on the virtue of honesty is the best policy. And this alternate version of Fletcher we're describing does *not* inherit the difficult divorce case because of his reputation of nobility, *nor* does it fall into his lap by random selection or a strange twist of fate. Finally, the movie does *not* begin with him demonstrating a strong sense of priorities, sacrificing a potential win at the office in favor of spending as much time as possible at home with those he loves.

On the contrary, the exact opposite of all of those things happens or is true.

Liar Liar's Fletcher Reede enters the movie divorced and with a long-standing reputation of dishonesty and bent ethics he uses to win law cases. The opening scenes establish that his son Max thinks his dad is a professional "liar" because he puts on a suit and goes to court. We can assume Max's confused terminology comes from things he's overheard his mother say. And once Fletcher breaks Max's heart by failing to show up for the boy's birthday party, Max spends his birthday-candle wish asking that his dad to not be able to lie for just one day.

As we have already discussed, the Primary Situation of *Liar Liar* is that Fletcher gets presented with an *Opportunity* to advance his career if he can win a divorce case on behalf of a cheating wife and neglectful mother over her wealthy but decent husband, a man who loves his kids. The only clear way forward to winning this case is to distort facts and suborn perjured testimony. That is the *new* thing happening in this story.

What about the son's magical wish that prevents Fletcher from lying for a day? Certainly, *that* is also *new*. It's definitely more incredible than simply being assigned a law case.

Here you must really resist the temptation to conflate new with *outstanding* or *unprecedented*. *Liar Liar* is a fanciful fairytale at heart. The forces at work that empower the magical wish are never explained. It's a birthday wish. It comes true. And we are not invited to explore the mechanics of that event. The story asks us to simply accept it.

The reason the wish aspect of the story stems from the B-Story and should be seen as coming from the Momentum supplied by the story's Hidden Past is that the wish comes from his *son*. As we already mentioned above, the son is already disappointed with his father; he's already prepared to make the wish and just needs to be let down one last time (which his father delivers because of the A-Story).

The audience accepts that the "magic" in the wish comes from the purity of a little boy's heart. The Desire for the wish is born from years of broken promises of a father continually disappointing his family. The wish is just the *latest* attempt by a family burned time and again attempting to get Fletcher to reorganize his priorities and put his family first.

Fletcher is divorced from his son's mother. She has done the pleading and has exhausted her willingness to argue. And now their son, Max, is making *his* appeal for his father's attention and love in a way that makes sense and feels available to him: spending his birthday wish on it. It's the endpoint of a crisis that has been building and leading here. Max's mom has moved on from Fletcher (although bound to him through Max). She has a new fiancé and plans to move with him to Boston and take Max with her.

It would be different, for example, if the mechanism of the magic were explained *and* the Resolution to the Problem involved some action by Fletcher to appease or conquer the magical force. If the Primary Situation was that Fletcher falls victim to a curse placed on him because his son acquires some enchanted talisman and there was no time limit element to it, it may not even matter what Fletcher's job was. He could do anything for a living. Or, if he's still a lawyer, the Author-Storyteller could just as well show Fletcher lose his case, get fired, and then never need to go back to his life as an attorney again. The focus of that story would be Fletcher figuring out *why* this magic spell works and what he needs to do to redeem himself in order to break it. The Primary Situation *could have been* defeating the magic.

But Fletcher does not defeat the magic. It's not the point of the story. The wish has a time limit, and once set, there is nothing to do but ride it out until the time expires on the wish. For the duration of the Revealed Story of *Liar Liar*, all Fletcher can *do* is take action to address the Opportunity in the A-Story Primary Situation. The B-Story's Underlying Cause is a major obstacle to being successful in handling the Primary Situation. He is powerless to take action with respect to the B-Story's Problem, except to confront *himself,* reprioritize his life, and establish a new relationship with those he cares about moving forward.

How about Fletcher's *job*? If the A-Story Primary Situation is about his job, doesn't *that* contradict the idea that there are two main stories at play? Isn't the A-Story already in Fletcher's life before this movie begins?

Answer: *no*.

We must exercise discernment as we parse the Elements of a story. Granted, the story of *Liar Liar* does not begin with Fletcher being hired or becoming a lawyer because he is already a lawyer before the Revealed Story begins. Specifically, however, the Primary Situation is the *law case*. Anything that describes Fletcher outside of the context of the law case itself is part of his life, and therefore, is B-Story.

Fletcher's reputation as an up-and-coming lawyer with the moral flexibility to do what it takes to win a case exists *before* the movie begins. As does his relationship with his secretary, which is another major Subplot in the Underlying Cause that contributes to the **THEMATIC LAYERS**. Fletcher has a great secretary. She has put up with his flaws and often compromised her own integrity to cover up his dishonest actions. She is his ultimate support system. But he has treated her in the same utilitarian, self-serving way that he has treated everyone important to him. He's taken her for granted. And once she discovers that there is a hex that keeps him from lying, she learns an insulting truth: despite her loyalty, Fletcher has lied *to her* about the reason why he denied her request for a salary increase. Of course, she quits on the spot, leaving him in the lurch, further impacting the A-Story case. More foundational material from the Hidden Past coming to wreak havoc on the unfolding Now.

So with all of this understanding about the Momentum from the B-Story Hidden Past creating an explosive Situation for the Revealed Story in the unfolding Now, here is the graphic representation of *Liar Liar's* major story threads plotted through time:

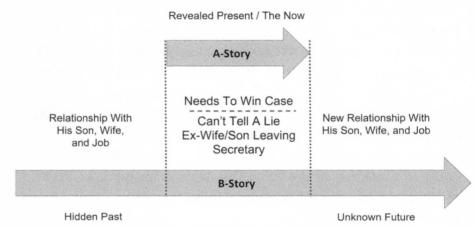

Figure 15: The Revealed Story of *Liar Liar*

This graphic emphasizes the concepts but obviously isn't exhaustive. There are more Subplots that add expression to the Thematic Layers of the A-Story/B-Story Convergence.

But you see how three of these four major components come from the B-Story while only the law case comes from the Primary Situation A-Story.

So what is the Premise of *Liar Liar*? What is the Foundational Idea?

We can strip the story down to its root in a single simple sentence:

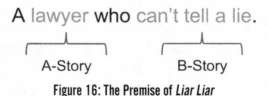

Figure 16: The Premise of *Liar Liar*

Bear in mind these are the simplified core concepts of the A and B Stories. As we have explained, the entire A-Story Primary Situation is truly a lawyer who must win *a specific case* on *a specific day*. And the B-Story's Underlying Cause is the Main

Character's major flaw that he is a pathological liar, which colors all of his relevant Hidden Past.

Powder Kegs and Premise Case Study II: *Star Wars*

Star Wars is a fantastic IP to consider for illustrating the principles of storytelling.

As noted in Chapter One, the very first *Star Wars* film from 1977 is subtitled *"Episode IV."* With the overt promise of an entire trilogy of prequel films, can there be any doubt just how important the Hidden Past of this story is? We absolutely know from Frame One of the movie that there is some sense we are joining this action *already in progress*.

"If there's a bright center to the universe, you're on the planet that it's farthest from."

Luke Skywalker laments his life with these words to his newly acquired robotic android companion C3PO on the day they meet. He could hardly announce his belief that he is a nobody, making no difference, any clearer.

Out there is a great, big galaxy where the action is. By this point in the story, we know there is an evil Empire. There is some black-armored space knight named Darth Vader who is a principal bad guy who ranks highly in that Empire. There is also a princess named Leia who has secreted away some unknown information into the pair of "droids" (in *Star Wars* lingo) now in Luke's possession. We also know that Luke is a lowly farm boy on what seems to be an insignificant backwater desert planet, helping his aunt and uncle to harvest whatever form of crops that grow in such barren conditions. It looks like a thankless, hard life. And he yearns for significance. He begs his guardians to let him apply to the academy so he can join the resistance, as his boyhood contemporaries have all done.

By all appearances, Luke *is* a nobody.

Spoiler alert for readers who've been in a coma since the 1970s—Luke, it turns out, is not just the soon-to-be hero of *Star Wars, Episode IV* (further subtitled *"A New Hope"*). Luke is about to discover that he is extraordinary. The absolute lynchpin to this entire galactic conflict. As a Skywalker, he is heir to a lineage with a special relationship to the mystical Force—a type of transcendent energy that flows from all living things, binds all things in existence, and has a powerful duality: Light and Dark. Over the course of the next two stories in the series, Luke will find out that his life on the desert world of Tatooine was not happenstance; he will have multiple mentors training him in the Force-mastering ways of the Jedi Knights, and he will learn a shocking truth about his relationship to Darth Vader.

The greatest parts of Luke's own B-Story are unknown to him at the beginning of Luke's adventure in Episode IV, but they already exist **before** the movie starts.

You should be thinking about stories in terms of an ongoing Underlying Cause, a B-Story that represents the major Elements of a Main Character's life. As the central figure of the original trilogy arc that defines what has become the greater *Star Wars* IP universe, it cannot be overstated how significant Luke Skywalker's family tree is. The SIZE to which that tree has grown, accounting for the canonical films and extended world of the associated novels and stories, is mind-boggling.

So what, then, is the Primary Situation of *Star Wars, Episode IV*?

Luke's Desire is to join the rebel alliance and make a difference in the fight against the evil Empire, and that specific A-Story begins with the *Opportunity* to get involved when his uncle purchases two droids salvaged while wandering the deserts of Tatooine. The droids, C3PO and R2D2, have some kind of data crucial to the rebels' chances of striking an important blow against the Empire. Fearing capture by the sinister Darth Vader, Rebel leader Princess Leia rids herself of the incriminating stolen data, smuggling it off her spaceship in the droids. She commissions them to bring the data to a man she knows should be an ally to the Rebel cause, a hermit on the desert planet Tatooine named Obi-Wan Kenobi—it's an act of faith and desperation. By pure chance (or will of the Force), the droids end up in Luke's possession, and he follows them to find Kenobi, ultimately leading to his joining Kenobi in his quest to deliver the droids to the Princess's allies.

Obtaining the droids and following them on their Journey to meet up with Obi-Wan Kenobi is the thing that is *new* in Luke's B-Story life. It's a Journey that does not complete until Luke becomes an indispensable part of the Rebel fighter corps and ultimately is the one to use the data stolen from the Empire to destroy its devastating *new* weapon, the Death Star. The Empire's construction and deployment of the Death Star is the Primary Situation that Luke must confront through the course of the Journey.

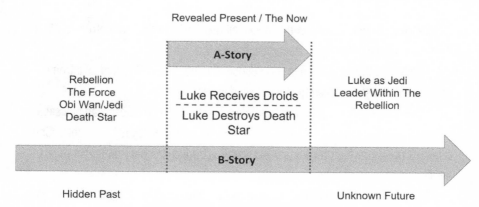

Figure 17: The Revealed Story of *Star Wars*

How about the Premise of *Star Wars, Episode IV*? What's the B-Story Foundational Idea upon which the story is constructed?

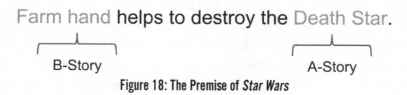

Figure 18: The Premise of *Star Wars*

As with our examination of the Premise in *Liar Liar*, we can expand the simplified Underlying Cause to encompass its entirety: *A farm hand with great potential in powerful mystical arts joins the forces opposing oppression in the Galaxy*.

Powder Kegs and Premise Case Study III: *Die Hard*

"Good Guy(s)" versus "Bad Guy(s)" action-adventure stories make it a bit easier on average to see the moving parts in the Your Storytelling Potential story model. The stakes are generally very clear. The audience easily identifies who the Main Character is, what the Primary Situation is, and understands the goals and **OBSTACLES**.

Nowhere is this more true than with the now-classic 1988 Bruce Willis star-maker *Die Hard*. Widely considered one of the all-time great action flicks, *Die Hard* features a deceivingly simple **SET-UP** or Introduction that allows it to move quickly into the action its audience pays to see. But the analysis of this film related to our various concept discussions in this book will demonstrate the story strengths in it that make such a powerful connection with viewers.

Relative to the discussion in this section, the focus is on *Die Hard* as a tremendous exercise in streamlined RELEVANT Hidden Past.

Willis's Character is John McClane. He is a New York cop whose wife has separated from him and moved with their children across the country to Los Angeles. She is now working for a high-tech financial securities trading company under her maiden name.

Truly, this is all the B-Story Introduction *Die Hard* requires. It absolutely sets the stage for the Revealed Present story.

What is the stage? A corporate Christmas party in an office high rise.

John is a blue-collar, old-school, bare-knuckle, technophobe. A real street cop. The life his wife has chosen is the polar opposite. Opposite coast. High tech firm. The glitz of LA steel and glass over the old world grime of New York.

We meet John on the flight to LA, where he's shown dealing with flight anxiety. Being out-of-sync with modern life will be a constant Theme for him throughout the series as he continually finds himself up against tech-savvy terrorists. In this first film, advice from a fellow traveler on a technique for coping with air travel anxiety causes him to remove his shoes to perform an exercise—significant as he ends up battling barefoot in a building littered with shattered glass. The fact McClane pushes himself out of his comfort zone from the get-go underscores his Desire to heal his marriage, speaks to how much his wife means to him, and humanizes him with an easily relatable goal that pulls the audience in and makes them care about what transpires. He's flawed, but he's trying. Hard. (Don't roll your eyes. Lighten up.)

He is there to capitalize on the goodwill and cheer of the Christmas season in an attempt to reconcile with his wife. The stage is significant: the Christmas party forces him to confront everything about her choices and new life. It's also the reason the building is so sparsely populated with fewer security personnel on duty, making it a target for the thieves posing as terrorists who seize the building. Be aware of Elements that accomplish multiple objectives in this way. Notice *Convergence*.

The Primary Situation in Die Hard could not be more front-and-center. Of course, it's Hans Gruber's team of thieves using terrorist tactics to isolate the Nakatomi Building and take the employees hostage.

Unlike steadfast heroic Characters like James Bond and Sherlock Holmes, John McClane **does** undergo a Transformation over the course of the story. As much as it is laudable that he makes the trip to reconnect with his wife and unify their family, his *initial goal* is to get her to give up her LA life and return to New York. Interestingly, the B-Story relationship that influences and expresses the progression of McClane's evolution is not his wife, Holly. The circumstance of the Primary Situation keeps John and Holly separated from one another with no means of communication for the majority of the film. Instead, after John makes contact with the authorities outside, he begins to form a connection with the first responding officer on the scene, Sergeant Al Powell. Knowing their conversations over the radios are not secure, McClane and Powell have a coded, heartfelt bonding conversation in John's most desperate and hopeless moments. And not only do we know he has shifted in his relationship with Holly, but we witness a lasting bond forged between the two men as well.

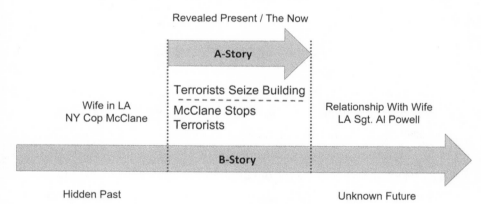

Figure 19: The Revealed Story of *Die Hard*

Many of the IPs we are studying in *Your Storytelling Potential* have strikingly unique Premises. At least they were groundbreaking at the time. Here, with *Die Hard*, we see a fairly simple Introduction that pits a cop against a gang of thieves making a heist. At that level, there's very little to it that's unprecedented. The film even makes reference to the long, long history of white-hat versus black-hat Western movies, with McClane adopting the satirical moniker "Roy"—for golden age movie legend Roy Rogers—while the terrorists don't know who he is.

As it turned out, *Die Hard* became a seminal film in the action genre, establishing a trend of action films pitting lone heroes against long odds in contained situations analogous to the Nakatomi Plaza building. It spawned the now-cliched story pitch in the form of "this is *Die Hard* on a cruise ship" or "this is *Die Hard* on a space station," etc.

But what truly separated this movie from the pack was its flawed, vulnerable hero with a clear, relatable goal. It has to be this *specific* Main Character in this *specific* Situation. The B-Story Elements are not complex, but they are rich. And they are very well executed by director John McTiernan and engaging performances by star Willis, Alan Rickman as bad guy Gruber, and Reginald Veljohnson as Powell.

A straightforward story, well told. As we see in the Premise breakdown:

NY COP visits his wife **when** terrorists seize a building.

B-Story   A-Story

Figure 20: The Premise of *Die Hard*

Our concentration in this chapter is seeing the Your Storytelling Potential model in practice. We are still at a fairly high-level conceptual viewpoint. *Die Hard*'s basic story Elements are easy to identify, but when we return to look at it in the context of further discussions on Theme and the Core Elements that give Structure to the Main Character's Journey—which we call the **CHARACTER WAVE** in this system—we will see the film has surprising depth and extremely well-integrated Thematic Layering.

Powder Kegs and Premise Case Study IV: *Rocky*

Sylvester Stallone has been a household name in movies for over five decades. With five direct sequels and a growing spinoff series of films, it is hard to think of *Rocky* as a small independent franchise. Each subsequent release has upped the ante on budget and scope of the story. It conjures images of grand battle royales and the opulent world of elite athletes. Very easy to associate *Rocky* with major tentpole franchises.

The original 1976 Best Picture winner was anything but a major tentpole film. With a modest budget, even for its day, at just $1.1 million and boasting a then-unknown star, *Rocky* was sold as a small tender love story featuring a down-and-out blue-collar palooka and an unglamorous introverted pet shop clerk. The original trailer features the rousing score by Bill Conti and plays the hook of Rocky's shot to fight for the world championship as an uplifting testament to the American Dream. But very little is made of Rocky's opponent. Carl Weathers' Character Apollo Creed, the heavyweight champion inspired by boxing legend Muhammed Ali, barely appears in the ad. From the first audiences learn about the film, there is no hope that Rocky will actually compete against Creed. Creed is an unclimbable mountain. Rocky's battle is with himself, just to survive and prove something to himself.

If the A-Story in *Die Hard* is prominent and easy to encapsulate, the A-Story in Rocky is the opposite, nothing but a date circled on the calendar in an inevitable finale.

Apollo Creed learns his next opponent has been injured while training for their upcoming title fight. Needing to scramble for an opponent to honor his obligation to defend the belt and lacking any bona fide contender ready to step in, Apollo hatches a plan to turn the fight into a curiosity by giving an unknown boxer a shot. There is no personal animus. Rocky's Opportunity arrives almost at random, with Apollo merely delighted by the unknown fighter's nickname, "The Italian Stallion." There really is no ongoing confrontation with the Primary Situation. A date is set. And as with all athletic competitions, all there is to do relative to the upcoming boxing match is to get prepared for it. For boxing fans, the spectacle of watching a live match holds its own engrossing drama. But as a story (where we realize the competition is necessarily fixed according to the needs of the Plot), there may be *some* suspense to see what happens in the fight, but there's little to engage the audience if they don't grow to care about the Character(s) engaged in the fictional event.

In other words, *Rocky* is almost *all B-Story*. It really underscores the appropriateness of thinking of your Main Character's B-Story, their personal ongoing life story, as an *Underlying Cause*.

Underlying Cause is the total focus of *Rocky*. Arguably, if Rocky's title shot were taken out of the film, there could be an equally compelling story about a struggling blue-collar ex-boxer finding love with Adrian and perhaps establishing a new identity outside of sports.

As we meet the titular Character, his life is in the gutter in so many ways. He lives on the tough streets of Philadelphia. He makes a living as low-level collection muscle for a second-rate loan shark. The loan shark's driver/bodyguard routinely skewers Rocky with degrading insults, seemingly just for the fun of getting a rise out of him. Rocky frequents a crummy neighborhood watering hole with his best friend, an ill-tempered drunk named Paulie. We meet Paulie in the bar's filthy men's room, as the stubby man grouses about having to comb his hair using the remaining shard of mirror still clinging to the wall. Their neighborhood is in decay. Rocky longs for Paulie's mousy sister, Adrian, who works in the little pet shop across the street from the boxing gym where Rocky trains. But with his eyes on the prize, this limited-skills boxer with low self-esteem works to rehearse jokes he hopes will win her attention and affection.

As a boxer, Rocky struggles. As he reveals to Adrian when they finally do go on a date, he was told from an early age that he doesn't have much of a brain, so he had better develop his body. His boxing is his identity. Yet, as the film opens, we see him lumbering along with poor technique, with another low-ranked club fighter getting the better of him until the man takes a cheap, illegal shot that enrages Rocky. Then the lion comes out, and Rocky quickly finishes his opponent with a burst of fury. He has heart and innate ability but has failed to develop himself—a symptom of not believing in himself. As an aging fighter going nowhere and a consistent disappointment in his criminal job, he loses his locker to a younger prospect when the gym owner and trainer, Mickey, has had enough with him.

Rocky is at his bottom.

Nonetheless, we root for him. Rocky's affection for Adrian is genuinely sweet. He defies his criminal boss and makes excuses about why he does not harm a delinquent paying client. He escorts home a teen girl he perceives is in jeopardy and running with the wrong crowd. He takes care of two turtles and a dog from the pet shop. He weathers insults from people he bears no ill will with indefatigable cheer. He's upbeat on life even while down on himself.

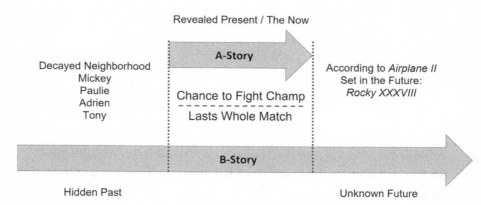

Figure 21: The Revealed Story of *Rocky*

As we noted before, the entirety of the Primary Situation of *Rocky* is (1) he gets offered the boxing match, (2) he trains and prepares for it, and (3) he shows up and fights with the hope of simply surviving until the final bell. The intensity and magnitude of the Opportunity and exertion needed to meet the challenge is all the transformative potential this particular A-Story needs.

All else in the movie is the exploration of his Underlying Cause. It's his ongoing B-Story life.

In this way, *Rocky* might be the structural and conceptual opposite of *Die Hard*. Recall in *Die Hard* we find the *relevant* B-Story to be quite simple and straightforward yet powerful. The A-Story is easily identified but involves a well-organized, ingenious criminal scheme and many life-or-death hurdles to overcome for the Main Character. That story works masterfully to get us to identify with the Main Character's life in a simple stroke, which creates the depth of story to elevate the material above its pulpier, complex, action-forward Primary Situation. By contrast, while the boxing action in *Rocky* has a certain thrill to it, the ultimate stakes in the greater game of life are low— it's *just* a sporting event. And it only takes up a few minutes of screentime, mostly all at the very end. But this story spends its time developing the complexity and depth of many B-Story strands to really bring the audience into its Main Character's limitations and what he must do to transcend them.

Now, to the Premise:

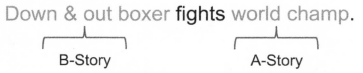

Figure 22: The Premise of *Rocky*

Our B-Story side of the equation really carries the load of the foundational *idea* "down-and-out boxer" in the simplest terms. But that summarizes the majority of the film, as we have just seen.

Powder Kegs and Premise Case Study V: *The Harry Potter* series

Much like the undeniable seminal quality of George Lucas's *Star Wars* franchise and its influence on the course of cinematic history and the rise of the popularity of the space opera, J.K. Rowling has ushered to the stage a fascination with young adult fantasy properties with her landmark Harry Potter book series.

We will revisit all of the IPs in this chapter for examples as needed in future discussions of new concepts as we build your understanding of the complete Your Storytelling Potential Method. Likely that will mean focusing on small story beats within individual Harry Potter books. For *this* discussion, however, we want to consider the Harry Potter story from the Beginning to the end of all seven books (or the eight movies based on them), namely the *superstructure*.

As with any series, the Potter series tells a single unified tale over the course of seven episodes. The series has a main overarching A-Story that unfolds by way of smaller A-Stories. Any single book is a complete story all its own—a new Situation arises and gets resolved, even while there is something *larger* that remains unresolved. And Rowling had the entire spine of it planned out before typing page one of the first book, *Harry Potter and the Sorcerer's Stone*. This is a tremendous example of A and B story Convergence. In the grand scheme, what links the seven episodes together is Harry's ongoing life. But the total saga of Harry Potter versus "He Who Must Not Be Named" (Voldemort) is itself the Primary Situation, namely the A-Story. The confrontation with The Heir of Slytherin is so central to the saga, it is practically inseparable. (Not unlike another example we already looked at, that of Luke Skywalker confronting his own father, Darth Vader!)

The first chapter of the first book chronicles the circumstances of how orphaned Harry comes to live with his abusive aunt and uncle, the Dursleys. Many B-Story seeds are planted in the form of context-less information that suggests there is more going on than ordinary folk like the Dursleys know about. Cats who can read maps and magicians who can sap light from street lamps. We realize we have entered a world of witches and wizards. There are allusions to a "You-Know-Who" having been killed while murdering two people, and that this baby, Harry, somehow miraculously survived the powerful attack.

So much boiling in the Hidden Past witch's brew of the Underlying Cause.

Beyond that, the story fast forwards to Harry at ten years old. He is ignorant of his wizard heritage. His world shifts radically when a giant named Hagrid visits with an acceptance letter to the wizarding school Hogwarts Academy. The remainder of the first book relates Harry growing to accept his place as a famous young wizard, making important connections that will aid him in his inherited duty to defeat the dark wizard to whom he is bound, and pursuing the legendary Sorcerer's Stone—which it is told can restore Voldemort's body.

The Big Picture of the Harry Potter series looks like this:

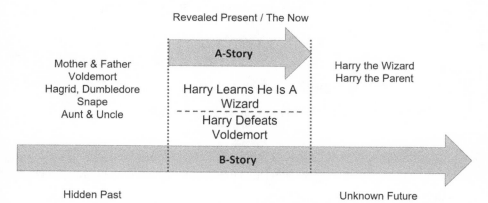

Figure 23: The Revealed Story of the *Harry Potter* Series

Each subsequent novel in the series moves forward incrementally in time to cover an adventure as we follow his struggle against Voldemort year-by-year progressing through Hogwarts. From the perspective of the *big picture* series story, the first book is merely the Introduction. If the major A-Story is "Harry must defeat Voldemort," it's noteworthy that Voldemort is virtually absent from the first book. He is talked about, and his presence is felt very late in the game. But the "Dark Lord" remains disembodied for a good portion of the series. He does not actually return incorporated until the end of the fourth book.

Obviously, the *rules* are subject to being bent when the story involves supernatural beings wielding mystical powers. There's little denying that Voldemort's presence is felt and his will impacts events throughout the entire story. But there is also no denying that the story of Harry Potter begins with a full head of steam powering the trains long before Harry arrives on Platform 9 ¾ for the first time.

The wizarding world, Hogwarts, the rise of Voldemort, the death of Harry's parents, the histories of many central Characters such as Dumbledore and Snape are all Subplots of Harry's B-Story in motion from before the Beginning of *Sorcerer's Stone's* Chapter One. A lot of Harry's Journey involves uncovering important events from his unknown past. This past is much more than a fun-to-read descriptive backstory. It rushes like a river down a mountain from a starting point we cannot see from here in the Now, driving the story forward in innumerable ways. Hidden Past impetus. (Rather similar to Luke Skywalker's own Hidden Past!)

Our final example of Premise coming from the B-Story for this chapter:

Figure 24: The Premise of the *Harry Potter* Series

The goal for these Premise breakdowns is to capture the foundational idea from the B-Story and the Primary Situation from the A-story. Both of which involve a Problem or Opportunity.

The Beginning Is Not the Beginning

Earlier in this chapter, we said the traditional **PLOTLINE GRAPH** label *Beginning* is misleading. A far more accurate idea is *Introduction*.

We have taken a look at five major IPs and have seen there is *so much* story already percolating before Chapter One of your novel, "Fade In" of your screenplay, or the lights go down and you step to the stage in front of an audience. The Primary Situation merely arrives as the pin to pop it or the match to ignite all the already existing energy. A *powder keg* ready to explode.

At the end of the A-Story—the Revealed Story—the landscape is changed forever.

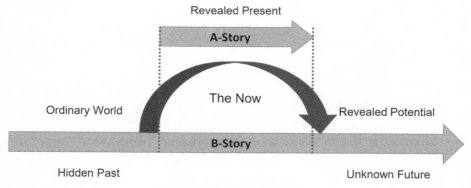

Figure 25: The Revealed Story

That "arc" is the period of Transition taking place in the Now of your story. It links the Hidden Past with an Unrealized Potential future. Creating that successfully is why an audience feels a level of fulfillment at the end of a well-told and complete story. The Author-Storyteller must know from where the story comes and where it is going.

The Introduction of your Revealed Story is not a place for events to start rolling. It's really a place where you *introduce* your audience to Characters and events already in motion.

————————

In this chapter, we examined the B-Stories of five IP examples to see how the Main Character's Hidden Past is already at work before the Transformative Event of the Now in the Primary Situation converges into a transformative experience resulting in an Unrealized Potential. We have also seen that Premise is a function of the B-Story.

In the next chapter, we continue the analysis of our foundational concepts as we consider the relationship between the Main Character's Personal Goal and your story's Theme.

CHAPTER 3:

Theme: The Conceptual War

In the previous chapter, we used our five major IP examples to discuss the Momentum your story receives from a properly fleshed-out Hidden Past in the B-Story. We saw how when the B-Story collides with the Primary Situation of an A-Story a Transformative Event occurs during a Period of Transition. And we also identified that a story's Premise comes from the B-Story, and we saw it in action working in our examples. Now we have a solid conceptual grasp of the interplay between the A and B Stories.

We're now ready for the third universal storytelling truth: Theme is not the *message* of a story, nor is Theme *some transcendent universal truth*.

In this chapter, we want to turn our attention to the third "blade" of the Revealed Story "propeller": *Theme*. Recall this image from the first chapter:

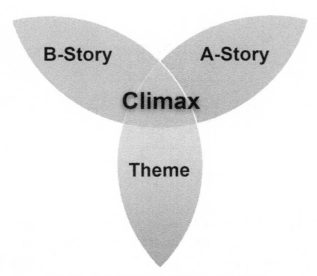

Figure 26: The Revealed Story/Inner World

This is the most challenging concept of how stories operate in the Your Storytelling Potential Method. The spotlight in this chapter is on Personal Goal and Theme. The Thematic element is the expression of the Main Character's Personal Goal.

We just said at the top that the material in the previous chapter gives you the conceptual mechanics for how the A and B Stories interact. That is true on a functional level. We need to go back to something we said in our brief overview discussion from the first chapter: while it's easy to understand that a Personal Goal *comes from* the Main Character, it is less intuitive to grasp that the Personal Goal is *expressed through* Theme, and that Theme itself finds expression in the intersection between the A and B Stories.

Recall that the propeller image is something created by the Venn-diagram overlap of our three Branches: Main Character, A-Story (or Primary Situation), and B-Story (or Underlying Cause). The top two blades of the propeller image come from the Character-Branch circle intersecting with the two A and B Story circles. Yet the Theme blade that extends below is produced by the intersection between only the A and B Branches. The reason this blade is formed by the overlapping of the A and B Stories is because Theme is the *glue* between the Primary Situation and the Underlying Cause.

So how does the Personal Goal get involved? Understand: we say that the Personal Goal finds expression *through* Theme. However, the Personal Goal is *not* the Theme! As a matter of fact, they are *opposites*: polar ideas arguing.

This concept will become more clear as we work our way through this chapter, but this is the critical area where the Author-Storyteller weaves their magic and demonstrates the complete understanding of their own *complete story*.

Let's start looking at what a Personal Goal is and then address Theme.

Personal Goal is rooted in the B-Story. It is the deepest Desire of the Main Character as it relates to the B-Story. The unique aspect of the Personal Goal is that it is specifically a function of the Main Character. The Personal Goal represents what we call an Opposing Idea.

Opposing Idea to what? Opposing Idea to the Theme, which is a function of the A-Story. In other words, this is how the B-Story opposes the A-Story on a conceptual, **THEMATIC LEVEL**.

By now it should be understood that the B-Story is the ongoing personal life of the Main Character. It stands to reason that if the Main Character has a Personal Goal, that goal has something to do with the course of events unfolding in their B-Story. As we described in the opening chapter, that goal may or may not be something tangible. More often than not, it is a notion—some type of Value they want to see win out and become a lasting part of their own personal world and experience. The B-Story reflects the Personal Goal simply because the B-Story *is* the Main Character's life story. And we would expect that a person's life story is largely shaped by the choices they make as they take positive action and/or react to their circumstances and events, assuming those choices are informed by their Desire.

Even when your Main Character is a self-destructive sort, as story analysts, we take the Values they *act upon* (self-destruction) as truly reflective of what they want rather than anything they espouse but do not live up to. It is less important what a Main Character *says* they want than what they actually pursue. Actions speak louder than words, right?

Now you may be asking the question, "From whence cometh Theme?" (You don't really talk like that, do you?)

If the Personal Goal arises from the B-Story as a function of the Main Character's life choices, what is the engine that provides the Opposing Idea? What drives the Theme?

Short Answer: *you!*.

The longer answer is this is the illusion of storytelling. A story has the appearance of randomly unfolding events. It is an artificial simulation of real life. But ultimately it is a craft. Would-be Author-Storytellers must develop skills weaving their tales. Learning the proper application of Theme is a challenge. It is easily overdone and far too often not done at all. The type of thing that, if it were easy to master, everybody would be doing it.

Making people conscious of this model for well-told stories is our true aim. Master these concepts, and you wield a great deal of power for increasing your odds of constructing amazing stories. It is not a guarantee. *You* remain the X-factor in the equation.

On a more practical level, the presence of Theme is a byproduct of well-built and *integrated Subplots*. Never forget the First Takeaway: *Convergence*. Deeper still, a Convergence that creates *Relevance*. Relevance is key. Theme is almost like a force of fate or a mystical hand in action in your story. It's an ethereal idea that shapes the unfolding of events in the A-Story in such a way as to challenge the Personal Goal in the B-Story. We are not talking about the presence of a deity in your story's world—except *you* as the creator of that world.

Properly integrated Thematic-based Subplots complete the trifecta of three-dimensional storytelling. A-Story, B-Story, and *relevant* Theme. *All* Subplots are linked to the A and B storylines through a relevant Theme, meaning all Subplots are a byproduct of the Theme Branch of our propellor image:

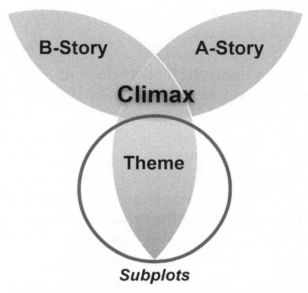

Figure 27: Subplots a Byproduct of the Theme Branch

This all folds back in on itself as we must understand that our task is placing the *right* Main Character into the *right* story. Therefore, although the Main Character's Personal Goal has the appearance of springing from within them naturally, as Author-Storytellers, we must remain conscious of creating our Main Characters with *relevant* Personal Goals. We create our Main Characters to have the semblance of life. To be three-dimensional, flesh-and-blood. In some way, we need our audience to connect with our Main Characters. And we want the Main Character's choices, reflecting their Personal Goal, to feel natural. However, we must engage in a bit of reverse-engineering to ensure that, whatever the Personal Goal, it is something that can and will be tested by the Primary Situation.

In reality, *most* stories are going to be constructed from an idea that begins at the A-Story level and we dig down to the deeper B-Story and Thematic levels. So we find Main Characters and infuse them with Personal Goals that *matter to* the A-Story. In the end, we are going to find this is all a very creative, iterative process—continually modeling and reworking, like a sculptor with clay. It's a process guided by this awareness and *not* a linear beat sheet formula.

Theme and the Core Elements

We have to fast-forward here a bit for this next portion of the discussion. As integration is a theme of the Your Storytelling Potential Method, it should come as no surprise that one of the challenges presenting this material is knowing where to start. Good storytelling requires every part to contribute to the Structure, and removing any one part causes it to fall. Or if you think of something that is integrated as a feedback loop, then you see why sometimes, to get a conceptual grasp, you just have to jump in at various points and discover what is going on.

We must emphasize this very important point, because this method is about the interplay of many Elements, and the only way *in* (so-to-say) is to jump into the story somewhere and see what is going on. Most writers struggle because they are trying to fit things into a procedure, and that is *not* what this is. It is also why most other writing books and systems leave one dazed and confused with all the stuff about "acts" and "beats" because approaching your stories that way is like trying to drive across a country without a map or any navigation.

Since we take our first immersed look at Theme in this chapter, we need to introduce the entire Core Elements "tree." Obviously, there are more in-depth discussions about the Core Elements to come. For now, let's take a look at the Twelve Core Elements as we think of their relationship to the three Branches of a story:

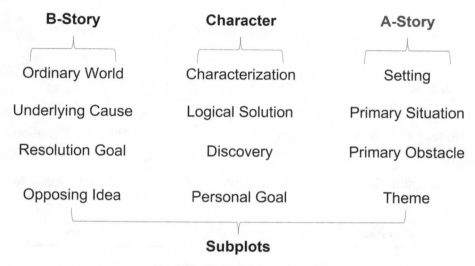

Figure 28: The Twelve Core Elements

What you should notice about the Twelve Core Elements tree is that there are four Core Elements in each Branch. As that would suggest, each Element has a relationship to the corresponding Elements in the other Branches at the same level. For example, Ordinary World (B-Story), **CHARACTERIZATION** (Main Character), and **SETTING** (A-Story) all represent Elements of the Revealed Story.

But these are not the only relationships that exist among the Elements. For the purpose of this specific discussion of Theme, we're going to focus on just five:

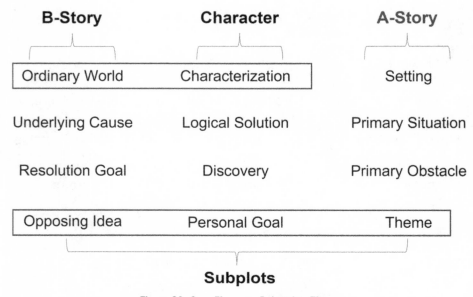

Figure 29: Core Elements Related to Theme

Notice the following highlighted Elements from the tree.

- Ordinary World
- Characterization
- Opposing Idea
- Personal Goal
- Theme

These are the Thematic Core Elements.

Don't get us wrong. Because of the principle of Relevance, Theme impacts all aspects of a truly well-told story. But these five Elements are the most closely, *most directly* related to the Theme blade of the Revealed Story propeller.

As we build out our stories, we likely begin at an A-Story level and work out a relevant, rich B-Story. We *find* our Theme emerging in the interplay between the two.

On the time graph we see:

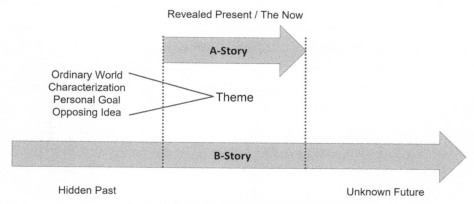

Figure 30: The Complete Story Theme Time Graph

This identifies the four Elements present in the Hidden Past, all of which converge in the Thematic idea in the Now. Rather than attempting to develop these Elements separately, the more profitable path is to discover that Thematic Idea while looking through the window of the A-Story at the B-Story. Once the Thematic Idea is defined, then you want to build backward towards these four supporting, interrelated Elements. Theme informs choices while building a *relevant* Ordinary World, a *relevant* Characterization, a *relevant* Personal Goal, and a *relevant* Opposing Idea.

More than once we have spoken about key differences between the Your Storytelling Potential Method approach and the vast majority of story building instruction systems. Certainly, for those who have studied screenplay writing, there is a near-universal mandate to keep dialogue lean. Likely you have encountered admonitions about keeping dialogue terse, with every line moving the story forward.

Is this what we actually observe in the best well-told stories? Certainly not.

Understand that what we are about to say here is *not* permission to load stories with inane, rambling dialogue. Dialogue works best when it is on-point. And there is a danger for neophyte storytellers to want to assert their originality by "breaking the rules" right out of the gate. It's seductive to look at a scene like the "subtle differences between America and Europe" conversation between Jules and Vincent in Quentin Tarantino's *Pulp Fiction* and make the mistake of thinking it justifies giving your Characters license to blather about nonsense. Crawl before you walk. Walk before you run. Tarantino is a master who accomplishes much with such flourishes. And it has to be handled so very well to work. Definitely an exception to the "rules."

That said, we do have a contention that runs a bit counter to the traditional view: there really are *two* types of dialogue. There is **A-STORY DIALOG** and there is **B-STORY DIALOG**. And it is the Thematic Core Elements that provide the true depth and richness to the B-Story that can then be expressed with rich, deep, *relevant* and meaningful dialogue.

Understanding the difference between the two types of dialogue is key to unlocking the potential to write great dialogue. With A-Story Dialog, you do want to give preference to terseness. Efficiency without losing the humanity in it. But there are countless examples of truly indispensable conversations in great movies that do little in a practical sense to move the story forward; this is characteristic of a thematically rich B-Story Dialog.

There really is room for thematic dialogue. Of course, the absolute sweet spot is dialogue that manages to accomplish both simultaneously. But that is often dictated by the needs of the story, the organic unfolding of events at a given moment. There are going to be moments in a story where the Main Character needs a tool (literally or figuratively) to accomplish a task. And in those moments there is little room to say much of anything that is not to-the-point. Other times, there may be respites from the driving Plot. The Main Character and their compatriots have just left the field of battle, perhaps they are in-hiding licking fresh wounds. And the time has come for deep soul searching and exchange of viewpoints. A mentor gives counsel. Depending on the type of story, there may be a need for an infusion of a fresh perspective, sometimes by way of a seemingly unrelated conversation topic. Possibilities are endless. *At times* it is appropriate for Characters to talk at-length and in-depth.

Remaining conscious of these thematic ideas affords the Author-Storyteller the ability to employ double entendres that accomplish something practical *and* consciously or subconsciously touch on thematic ideas at another level.

Theme: The Conceptual War

Theme is an expression of an *idea* and *value* that comes from the A-Story.

The Opposing Idea is the opposite of the idea expressed in the Theme and represents the *opposing value*. The Opposing Idea comes from the B-Story and informs the Personal Goal. The A-Story offers one idea but the Main Character believes something else. The outcome of this polarity war for the Main Character's belief system—perhaps for their soul—defines the nature of the period of Transition.

The "battleground" where the struggle between the Theme and the Opposing Idea takes place is in the Subplots.

Positive and Negative

The Theme and the Opposing Idea each express a *Value*. One **POSITIVE VALUE** (good for the Main Character) and one **NEGATIVE VALUE** (bad for the Main Character).

These are not necessarily moral judgments. When we say "positive" or "negative," there is no appeal to social norms, or philosophical arguments, or religious pronouncements. It is up to the Author-Storyteller to assign these Values. How this **THEMATIC CONFLICT** is framed and how it plays out provides the forum for the storyteller to make *their* point, to deliver *their* message, or to contribute *their* insight to an ongoing public discussion of a topic.

Earlier we identified the five **THEMATIC ELEMENTS**. And we said that *four* of them exist in the Hidden Past. The Main Character enters the Revealed Story in the Now bringing with them a pre-existing Personal Goal. Their outlook relative to the B-Story Underlying Cause. Once the Revealed Story gets rolling, we see the conceptual timeline shift to this:

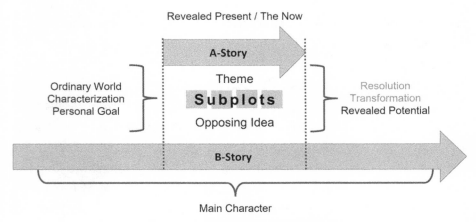

Figure 31: The Theme Revealed in Subplots

Resolution and *Transformation* are actually a part of the ongoing Revealed Story, meaning that they are not truly unknown (as will be explained fully in Chapter 9). The Revealed Story concludes with answers for these, which act as a springboard into the Unknown Future. The effects of the Resolution and the Main Character's Transformation are felt in the Revealed Potential of the Unknown Future. They are both part of the story's conclusions *and* the future we extrapolate after the story concludes.

We reemphasize the idea that A-Stories are windows to larger B-Stories. The Author-Storyteller's mission is to bring their audience into the world of the grand B-Story by glimpses looking through the limited A-Story. In the above graphic, we now see that the Opportunity to peek at the B-Story comes by way of Subplots.

The Your Storytelling Potential Method pushes you as a story creator to expand your thinking about the size and scope of your stories. All of this Hidden Story construction and reliance on Relevance may feel like a lot of "work." The *payoff* for this expanded work comes when you recognize that you don't need to struggle so much with Subplots. When you see them as essential and understand how they function—not as secondary threads to divert action from the main story, not just interesting interlude breathers from the main action—the challenge becomes *editing* your story *down*. Screenwriters know the Second Act struggle to fill the expanse of

45-60 or so pages between a Beginning they know well and an ending they know well. There is *much* more to learn about the practical nuts and bolts of executing your A-Story, but even now you should begin to see that delivering a well-told story demands a lean, effective technique. No padding and nothing irrelevant.

Subplots function as an intermediary between the A and B storylines with Theme functioning as the relevant binding agent. These opposing thematic forces push and pull on the Main Character throughout the period of Transition.

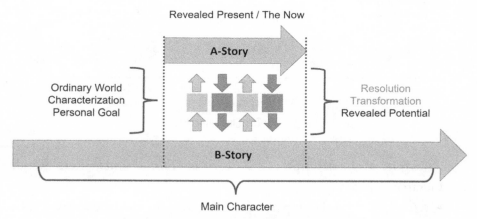

Figure 32: The Opposing Thematic Forces in Subplots

The motion created by that conflict of Theme versus Opposing Idea acting on the Main Character during the forward Momentum of the story creates what we think of in this system as the *Character Wave*.

Traditional methods call this concept the "***CHARACTER ARC***." Either way, we are describing the Protagonist's *transformative Journey* from the Beginning to the end of the story. Our belief is that the *Character Wave* is a superior notion. An "arc" suggests a smooth curve between a Beginning point and an ending point. Proponents of Character Arc might say it is just a way to broadly speak about Transformation without regard for the actual path of the intermediate Journey. But it certainly holds the danger of implying to writers that all *Character Arcs* are essentially the same.

A full understanding of the Character Wave requires a much deeper detailed discussion. That is coming in later chapters. The thing to hone in on for now is this Main Character mindset motion created by the Thematic Idea conflict:

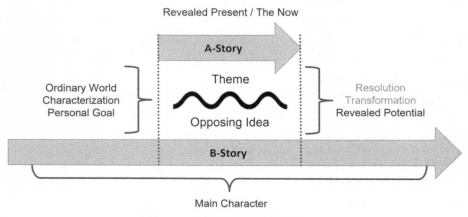

Figure 33: The Character Wave

Take note of the descriptor of B-Story as *Main Character* here. Recall the hierarchy of sorts:

- A-Story is the Now part of the B-Story (defined by a new Problem or Opportunity through to the Resolution of that Problem or Opportunity, which occurs at the story's Climax).
- The grander B-Story is truly the Main Character's ongoing life from before the Revealed Story begins and persists after it ends. And for darker stories where the Main Character does not survive, then it becomes the impact of the Main Character on their world and the lessons that we take away, which survive past the Main Character's death.
- The underpinning of the B-Story is therefore the Main Character. Their Personal Goal and Characterization shape their choices and actions, shaping the course of the B-Story. They are therefore indispensable to an effective A-Story.

It comes down to a **UNIQUELY EXTRAORDINARY MAIN CHARACTER**.

The goal in this process is to identify a Main Character who is *Uniquely Extraordinary*. Great stories are not about just anyone, rather they are about a Main Character that is ideal for the story you are telling.

We start with the ideas that light the A-Story powder keg and drill down until we find the *relevant* Main Character. From this point of view, the Main Character is the bedrock of well-told stories. We get to shape the Main Character by going through the A-Story to the B-Story by way of *relevant* Subplots. And again, this is all a creative process of *discovery*—we are not saying that you must have a perfect and complete A-Story before you can begin to shape the B-Story and ultimately the Main Character. The A-Story is a starting point and we use these concepts as a compass as we work and rework our story towards coherence.

Let's take a look at the relevant Main Characters from our major example IPs.

Uniquely Extraordinary Main Character Case Study I: *Liar Liar*

We have been discussing the principle of Relevance that *must* be present at the *Thematic Layer* of a well-told story. Relevance lies at the heart of every aspect of a story in the Your Storytelling Potential Method view. But here we are narrowing our focus to Theme. With the example case studies in this chapter, we aim to illustrate the necessity of *relevant* Main Characters with *relevant* Personal Goals and how they are integral to a functioning Thematic Conflict.

For each of these examples, we want to identify the Theme and its Opposing Idea. We name the Personal Goal for the Main Character in each IP. And we see the A-Story's Primary Situation Theme expression versus the B-Story Underlying Cause Opposing Idea expression at odds with one another. And it will be clear that the conflict between the Theme and Opposing Idea informs the Main Character's relevant Personal Goal.

As usual, we begin our example examinations with Liar Liar

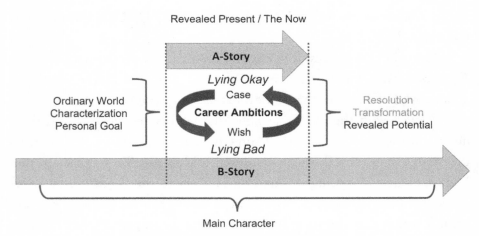

Figure 34: Main Character Thematic Conflict in *Liar Liar*

Why is Fletcher Reede a Uniquely Extraordinary Main Character?

It's no secret the Theme of *Liar Liar* is *honesty*. Recall the first chapter discussion about logline vs high-concept vs Primary Situation? We said the high concept for *Liar Liar* is "a lawyer who can't tell a lie." You can practically hear the writers in the pitch meeting and feel the buying executives' excitement. It's fair to say the general public holds a dim view of the legal profession. From that high-concept pitch, the temptation is to think an Author-Storyteller could literally fill out the Main Character's backstory any way they wish at random—so long as the Main Character passed the *bar* exam— and they would have the makings of a successful comedic tale.

For many reasons, this is just not true.

First off, unless we allow ourselves to be blinded by our ugliest prejudices, we do not profit by painting any demographic with a broad brush. It's simply unfair to hold a position that there are no ethical attorneys. Even if we believe the modern justice system promotes dishonesty, as a rule, we also accept there are always exceptions to the rules. And there is nothing to communicate if the issue is so thoroughly settled at the outset. Lawyers are people. They represent a cross-section of us. If their stories are worthy of being told, it is our task to find their relatable humanity and represent it as fairly as possible. Hopefully, this isn't truly an argument that needs to be made.

If the concept of a lawyer who cannot tell a lie has comedic promise, then the A-Story Situation that exploits that concept *must* place honesty at the center of its

Premise. There is no problem for a lawyer committed to unvarnished truth if there is no demand to lie. The ideal way to exploit the concept of a lawyer who cannot tell a lie is to place them in a Situation of having to argue a legal case that (at least seemingly) cannot be won on the merits of the facts. The clear way forward, in this *case*, is to suborn perjury and distort facts. A serious obstacle for an ethical attorney, but a cakewalk for a pathological liar.

We have already established in previous chapters' discussions of *Liar Liar* that Fletcher's son's birthday *wish* comes from the B-Story. It **is** the Underlying Cause. Yet, it can be safely assumed that the spark of inspiration for this story did not begin with the magic wish, rather it likely began with the "lawyer who cannot tell a lie" concept. The specific mechanics of how some attorney became unable to lie was likely a part of a creative discovery process.

And if we imagine that the development of this story began with the A-Story's difficult court case before writers Stephen Mazur and Paul Guay came up with any notion of a fanciful birthday wish, then the possibilities for how Fletcher's disgruntled son might have dealt with his frustration over his father's screwed up priorities become limitless. Rather than a magic wish to prevent his dad from lying, his son might just as well run away from home. Or hide Fletcher's case files in a treehouse. Or set booby traps to prevent his dad from making it to work.

It quickly becomes clear how perfectly matched the Primary Situation and the Underlying Cause should be at the Thematic level.

And we must have an equally well harmonized Personal Goal. Fish-out-of-water stories are compelling. Protagonists-in-the-wrong-story stories are not compelling. We said it in the initial *Liar Liar* discussion, and it bears repeating: all of the trouble this magic wish gives Fletcher Reede in his ability to win the case that will further his career does not mean much if Fletcher doesn't really care about his career.

There are things Fletcher cares about outside his career. The audience doesn't much care about a thoroughly unlikeable and irredeemable Main Character. He does want to bond with his son and is a fun dad to be around. He's not a violent guy nor does he have a laundry list of ugly habits. He simply places his career in the #1 slot on his priorities list, and he justifies unethical, dishonest behavior to achieve his career goals. It's very likely that, in Fletcher's Mind, he is doing right by his family and those he cares about by achieving as much as he can in his career. *Career ambitions at all costs* is his Personal Goal and makes him the perfect Main Character for *Liar Liar*'s Theme.

As the graphic above illustrates, the Opposing Idea of *Liar Liar* is that lying is justifiable in certain circumstances—such as winning an important law case—versus the Theme that lying is wrong—embodied within his son's wish. And this conflict revolves around Fletcher's career ambitions, which he sees as Priority #1 supporting all other priorities in his life.

To reinforce this point on relevant Main Characters with relevant Personal Goals to express a Theme, let's run a thought experiment:

What if...

*It was just about some random lawyer who can't
tell a lie for some other reason?*

Is *Liar Liar* the same movie if the lawyer is basically ethical and only occasionally bends the rules in extreme circumstances? The type of person who may make a compromise but agonizes over it?

Part of what makes Jim Carrey's performance so funny is the absolute cavalier way he sees truth as completely dispensable for the most trivial reasons. Fletcher is an extreme pathological liar. This is a guy who desperately *needs* this cosmic lesson.

How about the wish? What if we keep Fletcher more or less the same, but instead of knowing anything about his family life, we simply see him run over the foot of a carnival mystic who places a curse on him, and that is why he cannot tell a lie? Or if he has to argue the case in front of the judge with lie-detecting powers, as we mused in the first chapter discussion? There are countless ways to craft the story to capitalize on the "lawyer who can't tell a lie" concept.

Doesn't the purity of a child's wish and the family connection truly lend this story an immeasurable amount of resonance? Don't we truly root for Fletcher to have the moment of **CLARITY** this Situation offers and make the Transition to honesty as the best policy *because* of the connection to his son? Doesn't this speak to our near-universal Desire to see families come together?

Fletcher is the right Main Character to undertake this particular transformative Journey. He is the Uniquely Extraordinary Main Character to explore these **THEMATIC IDEAS**. It *has* to be Fletcher and *nobody* else.

Uniquely Extraordinary Main Character Case Study II: *Star Wars*

When we say, "it **has** to be *this* Character, and no one else," it *really* applies to Luke Skywalker. He is one of two Main Characters in the five major IP examples we feature throughout this book we might consider to be an *Anointed Main Character*.

In the broad scheme, the idea that the Main Character must be indispensable to the story must be *figuratively* true. The makeup of the Main Character and their Personal Goal is perfect for the Thematic Idea. They are suited to experience this Transformative Event.

But Luke Skywalker is a breed of Main Character that enters the challenge of the A-Story as a birthright. In his case, it is *literally* true that no one else can be the Main Character of *Star Wars*. The audience does not know it at the outset, but there are mystical forces at play long ago in the galaxy far, far away. Luke comes from a special lineage. He is the fulfillment of ancient prophecy. Interestingly, we know this because of events that unfold in the further adventures after *Episode IV*, the first-released film from 1977.

The temptation, therefore, might be to question whether Luke is a relevant Main Character. If he is born into this, is there freedom to mold such an anointed Main Character any way we choose and ignore the Thematic concerns?

Definitely not!

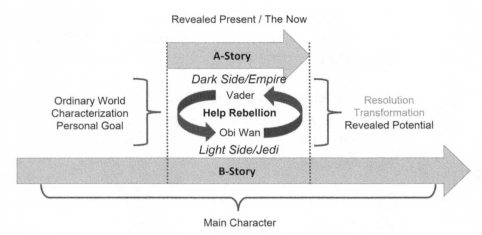

Figure 35: Main Character Thematic Conflict in *Star Wars*

Luke has no idea he is special. He does not know who his father is. He has never heard of the Jedi or the Force. He has never seen a lightsaber. "Ben" Kenobi is a crazy old hermit everybody knows lives by himself in a remote location. The Empire is some distant reality. It's an oppressive government and there are stories of rebel fighters opposing it. He lives an unremarkable life with an aunt and uncle struggling to make a living as farmers on an out-of-the-way barren desert planet. As a young man coming of age, Luke is simply eager to break out of this small life into a larger world of adventure. He wants to matter. He supports the idea of rebellion and longs to follow in the footsteps of his peers, who have run off to join the forces in the fight.

Like any story, *Star Wars* has many thematic ideas running through it. But when we consider its main Theme in the way we do within *Your Storytelling Potential*, there are no ideas larger and more prevalent than war. Conflict itself.

Star Wars is epic. Massive scale. What lies in the balance is not a border, or a dispute between countries, or the fate of everyone on a given planet. It is literally a war for the freedom of the Galaxy! The sides are clearly drawn: Empire vs Rebels, tyranny vs freedom, *evil vs good*. Darth Vader and his master, the Emperor, mean to rule with an iron fist. They command vast resources. They are cloaked in black. And they wield a mystical power called the Dark Side of the Force. Their opponent, the Rebels, is a ragtag outgunned and outnumbered alliance. They are the marginalized remnants of the Old Republic where freedom and democracy were cherished. And there are but a handful of masters of the Light Side of the Force—the Jedi Knights—remaining.

Distill it down to its core, and it is clear that the true Theme of *Star Wars* is *The Force* itself. This becomes even more evident in the follow-up episodes once Luke learns Darth Vader is his father and that Vader and The Emperor are engaging in a psychological campaign to turn him to the Dark Side. In this introductory *Episode IV*, the Dark Side is represented by Darth Vader and the Light Side is embodied by Luke's mentor Obi-Wan Kenobi. Kenobi, we learn, was once Vader's teacher in the ways of the Force before Vader turned to the Dark Side.

The Force, as George Lucas defined it, stands for religious mysticism in this Galaxy. It is akin to Eastern religious traditions here on Earth, where the view is essentially pantheistic—everything is one in a spiritual sense. The proponents of The Force in *Star Wars* describe it as an energy field generated by all living things that unites the universe. It should come as no surprise that the events in these stories unfold according to a principle of finding and maintaining a *balance* in the Force. There are no coincidences in these stories. The Force orchestrates events as they should be.

Now that you have come this far into the Your Storytelling Potential Method and understand its two-story approach, what would you say is the Primary Situation of *Star Wars*?

It should be clear the A-Story of *Episode IV* is *to deliver R2D2 to the Rebel alliance*. That's it. R2D2 has the blueprints for the Empire's Death Star in its memory banks. Princess Leia has outrun the pursuit of Darth Vader's Imperial Death Star ship to the orbit of Tatooine, the planet where she knows the hermit Kenobi lives in exile. Knowing she is a prominent target of the Empire, in an act of desperation, she loads the crucial data into the little droid and dispatches it to the planet's surface with instructions to locate Obi-Wan. From there it is pure chance that R2D2 and his companion droid C3PO end up in Luke's possession.

Recall how closely Luke comes to never receiving this Opportunity to join the fight. R2D2 gets captured by Tatooine scavengers called Jawas who repair droids and equipment and resell them to the locals. When Luke's uncle Owen does business with the Jawas, he makes a deal for C3PO and a different R2 unit. And just as they complete the transaction, that R2 droid blows a circuit (or "motivator" in Lucas-jargon), and they are forced to settle for R2D2. It's a small, somewhat humorous moment that illustrates how The Force pulls the strings on events in this world.

Notice there is nothing inevitable about Luke's specific Journey. When we first meet Luke, he pleads with his uncle to allow him to leave to join the "academy" where he can become a pilot for the Rebels. Luke exudes youthful exuberance and idealism. Ironically, if Luke gets his way, it's likely he never realizes his potential. If he were to join the academy in the traditional way, as a nameless recruit, no doubt he would spend time in a training class learning traditional combat techniques and how to fly the Rebel's X-Wing and Y-Wing fighters. He would start at a low rank as a face in the crowd. A foot soldier on the front lines. He would neither learn about his heritage nor the ways of the Force and the Jedi.

Instead, a fate guided by The Force sweeps Luke up into high adventure. It brings him to Kenobi. It sets him on a crash course with Vader and the Emperor. It elevates him to a key position within the Rebel alliance. He acquires special skills and possesses crucial data. It also places him in the jeopardy of falling prey to the Dark Side—to either be destroyed by it or seduced into it. That starting point, Luke's Personal Goal of wanting to HELP THE REBELLION, which reflects his innate goodness and drive to take action, is the quality that will determine his fate.

BUT...

What if...

It was just some random space farmhand who came across the droids and brought them to Obi-Wan?

Or what if Lucas had a different concept for how The Force works—if it were merely passive magic that good guys and bad guys use—then perhaps that first R2 unit makes it inside Uncle Owen's place and R2D2 gets sold to the next family down the road. Or R2D2 might have been discovered by any random occupant of Tatooine traveling across the open desert before the Jawas capture him.

In some alternate reality, we can imagine Luke joins the academy and fades into obscurity. Han Solo is living on Tatooine at the time, and he's an enterprising guy looking to make a score. Maybe a Character like Han finds R2D2 and brings him to Kenobi looking for a reward. The film loses its young trainee and mentor dynamic in favor of a buddy adventure between a roguish space pirate and an old wizard dude.

Rather, Luke is not ordinary; he is *Uniquely Extraordinary*. His father is Darth Vader. His sister is Leia. Obi Wan is there specifically to watch over him. And *that* is his B-Story!

Without a sense of that larger B-Story, George Lucas could have had the essential bones of the Episode IV story with Han Solo and Ben Kenobi and no greater vision for a conflict with Darth Vader than two space wizards duking it out with lightsabers and magic. The significance of The Force could be lost in favor of the spectacle of brightly colored lasers blasting spaceships into oblivion.

For all the grand stakes of *Star Wars*—the outcome of a war for freedom of the Galaxy and what causes audiences to connect with it is—the idealistic purity of its naive young hero being placed at the center of a war for his soul. Will he become a master Jedi and restore balance to The Force, or will he follow his father's fate and be consumed by the Dark Side?

In the wake of *Star Wars* came countless rip-off space operas. Most of them have faded into forgotten film history. They make a buck because of an appetite for interstellar adventure stories whetted by the success of *Star Wars*. We have to wonder what its legacy would be without Luke Skywalker and the Force at its heart.

Uniquely Extraordinary Main Character Case Study III: *Die Hard*

"*Die Hard* is a simple action movie."

That statement is *false*.

On one level, it has all the essential hallmarks of an action movie. Good Guy with Guns comes up against a team of Bad Guys with Guns. Good Guy with Guns is going to shoot his guns better than Bad Guys with Guns, and keeps shooting Bad Guys with Guns until there are no more Bad Guys with Guns—and, of course, the Leader of the Bad Guys with Guns dies last. Simple, we've all seen that movie before.

Recall the second chapter discussion of *Die Hard* on Premise and the building of narrative Momentum coming from the Hidden Past. We said that the Introduction of *Die Hard* is uncomplicated and gets to the conflict action quickly.

We also said that *Die Hard* does an exceptional job with its Thematic Layering. It's here we believe this film elevates its pulpy popcorn-munching Premise to distance it from its peers and subsequent imitators.

Liar Liar has an extremely easy Theme to identify: Honesty. It's implied in the title.

If Vegas were taking bets today, however, we would place money that you would not successfully pinpoint the Theme in *Die Hard*. If you know the film—especially if you feel you know it well—think about what the Theme is before looking at our graphic breakdown of the Theme to follow:

Main Character Thematic Conflict in *Die Hard*

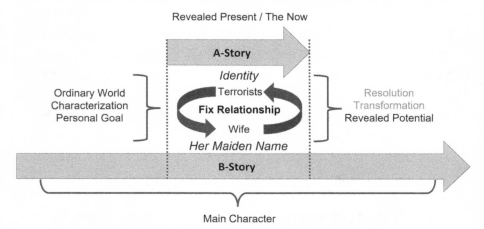

Figure 36: Main Character Thematic Conflict in *Die Hard*

How did you do? Did you get it?

In the Your Storytelling Potential Method, there is no question that the main Theme of *Die Hard* is *identity.* The whole movie is an elegant ballet of Characters wielding *identity* with power, concealing *identity* for protection, and digging to discover *identity* to gain advantage.

From the moment John McClane arrives, his entire B-Story is framed by his wife's use of her maiden name and the *identity* she has elected to use in her profession. He does not realize she has gone back to using her maiden name, Holly Gennaro. She explains in their one brief conversation before the hostage crisis that a Japanese company will assume a married woman to have other priorities than her job, hence the decision to present herself as single.

Hans Gruber's crew seizing the Nakatomi Plaza building and taking the corporation's employees hostage is the Primary Situation. For the majority of the cat-and-mouse conflict with John McClane, Gruber does not know *who* McClane is. Doesn't know his name, doesn't know his skill set, and, most importantly, doesn't know that McClane is related to one of the hostages.

John uses his skills to conduct a small-scale guerilla warfare to thin out the hostage-takers, seizes an automatic weapon to even the odds, and obtains one of their coded walkie-talkie radios to monitor their communications. Part of his strategy is reconnaissance: gather as much intel about who these guys are and pass that information to the authorities when he can. Once he decides the time has come to break radio silence, the first conversation he has with Hans is entirely preoccupied with *identity*. He calls Hans out *by name* and lists as many of his crew as he can. He wants Hans to know how far ahead of him he is. Hans's questions for McClane are designed to ferret out McClane's *identity*—he surmises this poison pill might be a security guard and then potentially a big-headed cowboy-movie fan. John's *concealed identity* is pivotal for his ability to stay in the game against superior numbers.

John's advantage begins to evaporate at the point an arrogant hostage, one of McClane's wife's co-workers, *names* John to Hans. Fortunately, Ellis, the hostage, lies to Hans and says McClane was *his* guest at the party. Next, Hans learns McClane's profession and place of origin (a cop from New York). When the two run into one another, Hans hides *his identity*, pretending to be an escaped hostage. Finally, Thornburg, an unscrupulous TV news reporter who heard the McClane-Ellis episode over the radio uses McClane's name to research him and discovers where in the LA area John's wife Holly and their children live. Thornburg's broadcast interview with the McClane children informs Hans of the last important piece of the puzzle: who Holly really is. Until that point, Holly's own *identity* and relationship to McClane had remained hidden.

The B-Story's Opposing Idea revolves around Holly's *maiden name* and, broader, her right to her own identity. Their relationship and separation are obviously B-Story. Ellis has clear designs on Holly, and his misguided attempt to resolve the Situation—which outs John and ends up getting himself killed—stems from the B-Story. Ellis challenges John when he first arrives by making a show of the gold watch Holly has earned for her efforts at Nakatomi—Ellis's point presumably being that the two of them have worked closely together and the watch is symbolic of her close ties with the company and, by extension, with Ellis. This same watch, symbolic of her marriage-independent *identity* in LA, gets unclasped as Hans dangles from her arm off the side of the building, thus sending the villain to his demise.

Now take another look at our graphic breakdown. One of our Thematic component labels is *incorrect*. Do you see it?

We made the same "mistake" in the last chapter's breakdown of the Premise: "**A New York cop visits his wife when terrorists seize a building**." And there is a reason we leave this mislabel here.

The wrong label is *Terrorists*. Yet another way *Die Hard* plays with the *identity* Theme. Most people would say that Premise description is accurate. We imagine many, if not most, would use the term "terrorists" when describing the story.

Except Hans Gruber and his crew are *not terrorists*! They are *thieves*. In the strictest sense, where "terrorists" commit violent actions to achieve political ends, Hans and his cronies are in it for the payday. They are *posing* as terrorists, namely hiding their real *identities*, to score that payday. As a matter of fact, it is central to Hans's plan. Nakatomi has hundreds of millions of dollars' worth of negotiable bearer bonds in its vault—a vault with 7 layers of security. One layer is code access. The next five are mechanical and can be drilled through. The final one is an electromagnetic one that Hans relies on the FBI anti-terrorism protocols to shut down for him as they cut power to the city grid. He also plans to cover up the theft by offering a hostage release by helicopter on the building roof, which he plans to blow up. While the authorities comb through the bodies and debris, Hans and company shall slip away. (Unfortunately for Hans, it doesn't work out.)

If you followed the directive to name the Theme of Die Hard before looking at the graphic breakdown and got it wrong, why do you think that is?

We suggest one reason might be the common misperceptions about Theme. It's hard to break out of the mindset that Theme is a grand message for the audience. When we hear Theme discussed, it can feel as though it should be some transcendent universal truth. *Die Hard* is a great example of Theme as a bonding agent idea. Arguably there are more "important" notions in the movie. "Family," for instance. Or "love." McClane and officer Powell both get the chance to redeem past wrongs and grow.

These are all thematic ideas running through the movie. But the "glue" between the Primary Situation and the Underlying Cause is definitely *identity*. It plays an important *practical function*.

So...

WHAT IF...

It really was just some random security guard who happens to be in the building that night?

There is nothing about the Primary Situation of *Die Hard* that demands the hero be a cop with a close personal relationship with one of the hostages. Unlike Luke Skywalker, John McClane is not an Anointed Main Character. His presence is random. The villains do not target this company because of him. Nor is he there in the official capacity of his job. He is not investigating a crime on assignment. He is not a first responder to the building takeover crisis. The genre demands a hero with the skills needed to engage the threat, but he is not *uniquely* qualified. He is the right "wrong" guy in the wrong place at the wrong time.

It is very easy to replace McClane in this story with any arbitrary person at a practical, functional level. A lesser film could have made McClane a moonlighting cop or former soldier hired by Nakatomi to work security for the evening. All of the major action beats could remain intact in this alternate version. McClane would have every reason to keep his identity from the villains simply for the tactical advantage. Reimagine him as a drunk bachelor and the story just becomes about defeating the plans of some bad dudes with hostages, perhaps affording our man a little redemption in the process. Maybe he just dies sacrificing himself at the end.

But gutting the film of the Thematic Layer cuts it off at the knees. Are we not invested so much more over the suspense of watching that thin thread supporting John and Holly's hidden identities and whether it is about to snap? Don't we care about his success, not just because random people's lives are in the balance but because he's trying to save his wife? Would we not feel the absence of the emotions we experience over Thornburg's ratings-grabbing exploitation of the McClane children and its effect on the Plot?

The point is this: it *has* to be McClane and no one else.

Uniquely Extraordinary Main Character Case Study IV: *Rocky*

Do you know the name Chuck Wepner?

If you're not a fan of boxing and a student of the sport's history, you probably do not.

On March 24, 1975, Chuck Wepner fought legendary heavyweight boxing champion Muhammad Ali and came seconds short of surviving the fifteenth and final round. Wepner's performance against Ali was considered an inspirational story. He was a ranked contender, but not highly. He was not making enough from professional boxing to earn a living and had to train around his schedule as a liquor salesman for his fights before Ali. Wepner eagerly signed for $100,000—by far his biggest payday as a boxer—against the $1.5 million going to the champ. Ali was expected to make quick work of the overmatched challenger known as "The Bayonne Bleeder," a somewhat derogatory nickname for the Bayonne, New Jersey native with a reputation for getting injured in his matches. Yet Chuck managed to push the great Muhammad to the final round in the fight with a gutsy performance that included a shocking ninth-round knockdown of the champ.

Rocky *is not* the Chuck Wepner story.

Then unknown actor Sylvester Stallone used the Wepner-Ali fight as inspiration for his own tale of a blue-collar palooka from the streets of Philadelphia. A year later, *Rocky* would earn Stallone a Best Actor nomination and take home the Best Picture Academy Award.

In our previous discussion exploring the Premise and Hidden Past of *Rocky*, we noted that the movie is mainly B-Story. The Primary Situation is a blip on the radar—it shows up, we know it is coming, Rocky remains immersed in his ongoing life with the expectation of the upcoming fight, and he puts on the gloves with the hope of lasting until the final bell. There is some choreographed boxing action in the tight third act, with the only suspense being whether or not he can last the full fight. We expect he will. There's not much drama to that aspect.

Let's take a look at *Rocky* as a story that's virtually *all Main Character*:

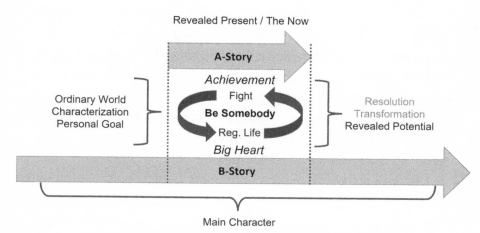

Figure 37: Main Character Thematic Conflict in *Rocky*

After a lengthy series of movies where Stallone's iron-willed prizefighter seems to only get more physically buff and defeats an increasingly gargantuan series of foes in the ring, it's almost tough to recall that Rocky Balboa was already an over-the-hill boxer in the very first film. He has over 60 matches under his belt before lacing up the gloves against Apollo Creed in *Rocky*. He loses his locker at Mickey's gym to a younger prospect. He *had* talent, the crusty old trainer tells him, but he became a leg-breaker for a two-bit loan shark instead of working to fulfill his promise.

Rocky lives in a world of constant reminder that he comes from nothing and is nothing. He is surrounded by people beaten down by hard reality. People who have grown to accept their station. Paulie lugs frozen sides of beef around in a meat processing plant. Gazzo is a lowlife loan shark taking advantage of poor blue-collar dock workers. Adrian is a smart woman making low wages feeding animals and selling pet supplies. Mickey trains long-shot fighters with little education in a rundown gym. When Rocky argues with the bar owner/bartender that Apollo deserves respect because he took his shot and became something, the man mocks the idea by "taking a shot" of whiskey. They work hard and expect little in return.

In our earlier analysis, we detailed many of the ways that Rocky demonstrates the size of his *heart*. He takes care of animals and people—drawn to those who are equally damaged, such as his friend Paulie, an abrasive boozer who may not deserve such loyalty. But Rocky doesn't prize the man in the mirror, doesn't celebrate his own good heart, and feels he has a long way to go to *be somebody*. The teenager Rocky walks home and offers life advice to, turns on him with a crude "Screw you, creepo!" Rocky slinks away admonishing himself, "Yeah, who are you to give advice, creepo?"

The Theme and Opposing Idea identified in our graphic breakdown above may not read as opposites at first blush.

With *Liar Liar*, *dishonesty* versus *honesty* is a clear dichotomy. In *Star Wars*, the *Dark Side* versus the *Light Side* of The Force is a clear dichotomy. In *Die Hard*, *revealed identity* versus *hidden identity* is a clear dichotomy.

But now we describe the opposing Thematic ideas in *Rocky* as *achievement* versus *big heart.* How are those conceptual opposites? The first point of clarification probably goes without saying, but it's important not to get too hung up on precise wording. We're attempting to boil often complex ideas into a one-to-two-word summary label. But that doesn't fully explain this duality.

As Character-oriented as *Rocky* is, understand that the Thematic Conflict takes place in Rocky's Mind. This is a conflict of *self-perception.* Rocky's internal conflict revolves around self-worth. *Achievement* refers to seeking out and seizing an Opportunity to prove his worth by performing something outstanding *externally*. To achieve validation, Rocky feels he needs to accomplish something the *outside world recognizes* as valuable. For him, this accomplishment is proving himself to be a worthy warrior in the boxing ring. On the other side of the Thematic Conflict stands his *big heart*—an intrinsic characteristic manifested throughout his daily life. *Rocky* is a love story as much as a fight story, and we sense it is his *big heart* that draws Adrian to him. This is a Thematic Conflict that is not about this *or* that but rather finding a balance between the two. We appreciate Rocky for the kind of person he is *and* we want to see Rocky get his chance to climb *his* mountain so that he can prove to himself that he is worthy and whole.

In case there's any doubt...

What if...

It was just some other random boxer who doesn't see himself outside of his own world?

Of all of our "What If?" thought experiments in this chapter, this one is easiest to fathom. We don't have to use our imagination to conjure an alternate Characterization of a potential serious underdog fighter getting the chance to battle the world heavyweight champion and giving an inspired effort beyond all expectations. As we stated earlier, *Rocky* is *not* the Chuck Wepner story.

If anything, *Rocky* is the Sylvester Stallone story. Not literally, of course. But the Main Character is plainly reflective of how then-struggling actor Stallone viewed his life: *undervalued*. Starving to find *his* shot at validation. It is now part of Hollywood lore (and something we likely shall never see again in the modern movie industry) how Stallone refused to sell the hot property of his coveted screenplay unless the purchasing producers agreed he would be cast in the lead.

Rocky is a story of personal triumph. The sequels would become tales of overt triumph, as the titular Character would not only claim the heavyweight title in a rematch but then go on to defend it, lose and rewin it, and prove himself time and again against bigger behemoths. Accordingly, Rocky's life would be a world-hopping rollercoaster of wealth and notoriety, losing his empire, and settling into comfortable golden years as an aging legend and restaurant entrepreneur.

Chuck Wepner, by contrast, never had a more shining moment in his professional boxing career than the legendary Ali fight. His pugilist star faded and he eventually ran into trouble with drugs. He auditioned to play a sparring partner in *Rocky II* but was passed over because of his addiction. He did inspire another notable part of the *Rocky* series when he took on wrestler Andre the Giant in an exhibition "fight," which became the basis for a similar scene in *Rocky III*. He successfully sued Stallone years later. Wepner served jail time for cocaine. He continued to work in liquor sales. And the movies have continued to be fascinated by his story as more than one production now features an eponymous Character directly based on him.

Nothing we know about Wepner's personal life suggests the similarities between Stallone's Character and Wepner extend beyond the boxing ring. Any essential change to the Main Character of Rocky Balboa could not help but profoundly alter the story of *Rocky*. This Primary Situation could intersect with any boxer's life. But the Thematic Layer of the film and its power to captivate audiences relies on just one immutable version of this Main Character.

It *has* to be Rocky, and no one else.

Uniquely Extraordinary Main Character Case Study V: The *Harry Potter* series

In the *Die Hard* discussion, we placed a bet against you correctly identifying the Theme.

Now we're betting that when we said two Main Characters in our five major example IPs can be considered to be *Anointed Main Characters*, you recognized Harry Potter was the second one after Luke Skywalker. Look at you! So clever.

As with Luke Skywalker, it is *literally* true that no one else but Harry can be the Main Character of the *Harry Potter* wizarding world saga. We are to understand that the wizarding society is many millions strong, but only one is "The Boy Who Lived;" Harry cannot simply be just another wizard. Our Thematic investigation with Harry must also dig into the ways he is a relevant Main Character. What is the primary Theme of these novels?

Take a look at the Thematic component breakdown graphic for the *Harry Potter* series:

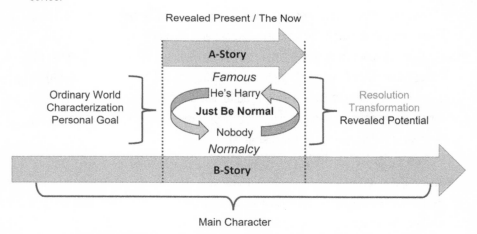

Figure 38: Main Character Thematic Conflict in the *Harry Potter* Series

For this analysis of the Theme, let's shift gears a bit and discuss the various potential interpretations of Theme versus the way we approach it in the Your Storytelling Potential Method. As we have touched on before, Theme is a slippery fish to grasp. Without question, every well-told tale has numerous thematic ideas woven throughout.

We have also acknowledged that there is much in this method that diverts from the path of most traditional schools of thought on storytelling. And it is not our contention that every great work follows this blueprint precisely—certainly, most of the storytellers who have crafted notable narratives are not versed in the Your Storytelling Potential Method philosophies. This is not dogma, and in many cases, the Author-Storytellers in question might argue with our perspective. We offer our breakdowns of these IPs to make the arguments we believe support the basic truths of storytelling as we see them. Every reader will draw conclusions about how correct these insights are. We believe the cases we lay out are compelling. You decide.

We say all of this as an opening to this discussion about Theme in *Harry Potter* in recognition of the volumes of analysis available. We assert that the primary binding idea in the series is **normalcy**.

The Harry Potter Wiki lists the IP's Themes as:

• Confronting Fears
• Death
• Love
• Fate
• Acceptance/Tolerance

Wikipedia's main "Harry Potter" page does list "normalcy" among the acknowledged Themes of the series, as put forward by at least some literary analysts. Throughout a lengthy series, many thematic ideas are going to arise. Rowling has stated that she doesn't consciously infuse Themes into her work, preferring instead to allow them to "grow organically."

Free form writing has its place. It can exercise creative muscles. It's a tool for sharpening skills. It holds the potential of producing some truly original and soul-inspired work. And there are genius Author-Storytellers who claim they begin some or all of their best-received material by simply sitting down with little more than a spark of an idea and just letting it flow. Please consider whether this is *your* most profitable course of action. However you make it happen, the proof is in the pudding.

Central to our goal for presenting the Your Storytelling Potential Method is arming students of the craft of storytelling with the tools that increase one's odds of producing memorable, resonant narratives without having to make endless revisions. Add to that everything we have described about the *iterative nature* of this approach—Beginning with the kernel of an A-Story idea and working down to Main Character, cognizant of the components of Revealed Story, *building and reworking*— and we trust you see the wisdom in identifying the possible *relevant* Theme(s) as soon as they present themselves. Hopefully before committing too much work to a manuscript, ideally during the planning phase.

Another thing to consider when considering if "Normalcy" is truly the Thematic Idea is our concept of Theme specific to this system. Remember, we're not primarily concerned with Theme as a transcendent, deep truth or as an important message your story is trying to convey. In our view, Theme is a binding agent concept between the Primary Situation and the Underlying Cause. It's the connection between the A and B stories. And it expresses the Main Character's Personal Goal.

Harry differs from Luke Skywalker in a significant, fundamental way. Luke is looking to enter the fray. Harry is a *reluctant hero*. Luke knows nothing about The Force and the Jedi, but he is aware of the Empire and the Rebellion, as all citizens of the Galaxy ruled by the Emperor are. Harry spends most of his childhood completely oblivious to the existence of wizards and magic. He doesn't know who Voldemort is. And he certainly does not know that there is a vast hidden society to whom he is *famous*.

Remember that Harry becomes an **ANOINTED CHARACTER**. Luke's special relationship with The Force is passed to him by his DNA. Harry's parents are wizards, but were it not for the events that shaped his destiny in his infancy, Harry might otherwise be a very "ordinary" wizard. Much like Luke, Harry is the subject of a prophecy. But the irony of the prophecy in Harry's case is it only becomes fulfilled because his destined foe takes action to prevent it but instead causes it to be fulfilled. If Voldemort had not attempted to kill baby Harry, the two would not have been bound and Voldemort would not be disembodied, essentially dead and requiring resurrection. Harry is thrust to center stage neither by choice nor by inheritance. Harry survives the attack because his parents sacrifice themselves and his mother's love powerfully deflects Voldemort's death spell.

The aforementioned Themes identified by the Harry Potter Wiki and by other analytical sources are all arguably present and find expression throughout the series. But what idea reflects the Primary Situation's conflict with Harry's Personal Goal? What is Harry trying to achieve in the broadest sense?

Much is expected of Harry not because he is an extraordinary wizard, but because he is famous for having survived Voldemort. It is assumed Harry's destiny is to defeat Voldemort because it is prophesied, but Harry is not particularly well equipped to face the challenge. He needs a lot of help. What particular special abilities he *does* possess were conferred on him through the melding with Voldemort. It's late in the game before the true nature of Harry's bond with the Dark Lord is fully understood. They *discover* what Horcruxes are—these scattered items infused with pieces of Voldemort's shattered soul, of which Harry is one. But there are more naturally powerful and capable wizards than Harry, yet he is the only one who can do the job.

On the other side of Harry's life, before learning about Hogwarts and who he really is, he is a marginalized boy living in poor conditions, relative to the social class of his adoptive family. They neglect and abuse him, and make him sleep in a closet beneath the stairs.

Here is the clear polarity of Harry's life: being an exalted hero with great expectations in one world versus being an invisible punching bag in the other. Both realities are a lot for him to deal with. He is duty-bound and has no choice but to rise to the challenge of vanquishing the evil wizard. To shirk the duty means leaving the world open to being conquered and overrun with the spread of Voldemort's darkness.

But we have no sense that the balance of Harry's life post-Voldemort will be devoted to seeking out new challenges as some guardian defender. On the contrary, the final book's epilogue details Harry and Ginny nineteen years after the confrontation with Voldemort happily married with children and sending them off to their alma mater—as *normal* as it gets for people with such extraordinary abilities and history. Harry's story is of a young man tasked by fate to overcome overwhelming odds to prevent mass devastation. He executes that duty to the best of his abilities, courting as much assistance as he can draw to the cause. Revealed in the latter parts of the story, arguably the success of that battle against the forces of darkness owes more to the efforts of Harry's secret guardian Severus Snape than to Harry himself.

As a story that explores the Desire to achieve a sense of normalcy for a young kid who can never be normal, Harry is clearly a Uniquely Extraordinary Main Character. So what, then, about our thought experiment?

What if...

It was just some kid finding out he was a wizard?

Of these IP examples, it's probably the most difficult to imagine an alternate version of this story *without* Harry as the Main Character.

This is not the only wizard story we can conceive. Beyond Harry Potter, J.K. Rowling and her fans continue to explore the wizarding world. There is a new series of related movies called *Fantastic Beasts*. And of course, wizards have been a part of human mythology as long as we have been telling stories.

At the most practical level, Harry is entwined in the events of the story long before he gains awareness that he's involved in it. More than half of the seven-book arc revolves around Voldemort's effort to reincarnate himself from the beyond. His long-term plan is to gain immortality and to cleanse the wizarding world of non-wizard ("muggle") blood. This necessitates Harry's death, as he and Harry are linked. So removing or fundamentally changing Harry means fundamentally changing the Primary Situation.

Thematically, it may be conceivable that Rowling could have created Harry as a different soul. But it's unlikely audiences would find him as a compelling Main Character (though many Harry Potter fans do claim other Characters in the saga as favorites over Harry). As we have established, Harry succeeds despite not being all-powerful and only through a great deal of assistance from supporting figures like Dumbledore, Snape, Hermione, Ron, Hagrid, Neville Longbottom (who makes it possible for Harry to defeat Voldemort) and a host of minor allies. He mines himself for the fortitude required to press on in his mission, but he does not enter the situation with a warrior-leader's ferocity. He's just an unprepared kid.

Further in the opposite direction, Rowling might have given us an uber-capable, extraordinarily gifted hero. Harry is not James Bond or John Rambo or Superman. He is not Camelot's Merlin nor Marvel Comics' Dr. Strange. Such a Characterization for Harry might have made for a spectacular battle royale with the Dark Lord. But at that point, the story risks losing the rich tapestry of its intricate setting and cast of colorful wizard-world inhabitants. It would no longer offer the audience the Opportunity to connect with a young boy overwhelmed by the enormity of his challenge, needing to grow beyond his perceived limitations just to have a slim chance to succeed. It would have fewer relatable things to say that reflect our own life experiences. Certainly, a profound change to Harry would alter the Theme and the *Harry Potter* books would *be about* different ideas.

You should now have the understanding that stories are fundamentally about a Uniquely Extraordinary Main Character. The Author-Storyteller tells a story to illustrate something about the human condition. To do that, they must have intimate knowledge of the life of the Main Character. They have to know what that person is about and what it is they are after in the context of the story—their Personal Goal. Primary Situations arrive into the Main Character's life to act as a catalyst for Transformation, and they allow the audience the Opportunity to identify with the Main Character or at least to get to know them by way of the glimpse into their lives that the Revealed Story allows. Personal Goals are expressed by way of Subplots, and Subplots carry the Thematic Layer of the story. We have demonstrated through our IPs that altering the Main Character makes them inappropriate for the story, or at least requires the story to change at a profound level.

A well-told story must be about *this* Main Character, and no one else, because the Character is a *Uniquely Extraordinary Main Character*.

In the next chapter, we want to reinforce everything we have been talking about and further bring the conceptual down to a more actionable, practical level. The thrust will be some new graphic models and a very simple but penetrating exercise for discovering a story's Layers.

CHAPTER 4:

Three-Branch Reasons and Thematic Connections

Back in the first chapter's introduction to the principle of Convergence, we promised to reinforce the ideas in this system in varied ways using numerous examples and visual representations. Authorities in education theory universally maintain that people learn in different ways. Hence the mandate to offer assorted presentations of the subject matter.

This brings us to our fourth universal storytelling truth: The bigger the deeply rooted *why* a story is happening and *why* that story is related to the Main Character, the bigger the *tension* at the Climax.

With that in mind, this short chapter's goal is to deepen the examination of Theme using new tools. In particular, the spotlight is on implementing Thematic Ideas with consistency and establishing Thematic Layering.

Reference this new *master graph* for this chapter's discussion.

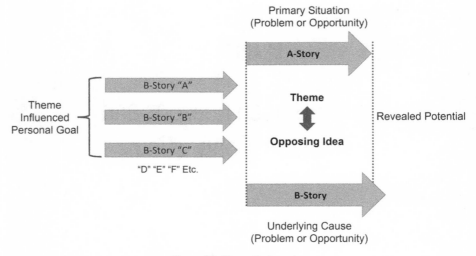

Figure 39: Thematic Layering

It is a slightly different version of our horizontal timeline graph that distills everything we have detailed thus far to its bare essence. Notice a Theme-influenced Personal Goal that is evident in multiple *B-Story* vectors, representing Subplot relationships existing *before* the A-Story, which presents the Revealed Story of the Now, begins, supplying Momentum. Notice the A and B stories, each offering a Problem or Opportunity and each supplying a Theme or Opposing Idea component; finally notice the Main Character moves on from the end of this Revealed Story episode into a Revealed Potential extending into the future.

We want to be clear, we are ***not*** suddenly saying there are multiple B-stories! This graphic is separating the strands of the overall B-Story (the Main Character's life) into parallel vectors representing as many different pertinent relationships the story requires to fully express the Theme and, on a practical level, move events forward. Think of it as analogous to the way a prism breaks a single stream of white light into its constituent color bands. (That there are three *B-Story* vectors in this graphic is an arbitrary number to illustrate the point. It could be two, five, or any appropriate number.)

Let's rotate the topic of Theme in our hands to view it from a slightly different perspective. We are talking about **THEMATIC CONNECTIONS.**

"The Reason We Asked *You* Here Today..."

In the last chapter, we said Theme is the expression of the Main Character's Personal Goal by way of a Theme Idea in conflict with an Opposing Idea. We used our IP examples to identify the Thematic Idea and the Opposing Idea and to demonstrate how they relate to the Personal Goal. But it may not be completely clear *how* the Personal Goal converges with the Theme Idea.

The choice of the tongue-in-cheek title for this section of the chapter relates to the emphasis in its Theme analysis: **REASONS.** Specifically, you are about to see that the *reason* the Main Character is *right* for the Problem/Opportunity presented by one side of the Primary Situation vs Underlying Cause equation is also the very same *reason* they are out-of-sync on the other side of the equation. Ironically, because they need the Transformational Journey in the story, being out-of-sync makes them *right* for both stories at the Thematic Level.

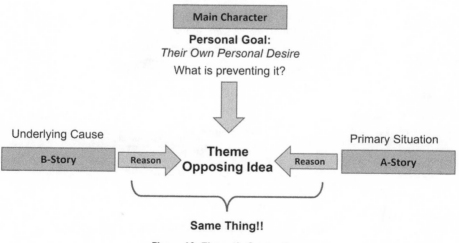

Figure 40: Thematic Connections

This graphic tool is a fantastic way to think about the Thematic Connections in your story and ensure a more thoroughly integrated Theme. Notice all three Branches contribute to the Theme.

The key here is understanding that the right Main Character for your Primary Situation has a personal *Desire* they cannot manifest. If it's something tangible, they cannot find it. If it's conceptual or spiritual, they hold Values that run counter to it but don't realize it. What is it that *prevents* the Main Character from reaching the *realization* of their personal Desire?

What we discover is that the very thing blocking the Main Character from reaching their Personal Goal is the *reason* they *now* face the Underlying Cause Problem or Opportunity *and* the Primary Situation Problem or Opportunity.

Let's take a brief look at this dynamic in action through our five major IPs.

Three-Branch Reasons and Thematic Connections
Case Study I: *Liar Liar*

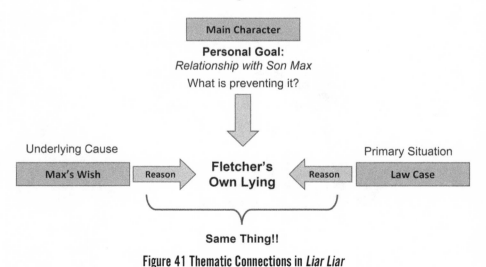

Figure 41 Thematic Connections in *Liar Liar*

What is the Main Character's Personal Goal?
Fletcher wants a relationship with his son.

Hey, wait a minute! Didn't you say Fletcher's Personal Goal in *Liar Liar* is *career ambitions*?

True. *but*, we also stated that Fletcher Reede's career ambitions are in-service to his Desire to do right by his family and, in particular, his son. The career ambitions are inexorably *linked to* the nobler aspects of his Character, the underlying Desire to be a success is to better provide for his family. At *heart*, Fletcher is a decent guy with screwed-up priorities. He wants to be a good dad. He believes that this justifies his dishonesty and misplaced priorities. The audience roots for him because he is not totally irredeemable. These are *not* career ambitions in-service to wanton greed. His love for his son is evident from the start.

What prevents the Main Character from attaining their Personal Goal?
Fletcher's very own lying.

What is the Underlying Cause Problem or Opportunity?
The Underlying Cause Problem is his son's birthday cake wish that prevents him from lying for one day.

What is the reason for the Underlying Cause Problem?
Fletcher's history of lying hurts those he cares about.

What is the Primary Situation Problem or Opportunity?
The Opportunity of being assigned a difficult-to-win big-money case that, if he does win, will advance his career.

What is the reason for the Primary Situation Opportunity?
Fletcher's reputation for being an unethical liar who is willing to do whatever it takes to win cases.

Notice how every Branch is linked to the Thematic Idea of lying, and that Thematic Idea finds expression throughout the entire story.

Three-Branch Reasons and Thematic Connections
Case Study II: *Star Wars*

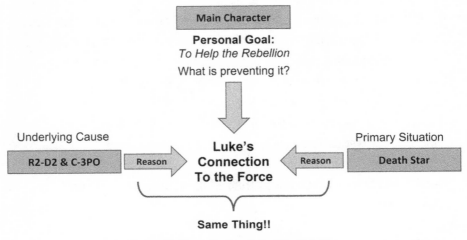

Figure 42: Thematic Connections in *Star Wars*

What is the Main Character's Personal Goal?

Luke's innate sense of duty and call to adventure makes him want to get involved and *help the Rebellion*.

What prevents the Main Character from reaching their Personal Goal?

Luke does not know it, but the reason he lives with his overbearing relatives on an out-of-the-way planet far removed from the action is that his relationship to Darth Vader makes him *vulnerable*. His guardian, Obi-Wan Kenobi, is keeping him out of harm's way by placing Luke on this out of the way planet. Knowing the realities of Luke's heritage and the danger of *who he might become if his father is able to convince him to turn to the Dark Side* as Darth Vader did, Luke's Uncle dissuades him from leaving home.

What is the Underlying Cause Problem or Opportunity?

Fate intervenes and delivers Luke the *droids* who have information crucial to the survival of the Rebellion, providing Luke with the Opportunity to join the action.

What is the reason for this?

There is no random chance involved in this *fate*, as we have already discussed. This is *The Force* at work orchestrating the lives of those who are *strongly connected to it*.

What is the Primary Situation Problem or Opportunity?

The Empire presents the Primary Situation Problem because it means to destroy the Rebellion with its powerful Death Star weapon.

What is the reason for this?

The ongoing galactic conflict pits the *Dark Side of the Force*, represented by the Emperor and Darth Vader of the Sith Order, against freedom-loving Rebel forces relying on the power of the *Light Side of the Force*, represented by the Jedi Knights Kenobi and Luke (later Yoda taking over for Kenobi as Luke's Jedi mentor in future episodes).

Notice how the *Force* itself is the central interconnecting point of the three Branches, the Force itself being the Thematic Idea at the heart of *Star Wars*.

Three-Branch Reasons and Thematic Connections
Case Study III: *Die Hard*

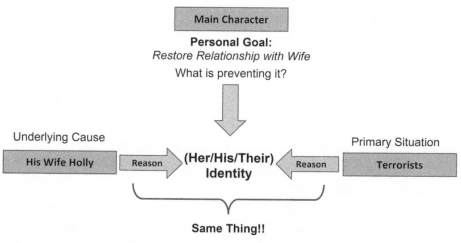

Figure 43: Thematic Connections in *Die Hard*

What is the Main Character's Personal Goal?
John McClane wants to fix his relationship with his wife.

What prevents the Main Character from reaching their Personal Goal?
Clash of independent *Identities*.

There is a certain implied chauvinism to John McClane. He rides into the picture from New York with a sense of entitlement and expectation. *He* is the man in the family, and *he* has this important job he can't just abandon. *He* is one of New York's finest. And if there is going to be a unified future for the McClane family, then obviously (in his mind) it is up to his wife Holly to give up her LA life, return to New York, and surrender her identity.

Holly has asserted her right to her own identity. She values the work *she* is doing. She has chosen to reclaim *her* maiden name for professional purposes.

What is the Underlying Cause Problem or Opportunity?
John McClane uses the Christmas holiday as an Opportunity to visit with his wife, to hash out the future of their marriage, and to reestablish their mutual *identity* as a married couple.

What is the reason for this?
The clash of asserted *independent identity* has caused them to separate.

What is the Primary Situation Problem or Opportunity?
A gang of thieves *posing* as terrorists seize the building where Holly works during a Christmas party, provide the Primary Situation problem by placing Holly in jeopardy while McClane does his sworn duty as a police officer to thwart criminals.

What is the reason for this?
John's *identity* as a New York cop with skills and a sense of duty that is unknown to the thieves. Holly's *identity* as a financial trading firm executive using her maiden name.

The criminals cannot connect their hostage Holly to McClane whose unexpected challenge disrupts their plans.

Notice how the Theme of *identity* forms a connection point for all three major Branches, and that Thematic link forms the basis for an action-packed story with rich and relevant Character depth.

Three-Branch Reasons and Thematic Connections
Case Study IV: *Rocky*

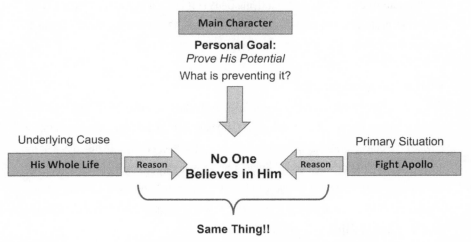

Figure 44: Thematic Connections in *Rocky*

What is the Main Character's Personal Goal?

Rocky wants to *prove to himself that he is somebody* even though it appears to the world that he is a nobody.

What prevents the Main Character from reaching their Personal Goal?

Rocky lives in a world of decay and Unrealized Potential. He *believes that he is a nobody bum*. His ambition is to be a successful prizefighter, but gym owner/trainer Mickey—from whom Rocky wants mentorship—believes that Rocky is an over-the-hill waste of his time and gives away his locker to a younger prospect. And everyone in his world either insults him or reinforces his view of life as one of lowered expectations.

When Rocky takes Adrian out for their first date, it is Thanksgiving Day. In order to get her to go, her brother Paulie throws the turkey she was roasting out the window.

Now she and Rocky will have to go find something to eat. She laments the lost turkey saying, "But it's Thanksgiving." Rocky replies, "To you. To me, it's Thursday."—he is a man who believes that he has nothing to be thankful for.

What is the Underlying Clause Problem or Opportunity?

Rocky believes that he must prove to himself that he is someone he can respect. *Rocky* is almost all B-Story. His Underlying Cause Problem is that everything in his life reinforces his lack of self-respect. Rocky's belief that he is a nobody doesn't come at any single moment. It's an established identity.

What is the reason for this?

Rocky struggles to respect himself. His defense of Apollo as a man who "took his shot" speaks to what Rocky values. During his date with Adrian, he describes the seminal advice he received from his father: essentially, "you weren't born with much of a brain so you better develop your body." Being a boxer is Rocky's identity. *Achievement in boxing* is his core Value, the measure of the man he wants to be. As Rocky tells Adrian, "All I wanted to prove is I weren't no bum." But all the messages from his daily life reinforce his belief that he is just a nobody.

What is the Primary Situation Problem or Opportunity?

Apollo Creed gives Rocky the Primary Situation Opportunity to *fight for the World Heavyweight Championship*.

What is the reason for this?

Apollo's legitimate ranked opponent gets injured while training for their upcoming fight. With no alternatives ready to step in, Apollo's strategy for promoting the fight is to turn it into a novelty spectacle by *giving an unknown a shot at the title*. He picks Rocky at random from a directory of local fighters because he is amused by Rocky's nickname: "The Italian Stallion." Over the objections of his handlers who don't like the idea of Apollo taking on a left-handed fighter, Apollo disses the unknown *nobody boxer*: "I'll drop him in three (rounds)."

Notice how the persistent Thematic idea of being a *nobody* radiates throughout all of Rocky's relationships and life, yet it is that very quality that lands him the Opportunity to fight Apollo for the championship because Apollo believes that Rocky is no threat to his champion standing.

Three-Branch Reasons and Thematic Connections
Case Study V: The *Harry Potter* series

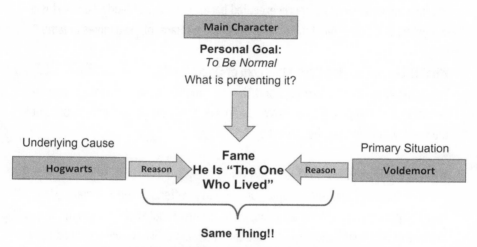

Figure 45: Thematic Connections in the *Harry Potter* Series

What is the Main Character's Personal Goal?

Harry wants *to be normal*.

What prevents the Main Character from reaching their Personal Goal?

Harry begins as a marginalized stepchild confined to living under the stairs in his neglectful relatives' house. He gets introduced to a fantastical hidden world of wizardry where he is *famous* for having survived as an infant the attack of an incredibly powerful, power-hungry, evil wizard. Tremendous expectations are saddled on his shoulders. Harry is actually a famous wizard. He will never be just a normal kid because of his true identity.

Rowling places extra attention on the idea of *fame* in the second book, *Harry Potter and the Chamber of Secrets*. Each of the seven books, covering the years Harry attends Hogwarts, features a different Defense against the Dark Arts professor.

In *Chamber*, that teacher is Gilderoy Lockhart, himself a *famous wizard* and author. Rowling depicts Lockhart as a fraudulent blowhard who's built his reputation through a series of embellished legendary autobiographical accounts. He and Harry take an instant dislike for one another—a somewhat one-sided clash of *famous* personalities. By the end, Lockhart undergoes a tremendous fall by means of exposed lies and self-inflicted amnesia from poorly executed backfiring magic. Clearly, Lockhart is a cautionary tale Character standing as an example for Harry of the dangers of *fame*.

What is the Underlying Cause Problem or Opportunity?

The introduction to the wizarding world, the realization of his wizard heritage, and the invitation to develop himself at Hogwarts provide Harry the Opportunity to become the great wizard he's prophesied to be.

What is the reason for this?

His wizarding heritage. From Chapter One of *Harry Potter and the Sorcerer's Stone*, Harry is special not just to the wizarding world in general, but specifically to the head-masters at Hogwarts Academy. They are the ones who deliver newly orphaned baby Harry to his relatives. Much effort is made to ensure Harry receives his invitation to attend Hogwarts. Because much expectation is placed on Harry due to his *fame* for being "*the boy who lived*," there is tremendous concern that he be tutored in the ways of magic to fulfill the prophecy and defeat Voldemort. The fate of the wizarding world depends on it.

What is the Primary Situation Problem or Opportunity?

Harry must solve the problem of how to defeat Voldemort.

What is the reason for this?

Harry and Voldemort are entwined through sorcery. Harry is *famous* in the wizarding world as "*the boy who lived*," which raises expectations that he is special and uniquely equipped to defeat the Dark Lord.

Notice how the Thematic Idea of Fame is rooted in each Branch, most notably Harry's very being. Fame is an aspect of Harry's reality that he is simply unable to escape, despite his Desire to be just the opposite: normal. But also notice that Voldemort himself is driven for his own infamous aspirations of *fame*.

If it is not yet clear how the Personal Goal connects with the Primary Situation and the Underlying Cause at the Thematic level, then hopefully this series of explanations has shed the needed light. Keep this exercise in mind as you build your own stories. This easy series of questions pays big dividends toward identifying Theme and clarifying its implementation.

And here comes another Theme-based exercise. This one should provide insight into our concept of Thematic Layering.

The "What Is It About?" Exercise

You want the greatest possible command of what your story is about. We don't need to convince you of the wisdom of that. If we have made the case for you to buy into the Your Storytelling Potential Method of story, then we're suggesting to you that you need to look at *four Layers* of your story to dig down from its basic Premise to the Theme. Being able to answer the questions in the following exercise is like a geologist taking a core sample of earth. This gives you the view of the foundational ideas on which you build your tale.

The essence of this operation is to ask "what is it about?" at these four levels:

- State the *Premise*
- State the *Primary Situation* Problem or Opportunity (A-Story)
- State the *Underlying Cause* Problem or Opportunity (B-Story)
- State the *Theme*

Believe it or not, what you just read is a fundamental paradigm worth *many times* the price of this book!

Despite its deceptive simplicity, storytellers routinely discover this short routine demonstrates that they do not fully understand their own story. And that is an immeasurable step towards filling the gaps that fix a broken narrative.

As you now expect, we are going to walk through this exercise for each of our major example IPs. At this point, we have stated the Premise, the Primary Situation, the Underlying Cause, and the Theme for each of these in previous topic explorations. And some of these may *read* a bit differently here, particularly Themes. Just know that we're continuing to expand on ideas and, in some of these cases, flesh out some details. Although it is helpful to have a succinct understanding of Theme (*lying* in *Liar Liar,* for example), let's please be clear that at times it's necessary to use a shorthand to refer to ideas with complexity. It's an ongoing conversation. And the more you can expand and deepen your Thematic Ideas, the richer your story inevitably becomes.

What is it about? Case Study I: *Liar Liar*

PREMISE: A lawyer who cannot tell a lie.

PRIMARY SITUATION: A lawyer has an Opportunity to advance his career with his firm by winning an important case but must lie to do so.

UNDERLYING CAUSE: A lawyer's son makes a birthday wish that he cannot lie for one day, and it comes true!

THEME: A lawyer who lies habitually and disregards his family in favor of his career.

What is it about? Case Study II: *Star Wars*

PREMISE: Luke Skywalker gets drawn into an intergalactic war when he acquires a droid with critical information.

PRIMARY SITUATION: The Empire plans to use its Death Star to destroy entire planets, thus eliminating the Rebels and all opposition to its tyranny over the Galaxy.

UNDERLYING CAUSE: Luke has the droids with the blueprint plans for the Death Star, which the Rebellion desperately needs if they are going to find a weakness they can exploit to destroy it.

THEME: The son of a renegade Jedi Knight who must learn the ways of the Force in order to oppose the Empire and destroy the Death Star.

What is it about? Case Study III: *Die Hard*

PREMISE: A New York cop must rescue his estranged wife and her coworkers after thieves seize the office building during a Christmas party.

PRIMARY SITUATION: Thieves seize the building, taking everyone hostage except for the cop whom they do not account for.

UNDERLYING CAUSE: The cop is in the building attempting to bond with his estranged wife who is living at the other end of the country with their children and working under her maiden name.

THEME: The thieves struggle to learn the true identity of the cop and his wife.

What is it about? Case Study IV: *Rocky*

PREMISE: An unsuccessful boxer fights the world champ.

PRIMARY SITUATION: A down-and-out aging boxer gets the chance to fight for the world championship when the reigning champion seeks to find a *nobody* to fight as a promotional gimmick.

UNDERLYING CAUSE: Rocky is washed up and his failed career is over.

THEME: No one ever gives him a chance in life. He and the world see him as a chump. Now he can prove himself and *be somebody*.

What is it about? Case Study V: The *Harry Potter* series

PREMISE: While just a boy, Harry Potter finds out he is really a famous wizard and that he must fulfill his destiny to defeat the Dark Lord.

PRIMARY SITUATION: Harry learns that, as a baby, he survived the attack that killed his parents by the power-hungry evil wizard Voldemort. And now the wizarding world looks to him to fulfill his destiny, become a great master wizard, and confront and defeat this Dark Lord.

UNDERLYING CAUSE: Because of his lineage, Harry has the chance to attend Hogwarts Academy to study magic.

THEME: Harry must accept the challenge of defeating Voldemort even though he would rather be a normal kid.

———————

Following our previous discussions about these IPs, you likely did not learn anything new about these stories through this exercise. In this discussion, the point is not to use this exercise to examine the IPs, but rather to use these IPs we have thoroughly discussed to demonstrate the beautiful simplicity and efficacy of this exercise in making sure that the story is coherent *because all the Elements are relevant.*

Don't lose sight of the goal here: use this exercise in examining your *own* undeveloped story ideas to see how well you know your story and how well your Theme is integrated into its Layers. These example IP stories are complete, produced, and distributed. Once you have satisfying answers to these *What is it about?* questions and the earlier Thematic Connections questions, it becomes infinitely easier to build out your stories with the assurance you have established important True North Thematic compass points leading the way on your Journey.

Again, story construction is a creative process—meaning you are constantly going over it and retreading ground as you piece it together. So these exercises are tools in the box to use as guides to see if you have all the parts and whether they're fitting together coherently. They assist in the process of reverse-engineering from endpoint goals you can establish early back to the seed-planting details needed in the Introduction and as your story moves along. Later on, we will get to an in-depth exploration of the Core Elements, and we will introduce very similar processes for mapping out a story across those Twelve Core Elements.

Before we get to the Core Elements deep dive, the next couple of chapters will break down the **COMPLETE CHARACTER WAVE**.

CHAPTER 5:

A Journey of Mind: Logic, Despair, Clarity

During the third chapter's discussion of the Thematic Conflict, we introduced the concept of the Character Wave. We said that the push-and-pull forces of the Theme Idea versus the Opposing Idea moves the Main Character through a wave pattern to create a pathway for Transformation and ultimately a Resolution.

As we said then, we believe this idea of a *Character Wave* is more useful than the traditional notion of a *Character Arc*. Many storytelling students struggle with the Character Arc because it is somewhat vague. It talks about where a Character starts in a story and conveys a generalized concept of change, but it says very little about what happens in between. It holds the potential of leaving the Author-Storyteller blind to the mechanics of how change actually operates. As though Transformation might be a mere accidental by-product of the significant or traumatic events taking place. Thinking of this process as a wave resulting from identifiable forces within your story offers the possibility of greater command of the course of your Main Character's Transformation.

This leads us to our fifth universal storytelling truth: All great stories are *Transformative Events*.

The place to start this dissection of the Character Wave, as usual, is with a graphic representation. Once again we modify our linear vector timeline model:

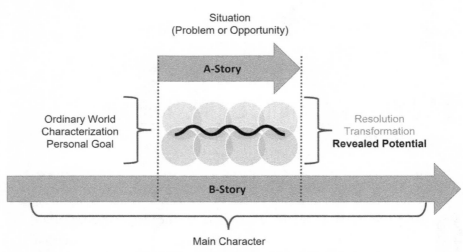

Figure 46: Character Wave Created by Transformative Events

You'll notice that as we move incrementally through the content in this system, our graph continues to get more complex as we add new Layers and information. Hopefully, you are starting to grasp everything depicted in this image, except for the new element in the very middle. Let's isolate that series of bubbles forming a new Venn diagram that we call the *Complete Character Wave*:

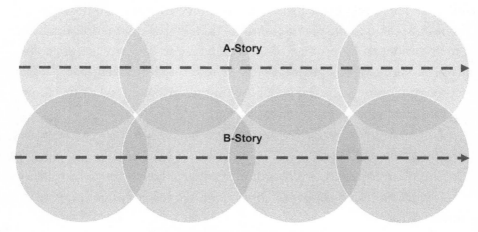

Figure 47: The Complete Character Wave

Bearing in mind this diagram is contained within the Now of the Revealed Story, you should see that each bubble represents a **MOVE-MENT** in the progression of the parallel A and B stories. As with all Venn diagrams, we see that each Movement of the Primary Situation not only corresponds to an analogous Movement in the Underlying Cause, but each Movement also feeds into the next circle in the progression through time. If it's not already evident, this Character Wave Movement through your story's timeline gives rise to the Your Storytelling Potential Method of **STORY STRUCTURE**, which is expressed completely with the **SIM-PLE STORY TIMELINE**.

For now, we have removed the *wave motion* line moving through the Movement bubbles. We must first consider the individual Movements for the A-Story and the B-Story. Then we will describe the movement of the Main Character through the progression and show how it results in a wave.

This is a good spot to reemphasize that B-Story and Underlying Cause *do not* imply a *subordination to the A-Story*. The Underlying Cause is *foundational*. It is the *larger* story of the Main Character's life. And that is why we begin this discussion with the B-Story Movements.

The Underlying Cause: A Journey of Mind

With the B-Story Movements, what we are concerned with is the Movement of the **CHARACTER MIND**. More specifically, the Main Character's mindset and Values.

The four Movements of the B-Story are:
- Reasons
- Motivation
- Transformation
- Commitment

Our timeline graph expands to these Movements:

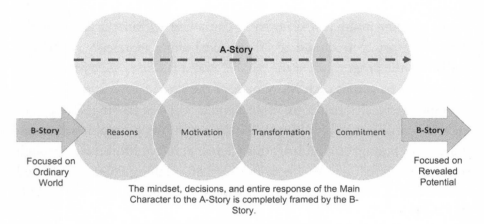

The mindset, decisions, and entire response of the Main Character to the A-Story is completely framed by the B-Story.

Figure 48:The Four Movements of the B-Story

Keep in mind, a story plays out—from your Main Character's *perspective*—as just another time period in the greater story of their ongoing personal life. The B-Story is framed by their Personal Goal. The Main Character is in pursuit of their Personal Goal, maybe overtly if it is something tangibly achievable or perhaps it stands as kind of a *true north* compass point in life if it's something more ethereal, like a core Value. And *then* this Primary Situation of the A-Story enters their world. It collides with their ongoing life. The Main Character must respond to the Complication presented by this new Problem or Opportunity. And that Situation offers a challenge to the pursuit of their Personal Goal.

The A-Story's Primary Situation is a catalyst for Main Character change. No matter how big a challenge it may be practically speaking, it can be life or death, a gigantic hurdle, or fate-of-the-world type stuff. But, at the end of it all, the heart and depth of the story come from this Movement of the Main Character's Mind.

Yes, explosive outward action displayed on promotional posters or book covers draws people in, but it's the inward Journey of mind and spirit that enables audiences to connect with your Main Character.

The early going of the story lays out the practical *Reasons* why the Main Character must deal with the Primary Situation of the A-Story. Further interaction between the A-Story and B-Story leads to the confrontation with the inner **MOTIVATION** that guides the Main Character as they navigate through the Primary Situation. More transpires to cause the Main Character to recognize the need for *Transformation* in a moment of *Clarity*. Finally, armed with this shift in perspective, they make a **COMMITMENT** to the action needed to resolve the Primary Situation—this lasting Commitment to their Transformation carries them forward into the Unknown Future of the Revealed Potential. The A-Story ends in a Climax while the Main Character's B-Story rolls on. And like a river shifting its banks, the direction of the B-Story is forever altered profoundly.

The Main Character has a *new Value* at the end of the story, different from the one they prized at the Beginning.

Transitional Doorways: Logic, Despair, and Clarity

In the above description of the four Movements of the Main Character's Mind, it was necessary to gloss over much of the mechanics of Transitions. It says things like "further interaction" and "more transpires." Be clear that we are *building* out the complete explanation of the Complete Character Wave. The B-Story Movements are an essential ingredient in it.

What drives and delineates the changeover from one B-Story Movement to the next?

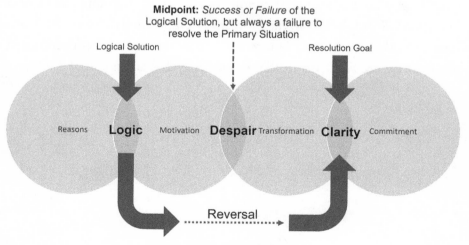

Figure 49: Transitional Doorways

As our Venn diagram suggests, it's *both* the overlap with the A-Story Movements *and* the impetus from one B-Story Movement into the next. The subsequent topic to focus on in this progression is the *transitional phases* between the B-Story Movements, the areas of overlap. We might think of them as doorways between subway train cars.

The story provides *Reasons* in the first Movement. These are the practical, factual aspects of the Main Character that make them the Uniquely Extraordinary Main Character for the story.

There are bad guys invading and endangering people, and here is a skilled law enforcement agent Main Character to combat them.

There is a geologic threat to a town, and *here* is a geological expert Main Character who's been predicting this sort of thing.

There is an interesting outgoing new person who just moved to this school, and here is an equally interesting loner Main Character whose world might get shaken up if they meet the right love interest.

You get the idea.

In the context of the B-Story, the *what happens next?* is that the Main Character becomes aware of the Primary Situation and applies **LOGIC** to deal with it. Whatever the Reasons that force the Main Character's hand into dealing with the Primary Situation, once they do, they *first* take the most Logical, straightforward action to address it. The application of a **LOGICAL SOLUTION** to the Problem or Opportunity creates the Motivation to *take action*. You might remember seeing Logical Solution among the Twelve Core Elements from the third chapter's discussion of Theme:

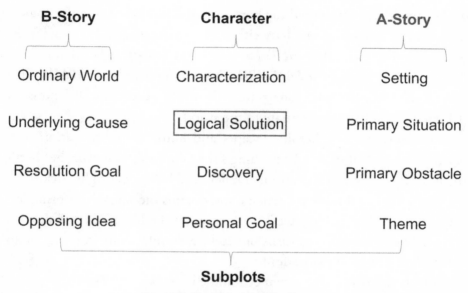

Figure 50: The Logical Solution Element

When we talk about a Logical Solution, we mean that it is Logical *to the Main Character*. It is consistent with who they are, how they think, and what it is they want out of life in the broad scheme. It may be the first thing they try that seems like the most obvious thing to do. On the other hand, given the right Main Character and dependent on the Primary Situation, that first choice might seem quite bizarre to the average person. Of course, a lot depends on the available options (or what seems to be available).

Is my Main Character a hothead who is going to rush in, guns a-blazin'? Or are they a seasoned veteran of war, taking a measured, tactical approach and looking to round up assistance?

Is my Main Character going to spark up a conversation with that new, intriguing individual? Or are they shy and far too withdrawn to be that open?

The Main Character has moved from Reasons to Motivation. They pursue the Logical Solution to the Problem or Opportunity in a way consistent with who they are, what they want, and relative to the available options. Then they hit a wall (the **MIDPOINT**).

At the Midpoint, everything bottoms out. They have taken the Logical action to its conclusion and have either *succeeded* or *failed*. But even if they succeed in their aim, they *still fail* to resolve the Situation! For that reason, the Midpoint is *always* a **FAILURE**. This Failure breeds **DESPAIR**. This does *not* mean the Main Character falls into a deep clinical depression (though, it could, if appropriate to the story).

The horror movie heroine escapes and finds the police station she's spent the first half of Act 2 searching for at the Midpoint, *but* the sheriff turns out to be one of the cannibal killers and brings her right back!

The hero spy thwarts the scheme and obtains the valuable information he's spent the first half of Act 2 working on at the Midpoint and delivers it to his boss, *but* his boss turns out to be a double agent working for an even more sinister organization!

Or the tried and true romance middle beat: *Boy loses Girl!*

The point here is whatever the Main Character initially tries does *not* work. This ends up being true for *all* the storylines. A-Story, B-Story, and all constituent Subplots. Everything bottoms out. And the Main Character is left to wonder, "Okay, *now* what do I do?" This is the end of the Logical Solution approach. Something must change for the Main Character to resolve the Situation.

This does *not* mean that the answers to Problems are always illogical. Remember, we're talking about the *Main Character's Logic*, a Logic born of their Commitment to the pursuit of their Personal Goal. The Personal Goal reflects their outlook. And the *something* that must change to resolve the Situation is the state of Mind. Some people will have skewed perceptions of life. Their Personal Goal needs adjustment. Other people may be internally conflicted, espousing one set of Values while doing things that run counter to it, and for them, they need to find the integrity to align with their Personal Goal. In the end, the shift enhances their ability to process the Situation better. (Of course, in a cautionary tale with a tragic figure Main Character, they may fail to learn their lesson. Or learn it too late.)

So *Despair* acts as the catalyst opening the potential for Transformation. That Midpoint bottoming out into Despair should trigger a **REVER-**

SAL. The Main Character has been doing things one way, now they must embrace the opposite approach.

The lone gun action Main Character realizes they *now* must accept help and be a team player to win the day.

The abrasive idealist Main Character realizes they *now* need to soften their edges to win people over to their cause.

The frightened, timid Main Character realizes they *now* must pick up the ax and battle the monster if they are going to survive.

Transformation is almost always a *process*. Change is hard. The more fundamental the change, the more resistant we tend to be. The same applies to your Main Character. And it is usually the case that at the **MIDPOINT FAILURE**, they are not armed with some crucial information. Our examination of the A-Story Movements to come will cover the *Discovery* Movement. The name alone suggests to you that before the Transition is complete, the Main Character likely needs to learn something they did not know before.

Despair triggers the Reversal and initiates a process of Transformation. The Main Character makes a Discovery along the way. Theme takes center stage once the Logic phase hits the skids. That Despair brings about uncertainty and the Transformative process, which leaves the Main Character wrestling with the Thematic Conflict. The Introduction of the Discovery brings about *Clarity* about what needs to be done.

The Transformation completes, and the Main Character moves to Commitment—Transformed, they have the new course of action to resolve the Situation, which we call the **RESOLUTION GOAL**:

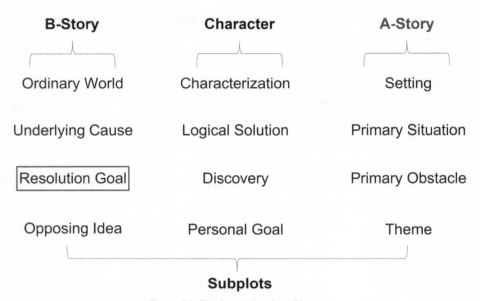

Figure 51: The Resolution Goal Element

The Resolution Goal is another one of our Twelve Core Elements. It stands to reason that the Resolution Goal is essentially the opposite of the Logical Solution. The Main Character starts off doing one thing to solve the Primary Situation and eventually discovers that they need to do the opposite.

Now let's see the Complete Character Wave in action from the B-Story side in our example IPs.

B-Story Movements Case Study I: *Liar Liar*

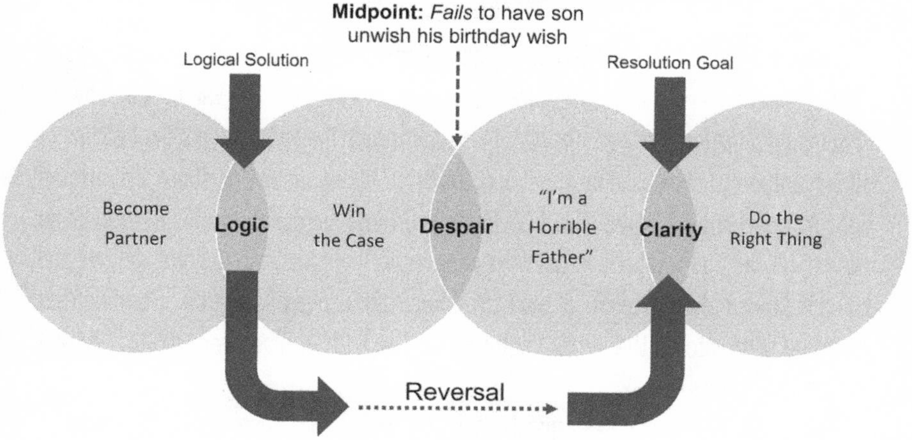

Figure 52: B-Story Movements in *Liar Liar*

Movement 1: Reasons

"Become Partner." The early part of the story introduces us to Fletcher Reede as an ambitious attorney who treasures his relationship with his son. *When he's there*, Fletcher is a good dad. He's fun, and his son enjoys his company. But Fletcher sees his profession as Priority #1. We understand that he's driven to succeed not for Reasons of pure greed, but because he believes it's the best way to provide. He's frustrated that his ex-wife, Audrey, and son, Max, don't cut him slack to do the things he feels he must do to get ahead at work. Honesty is not a Value for Fletcher at the Beginning of the story, so the truth becomes expendable in favor of whatever he thinks he must do or say to set their frustrations aside and to win law cases.

When presented with an Opportunity in the Primary Situation, Fletcher's Logical Solution would be to seize his career Opportunity and use any means necessary to...

Movement 2: Motivation

"Win the Case." We know the Primary Situation of *Liar Liar* is the *Opportunity* to win an important big money case and advance his career. The Underlying Cause is his history of dishonesty. Fletcher has burned his family so often, his son makes a wish that Fletcher cannot tell a lie for a whole day. So why is it we're saying the B-Story

Reasons and Motivation are about Becoming Partner and Winning the Case? Isn't that A-Story?

Be sure you follow the Main Character's Logic. Fletcher wants to become a partner because he sees it as his best way to take care of his son. His Values are skewed. His *Logical Solution* for the Opportunity is to embrace it and to use his bent ethics to his advantage to capitalize on the Opportunity. In *his mind*, at this stage, he is doing right by everyone he cares about by being the most successful in his career as he can be. (In fact, as we'll see in the next chapter, in this phase of all great stories, the A and B Stories align in terms of the Main Character's *Logical Solution,* meaning that whatever seems to be the correct solution for the A-Story also seems to the correct solution for the B-Story.)

However, Fletcher then slams up against the obstacle presented by the Underlying Cause: his son's birthday wish about his having to tell the truth for 24 hours. His effort to execute his Logical Solution gets hampered by his inability to lie. He makes many efforts to first understand what is happening and then to try to circumvent it.

Interestingly, in the very scene where Fletcher learns the source of his cursed inability to lie, he also receives a major challenge to his priorities. Audrey helps him retrieve his car from an impound lot and as they argue about her plan to move with their son Max and her new fiancé to Boston, Fletcher blurts out "I'm not a good father." This hits him hard because if he's able to say it, it must be his truth. His ex assures him that he *is* a good father... "when you're there." And then she tells him that he had better keep his promise to come to play with Max after work because the boy is so disappointed in Fletcher that he even made a birthday wish that Fletcher wouldn't be able to lie for one day.

As committed as he is to the idea that the important case cannot be won without dishonesty, Fletcher reaches a point where he attempts to have his son make an "unwish" to remove the hex. It does not work. Knowing that the wish only lasts for a day, he tries to present himself to the court as unable to continue the trial, and he goes to the lengths of beating himself up in the bathroom. The judge is ready to offer the continuance but asks Fletcher if he is able to continue, and Fletcher is compelled to confess that he can.

His back against the wall, he reaches his moment of *Despair*.

Movement 3: Transformation

"I'm a horrible person." Transformation is a *process*, as we have already noted. Without a doubt, the moment where Fletcher says he's a bad father is a significant step towards Transformation. *Reversal* takes shape. Yet it does not immediately bring about the recognition that honesty is the best policy.

It's still *after* that moment of self-perception that he tries having Max make the "unwish." He remains committed to his priorities as they stand, and he remains committed to the ends justifying dishonest means. He is not ready to place his family above his career nor is he ready to commit to telling the truth. But he is now *on the path*.

Ironically, it is at this moment when Fletcher finally relies on telling the *truth* to resolve the Primary Situation, that he reaches his moment of *Clarity*, completing his Transformation, which then propels him into his Revealed Potential. Fletcher does know the law. And because he is so sharp, he comes to realize that his client lied about her age to qualify for a marriage license and was therefore too young to enter into the binding prenuptial agreement. He uses his wits and *the truth* to win the case on a technicality. But then he witnesses the heartbreak of the defeated ex-husband—a truly good father whose children Fletcher's client now intends to use as pawns to further bleed the man. He realizes he is part of a broken justice system. The judge arrests Fletcher for contempt of court when he pleads to have the verdict overturned despite being the winning lawyer.

The A-Story of *Liar Liar* is complete at this point. But Fletcher has much to resolve in his B-Story: his future career, his relationship with his secretary, and, most importantly, his relationship with Audrey and Max, who are boarding a plane for Boston with a new father figure.

Movement 4: Commitment

"Do the right thing." The final act of *Liar Liar* primarily resolves the B-Story Plot threads. Once arrested for contempt, he issues numerous necessarily *truthful* proclamations about being a changed man. He counsels his jail cellmates about the dangers of avarice poisoning our souls and urges them to prioritize those they care about over leaving a material legacy. He mends fences with his secretary, pledging to open a small law practice for people in-need and confesses that he truly thinks she is wonderful. And he overcomes numerous setbacks as he races to the airport to head off Audrey's plane before Max is out of his life living in Boston.

The Clarity born from his A-Story-fueled Transformation enables the Commitment to do the *right thing* in all areas of his life. His profession, his relationships, and his family. Commitment to truth and ethics—doing the right thing—becomes Fletcher Reede's *Resolution Goal*.

B-Story Movements Case Study II: *Star Wars*

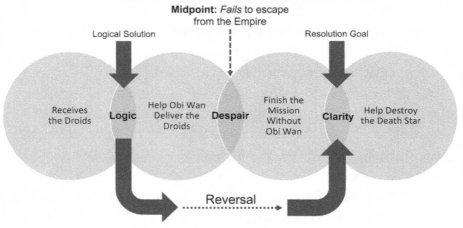

Figure 53: B-Story Movements in *Star Wars*

Movement 1: Reasons

"Receives the droids." Again, your mind might be screaming aren't the droids part of the A-Story?! I thought you said the Reason for Luke's involvement is his family heritage, that he is special!

Everything in great storytelling has Relevance. The droids seem to enter Luke's life by chance. They seem to lead him to his meeting with Obi-Wan Kenobi by chance. But it's *not* chance. The droids come to Luke because of his family heritage, they come to him because he is Luke. Luke's Journey must go from his innate Desire to get involved in the fight for freedom against the Empire to accepting his role as the Rebellion's central hope against the Dark Side power of his father, Darth Vader, and the Emperor. The droids, therefore, are the link bringing the A-Story into collision with Luke's B-Story. All of this is orchestrated by the unseen power of The Force as it seeks *balance*.

The droids definitely function as a *Convergence* device in the story. The essence of the A-Story is that the Empire means to squash the Rebellion and rule the Galaxy via their Death Star weapon, and the Rebels seek the Death Star construction plans smuggled in the droids so they can hopefully discover a way to destroy it. Luke's mission is simply to deliver the droids to Leia's people on her home world of Alderaan. Luke balks at this call at first. He is just a farm boy in his mind, and his guardians would never allow him to run off on an adventure. But the Empire's agents hunt down the droids' trail, follow it to Luke's home, and kill his aunt and uncle. Devastated but emancipated, Luke now takes the *Opportunity* to get involved, to deal with the Primary Situation *Problem*, and his *Logical Solution* becomes...

Movement 2: Motivation

"Help Obi-Wan Deliver the droids." He wants to get involved. He just learned that his father was something called a *Jedi Knight* and wielded special power through a mystical energy field called *The Force*. This Obi-Wan Kenobi can teach him these same skills and offers a pathway to join the cause he's drawn to in a more direct way than he'd been imagining. What else is there to do at this point *but* assist Obi-Wan in his mission to bring the princess's vital information to the Rebel leaders who need it?

Luke's Reasons lead to *action*. This is Motivation.

Luke and Obi-Wan charter passage from Tatooine to Alderaan aboard the Millennium Falcon, captained by Han Solo and copiloted by the wolfman-like Wookie, Chewbacca.

Little do they know that the sinister commander of the Death Star, Tarkin, intends to test the weapon's power on Leia's planet to psychologically torture her. The middle part of the film is a series of Failures from Luke's perspective. When they arrive at Alderaan's coordinates, not only is the planet destroyed, but the Empire forces capture the Falcon, and Luke suffers the loss of his mentor Obi-Wan to a lightsaber duel with Darth Vader.

In the exchange, Luke and Solo locate Princess Leia and make their escape, using her knowledge of the Rebellion to redirect their Journey to a secret Rebel base. Nonetheless, the odds have gotten longer. Luke's mission becomes more difficult. And he suffers *Despair* over Obi-Wan's death.

Movement 3: Transformation

"Finish the mission without Obi-Wan." Leia immediately recognizes that their successful escape means the Empire is tracking the Falcon and now their gambit to destroy the Death Star has an added time element to it, as they must find a way to destroy it before it reaches them. With Obi-Wan out of the picture and the Empire on the way, hope is a dim flicker. Vader gloats about this being "a day long remembered" because of Obi-Wan's death and the imminent destruction of the Rebellion.

Note the idea of *hope* in this movie. The actual title of *Episode IV* is *A New **Hope***. We believe the Theme of *Star Wars* is correctly identified as *The Force*, and more specifically the Light Side/Dark Side duality of it. But there's little denying that hope is also a major thematic idea. Leia's recorded message for Obi-Wan Kenobi famously pleads, "This is *our* most desperate hour. Help me Obi-Wan Kenobi. You're my only *hope*." Leia's plea comes on behalf of the entire Rebellion. It goes without saying that once Kenobi is lost, Luke becomes the titular *new hope* of the Rebellion. He reaches a new *Clarity* about his role in joining the fight.

So the mission he originally agreed to assist with—delivering the droids to the Rebel leadership—must evolve in two significant ways. First, he is no longer assisting Obi-Wan. **He** must become the Rebellion's hope. And, second, the mission is not just to deliver the droids, but to spearhead the Rebel's gambit to destroy the Death Star. This mindset shift would represent the *Reversal* in the story. It begins with Kenobi's death, which shoves Luke to center stage. Thematically, someone has to represent the Light Side of The Force in this galactic conflict, and now that falls to Luke.

Movement 4: Commitment

"Help Destroy the Death Star." *Star Wars* is such a cultural phenomenon and Luke so etched in the collective consciousness as the eminent Jedi hero of the original series saga, it's hard to remember that Luke's true first tapping into the power of The Force does not come until the very end of that introductory *Episode IV*. Sure, earlier as Obi-Wan trains him in lightsaber work with the floating remote ball aboard the Falcon, Luke has a momentary taste of his connection with his budding Jedi powers. But it's a fleeting moment that may or may not be *lucky,* as Han Solo dismisses it. The unambiguous first display of Luke's channeling of The Force comes while flying his X-Wing fighter enroute to the target point on the Death Star, hearing Kenobi's voice from the beyond, and shutting down his fighter's targeting computer in favor of trusting The Force to guide his aim. The Theme becomes expressed in the *Resolution Goal*. He gains the *Clarity* to see he can use The Force to help the Rebellion and destroy the Empire's Death Star. This Commitment and his Transformation catapults Luke from a relatively unimportant idealist to a leadership role front-and-center within the Rebellion.

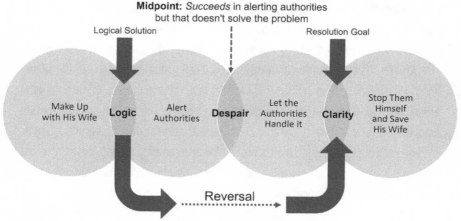

Figure 54: B-Story Movements in *Die Hard*

Movement 1: Reasons

"Make Up with His Wife." Well-trodden territory for us at this point, right? A New York *cop* travels across the country to mend fences with his *estranged wife* at Christmas time. Those two key pieces of profile information—cop and concerned husband whose wife gets taken hostage—inform his choices and define his options for action when the A-Story hostage crisis *Problem* arrives.

Die Hard is an action movie, but not a braindead one. John McClane doesn't just set up a sniper's nest and get to work taking out bad guys. He begins with careful surveillance. He assesses that he's outgunned with his lone sidearm against numerous apparent terrorists armed with automatic weapons. He evades detection and begins to learn the Nakatomi Building layout environment. He observes the leader Hans Gruber's demands of the company's CEO and subsequent execution of the man once

Gruber doesn't get what he wants. The audience identifies McClane's hesitance to do anything rash which might place his wife in additional danger.

Given his training and the parameters of the Situation, McClane's *Logical Solution* becomes...

Movement 2: Motivation

"Alert Authorities." The action that makes the most sense is to even the odds. Bring well-equipped law enforcement in sufficient numbers into the Situation. Hopefully, there is a way to provide them with as complete an assessment of the Situation as possible. But definitely, the thing *not* to do is to take on the team of terrorists solo.

Among the very first few things Hans Gruber's group does is to cut the phone lines to the building. Bear in mind that *Die Hard* was made in the late 1980s before the era of the ubiquitous mobile phone. Almost everyone at the time was dependent on landlines. As he speaks with his limo driver parked down in the underground garage, the line goes dead. This is McClane's first hint that something is awry. By the time the terrorists break-in on the Christmas party in the outer offices, McClane already knows he has no phone communication.

Following Gruber's execution of Nakatomi's CEO, McClane moves to a deserted floor and tries pulling a fire alarm. The quick-thinking terrorists use stolen badge ID numbers to call off the emergency crews and the alarm system data alerts them to McClane's location. Now he has no choice but to take on the one bad guy who comes after him. He defeats the armed thug, scoring a machine gun and a CB radio.

He next broadcasts to the emergency services using the CB, knowing the terrorists can listen in. And since the address is the same as the "bogus" fire alarm, the emergency dispatchers are skeptical of a prank. They send just one patrol car. Meanwhile, another of the criminal crew locates McClane, who is trying to break out a window to communicate with the LA cop below. After a lethal encounter with this terrorist, McClane's next best option is to throw the body out the broken window onto the cop's car just as the momentarily satisfied patrolman prepares to drive off. With their cover blown, Gruber's men open fire on the cop, who naturally calls for the cavalry to ride in and save the day.

So... mission accomplished! Right? At long last, law enforcement authorities outside the building are informed about the Situation and must take it seriously. A Midpoint *success*. But the Midpoint is *always a Failure!* Even when you win, you lose, sadly.

Movement 3: Transformation

"Let the Authorities Handle It." Up until now, the LA law enforcement community has frustrated McClane. Now that they truly are in the game, do they step up and handle the Situation with razor precision? Of course not. McClane's Logical Solution succeeds only in bringing in underwhelming tactical minds. Gruber remains perpetually a step ahead. And McClane finds himself trying to ride it out, but his hand is repeatedly forced into taking further action.

The fact that his effort to alert authorities fails to bring an end to the crisis causes McClane's *Despair*. The deeper he gets involved, the more he comes to the recognition that the help outside is no help at all, and this might just be all on his shoulders. It's the beginning of the *Reversal* in *Die Hard* that creates the mindset shift towards Transformation.

Remember, Transformation is almost always a *process*. There may be examples of great stories with instantaneous moments of epiphany and a Reversal into a 180-degree change. But the more common path is the Introduction of challenges to the Main Character's mindset and Values, slowly bringing them around to a new way of thinking about responding to the Problems and/or Opportunities they face.

In the case of *Die Hard*, there are multiple factors figuring into John McClane's Transformation. We have already discussed how his successful efforts to alert the authorities prove to ultimately be a Failure because the LA brain trust who arrive on the scene and the subsequent FBI agents who take over the Situation are not up to the task. McClane is witness to a series of their incompetent blunders. He ends up doing more than he bargained for to at least keep the "Good Guys" in the game. McClane's Despair Midpoint moment is really more of a ride from the success of getting his message out to a later true low where he has an emotional, resigned-to-Failure coded conversation with his remote ally, Officer Al Powell. The impetus to McClane's Transformation comes from A-Story Movement action that we will discuss in the next chapter.

Movement 4: Commitment

"Stop Them Himself and Save His Wife." Ultimately McClane achieves *Clarity*. No one is better equipped to confront and defeat Hans Gruber and his men than he. Not only does he find himself in possession of a crucial piece of the puzzle to Hans' plan that the outside authorities are not privy to, but McClane's wife's identity has been exposed. Hiding from Gruber no longer protects her. And waiting for outside action at this point will undoubtedly cost more lives, particularly Holly's. Hatching a plan to take out Hans and the remaining thieves becomes his *Resolution Goal*.

For McClane, the Transformational Journey to the Resolution Goal has kept him wrestling with the Thematic idea of Identity and assessing his relationship with Holly. By the end, *both* of the McClanes have moved *toward* reunion, with John ready to accept and support Holly's maiden name identity.

B-Story Movements Case Study IV: *Rocky*

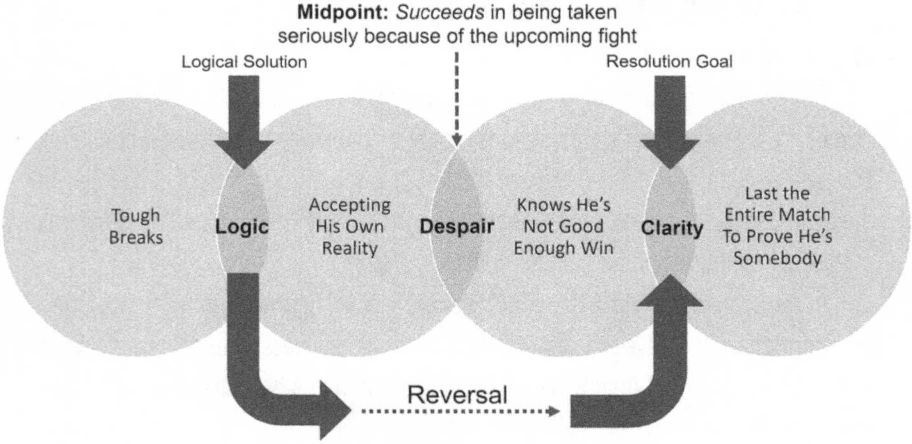

Figure 55: B-Story Movements in *Rocky*

Movement 1: Reasons

"Tough Breaks." *Rocky* is a story which illustrates that these *Movements* are not necessarily proportional to one another nor are they consistent from story to story. Each story has its own requirements. Even so, these Movements are *present* in almost every well-told story.

As we mentioned before in our *Rocky* examinations, this movie is *almost all* B-Story. The Movements of the A-Story we will discuss later are all there. But *Rocky* is a story with a highly functional, thin A-Story—he accepts, trains for, and arrives to participate in a scheduled boxing match. Other than that, everything that happens is B-Story. It's all Rocky's life and his relationships. Although the audience checks in with Apollo Creed's camp along the way, it is a very long time into the story before Rocky himself receives the offer to fight for the championship. *Rocky* has a *lot* of territory to cover exploring the Main Character's dysfunctional world.

We do not need to rehash Rocky's reality: by all accounts, including his own, Rocky is a *nobody*. A big-hearted, blue-collar, simple man of the streets struggling to find his way. He's drawn to a woman suffering from similar issues of low self-esteem, and most of his other relationships are with unsavory Characters, some of whom abuse and insult him. Boxing is his passion. It's the one thing that gives him a sense of pride, even if he is not very accomplished at it. And just before the promoter offers the fight to him, Rocky loses his locker at Mickey's gym. He's over-the-hill and not respected as a boxer.

Although it might seem reasonable to think the fight offer would be a tremendous boost, Rocky processes it in a way that makes sense *to him* at that moment, so his *Logical Solution* becomes...

Movement 2: Motivation

"Accepting His Own Reality." Defeating Apollo Creed is out of the question. An absurd notion. Creed is the greatest fighter in the world. Rocky is just a *club fighter*. As he describes himself, a "ham-and-egger." Apollo has beaten the best and remains undefeated. Rocky has piled up a lot of local fights (against "bums," as Mickey describes them), and has lost far too many to be considered a legitimate challenger. When fight promoter Jurgens makes the offer, Rocky immediately turns it down. "It wouldn't be such a good fight."

We don't see Rocky feeling ecstatic over the good fortune of getting picked. The movie does not show the moment where Rocky accepts the fight at all. Jurgens begins to manipulate him with appeals to his sense of patriotism, the fulfillment of the American dream. He goads Rocky, and we have to assume he probably clarifies the size of the payday if Rocky agrees to the bout. What we do see is Apollo alongside the Italian Stallion, looking like a deer in the headlights, on television, announcing the event. Mickey shows up at Rocky's place, contrite after having tossed the unwanted boxer out of his gym, and humbles himself for the chance to train Rocky for the Big Stage. Understandably, Rocky blows up at Mickey, angry that he never took an interest in him before. He mockingly offers to let Mickey move into his small, deteriorating apartment..."*It stinks!*" Rocky smashes his bathroom door to demonstrate the punishment he knows awaits him. None of this is cause for celebration for him.

Of course, he calms down and accepts Mickey's help. The fight is set. He needs a trainer. And boxing training is a very psychological process on top of the grueling physical one. We don't need to be professional fighters to understand that success as a boxer means having an unshakable belief in your ability to conquer your opponent. From his starting point, that's a massive uphill climb.

Movement 3: Transformation

"Be Somebody." In the broad sense, most of Rocky's life has been lived in *Despair*. From the point he receives the boxing match offer, he builds his belief in himself from scratch. Much of that comes from the powerful love story with Adrian. And a lot of it comes from the rigorous training the audience experiences through inspiring montages set to adrenaline-pumping music score marches composed by Bill Conti. Mickey really seems to believe Rocky has a shot!

Then the night before the fight, Rocky visits the Philadelphia arena where the fight is to take place. He goes through a personal crisis. Jurgens happens to be there, and when Rocky points out the banner with his painted image features the wrong colored boxing trunks, Jurgens dismisses the error. "It really doesn't matter, does it? I'm sure you're going to give us all a good show." It's trivia, but something that underscores how Rocky really doesn't much matter in the world. And that becomes his new focus.

The *Reversal* in this case is a mindset shift from the artificial psych-up of sports competition to a much deeper, personal exploration of self-worth. He's no longer fooling himself that he can prevail in the context of this 15-round boxing match. He has turned his attention to his greater Value as a man. The match grows to be a metaphor for life in Rocky's mind. And he resets his target. With this new *Clarity*, he knows what he must do...

Movement 4: Commitment

"Last the Entire Match." The reason no legitimate contender steps in to fill the void against Creed is the scheduled opponent's injury comes with only a few weeks to the fight. No one can adequately train to be in fighting shape at that level in so short a time. However, Rocky's entire life has trained him to take punishment. If nothing else, Rocky knows he can take everything Creed can dish out. Not only has no other boxer defeated Apollo Creed, but none have also gone the distance with him. To make it to the final bell of the 15th round would be a major accomplishment. This *Resolution Goal* offers Rocky the validation he craves.

B-Story Movements Case Study V: The *Harry Potter* series

As always, we conclude our IP examples with the *Harry Potter* series.

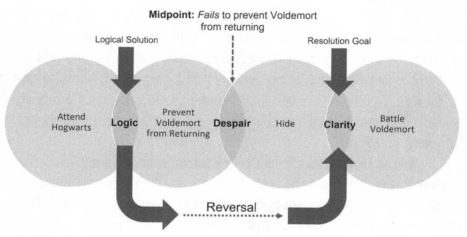

Figure 56: B-Story Movements in the *Harry Potter* Series

Movement 1: Reasons

"Attend Hogwarts." Do not forget that our discussions about *Harry Potter* are generalized to cover the entire seven-book series. We could also break down each book's narrative individually. Let's never lose sight of the interconnected and Layered quality of stories. Things can work on a macro level and the micro, substrata level. The series has a Theme and each book has a Theme, and we also acknowledge that every work has multiple Thematic Ideas at play within them. Similarly, an epic series has major

Movements composed of individual episodes, each with its own Movements. At the same time, as we've already talked about, we have to think about the *perspective* from which a story is told. The events of any tale carry varying significance, Themes, and Movements depending on which Character has been chosen to be the Main Character. Our work as Author-Storytellers is complex, to say the least. And hopefully this system gives you the framework and exercises to better think about constructing your tales.

The early part of *Harry Potter* introduces Harry to *who he is*. The B-Story is about his adventure attending Hogwarts, from Hagrid and the invitation letters on to the fantastic train ride, the sorting hat, and meeting the professors and classmates who become his allies throughout the saga. What it's all about is a young orphaned boy living a marginalized life who learns about his extraordinary heritage and fame within a secret underworld.

Previously we compared Harry Potter to Luke Skywalker in our example IPs as *Anointed Characters*—both have a special birthright destiny operating that truly makes them the *only* Main Character for the job. In Luke's case, destiny lends a hand by having the droids land in his lap. Harry, by contrast, is aggressively pursued to join the wizarding world. No invisible hand of fate here. Countless duplicate letters flood the Dursley household and then a *giant* shows up to ensure Harry gets the message: "Harry—yer a wizard."

With his Desire to escape the shoddy treatment of his guardian relatives, his Desire to know more about his parents' deaths, and essentially being ushered into his special station as "the boy who lived"—saddled with the expectation of confronting Lord Voldemort—Harry's only true *Logical Solution* option becomes...

Movement 2: Motivation

"Prevent Voldemort from Returning." Harry may be reluctant and require lots of assistance from his peers and professors, but the focus of the first several books in the series rests on preventing the disembodied Dark Lord from reincorporating. The failed attack that killed the Potters but left Harry alive backfired on Voldemort, leaving him splintered and without a body. Conversely, as Harry seems to be the fulfillment of the prophecy that a wizard child would destroy him, Voldemort spends much effort to attack Harry from the beyond as he seeks to reenter the physical world.

The *Philosopher's Stone* (or *Sorcerer's Stone* as it was known in the US edition) of the first book is a special object that supposedly holds that power. Thwarting Voldemort's servant, Defense Against the Dark Arts Professor Quirrell, from obtaining the stone is the Climax to the first story, but Voldemort is *not* the primary business of the book as much as introducing Harry to this wizarding world is.

The second book, *Harry Potter and the Chamber of Secrets*, features a diary authored by Tom Riddle, the former Hogwarts student who became Voldemort. The "Chamber" in the title refers to a hidden place wherein a monster resides that can be controlled by an heir to the Hogwarts House of Slytherin (again, Voldemort, of course). And while the focus is more on getting to the bottom of a mystery of who or what is causing many of Hogwarts' population to turn up dead or petrified—the light of suspicion falling on a few central Characters, including Harry himself—the eventual destruction of the diary entails the destruction of a part of *You Know Who*'s soul.

Third in the series, *Harry Potter and the Prisoner of Azkaban*, stands as the only story of the seven to feature no manifestation of Voldemort at all. The dark wizard's presence is felt, as always, through his cabal of supporters working against Harry and the good wizards of the world. *Prisoner* subjects Harry to something of a misinformation campaign, as much of it promotes the fear that Harry is the intended victim of the escaped murderer, Sirius Black. However, Black turns out to be an old friend of the Potters and proves to be an ally to Harry. One of the recurring motifs of the *Harry Potter* series is people believed to be friends turning out to be enemies and those assumed to be foes are revealed to be allies. One of the accepted pieces of lore around Black was that he betrayed the Potters to Voldemort, making him responsible for their deaths and the death of their close friend, Peter Pettigrew. The reverse is the case, as Pettigrew gets exposed as one of the Dark Lord's minions and not dead, but rather hiding out in alternate form as Ron Weasley's pet rat, Scabbers.

Most action taken by the so-called "Death Eaters"—followers of Voldemort—conspires to revive the fallen evil wizard. Voldemort's successful reemergence in physical form in the fourth book, *Harry Potter and the Goblet of Fire*, perfectly illustrates the *Midpoint*. Four-out-of-seven, precisely the middle of the saga.

Harry falls victim to another of the Dark Lord's disciples in disguise as yet another in the series of Defense Against the Dark Arts professors. This one covertly enters Harry in a tournament of champions, which seems innocent enough. But the prized cup at the heart of the contest turns out to be a "Portkey" which transports him and another competitor-ally to a remote location where Voldemort's lackeys capture them, kill Harry's competitor friend, and use Harry's blood as part of a diabolical ceremony that brings "He-Who-Must-Not-Be-Named" back to the land of the living. Without question, cause for *Despair*!

Also, the objective of Harry and the forces of good necessarily shifts from preventing Voldemort's return to survival, regrouping, and gathering the resources necessary to confront the threat: *Reversal*. And onto the next Movement...

Movement 3: Transformation

"Hide." Is it fair to say the action of *Harry Potter* turns into *hiding* after Voldemort's return? Perhaps more figuratively than literally. It may not be cowering in an underground bunker in white-knuckled fear, wishing the danger to pass, but Potter and his allies retreat out of the limelight to a fair degree while they figure out what to do next.

The fifth book's title, *Harry Potter and the Order of the Phoenix*, refers to Hogwarts Headmaster Dumbledore's re-activating of a defunct *secret* society. The Order holds clandestine meetings in Sirius Black's house where they discuss strategy for vanquishing the evil wizard and his cohorts *and* how to protect targeted individuals, particularly Harry. Aiding the Dark Lord's cause is the general wizarding world's unbelief that he has in fact returned. Harry and Dumbledore find themselves the objects of scrutiny and scorn. Eventually, Dumbledore is replaced as Hogwarts Headmaster by Dolores Umbridge, who is no fan of Harry and who ends the Defense Against Dark Arts program. This leads to Harry being recruited by the students to form their own *secret* training group: "Dumbledore's Army." This one concludes with a confrontation between the Death Eaters and the Order, who are obligated to ride to the rescue once Harry and his friends are lured into a trap.

Harry Potter and the Half-Blood Prince, the sixth book, continues to depict Harry and his allied wizards as under siege and scrounging for key insights that will turn the tide. The fledgling wizards of Gryffindor hunker down into their studies during an ongoing period of death and dread. The trials that test them and the awakening sexuality forge budding romantic relationships among the core teens. And as Harry's destined face-off with Voldemort looms near, Dumbledore shepherds Harry to important information about the former Tom Riddle's past secreted away in the forgotten memories of one of Hogwarts returning professors. Harry loses his mentor-guide Dumbledore when he is seemingly murdered by the inscrutable Professor Snape. Harry and his best friends, Hermione and Ron, all vow not to return to Hogwarts for their seventh and final year of study as the information they now have about Voldemort supplies them with a seek-and-destroy mission to end the vile wizard once and for all. Armed with *Clarity*, Harry is dedicated to confronting the Dark Lord's threat...

Movement 4: Commitment

"Battle Voldemort." The time has come for Harry to stand on his own two feet at last. His mother's interference saved him as an infant. Dumbledore has defended and guided him through the years but is now gone. Sirius Black has died. And Harry soon learns that his greatest protector may have been Severus Snape all along.

The last book, *Harry Potter and the Deathly Hallows,* chronicles Harry and his friends' search for the remaining objects entwined with pieces of Voldemort's soul, the Horcruxes. Snape's "murder" of Dumbledore was a plot hatched by an already-dying Dumbledore himself to mislead the Dark Lord. Snape dies early on and there is no one left more powerful than Harry to run interference on his behalf. The fate of Hogwarts and the wizarding world rests in his hands. The hardest pill to swallow is the realization that Harry and Voldemort's bond forged during that original thwarted attack means Harry is a seventh Horcrux and must die at Voldemort's hand for the sinister wizard to be defeated. There are many hard choices to make, but Harry's *Resolution Goal* stands clear before him.

––––––––––

Your grasp of the Complete Character Wave should now be firmer. We have looked at the broad scheme of the Main Character's Journey, the constituent Movements in the B-Story, and the Transitional doorways that lead from one Movement to the next.

The explanation of the Character Wave continues in the next chapter. We will look at the A-Story Movements, and with the complete picture of story events before us, we will see the "wave" formed by these forces playing off against one another.

CHAPTER 6:

Structural Connection Points

Our examination of the *Complete Character Wave* is incomplete. In the last chapter, we looked at the very important foundational four Movements present in the Underlying Cause of the B-Story. We characterized the B-Story transformative Movements as a *Journey of the mind*. We also noted that between the Movements are three key Transitional doorways: *Logic, Despair, and Clarity*. Now we must complete the picture by looking at the A-Story Movements and by following the Main Character's *complete* odyssey through the narrative and experiencing its wave-motion flow.

This steers us to perhaps the most important of our universal storytelling truths, the sixth: The A-Story does *not* begin with an "Inciting Incident," rather it begins with a *Proximate Cause*.

For a moment, think about your story as a road trip in a *borrowed car*.

In our first chapter's introduction to the Three Branches, we said it is somewhat challenging to separate the Main Character from the B-Story. It ventures into existential paradox to consider a person absent from the experiences and events of their life. And if you look back to our vector timeline graph at the beginning of the last chapter, notice the *Main Character* label applied to the entire broad B-Story vector. For just the next little bit, remarry those two Branches in your mind. Think of the Main Character as indistinguishable from the life they lead, namely their B-Story.

In the context of a road trip analogy, that Main Character and their entire B-Story get into a *borrowed vehicle*. The Main Character exists independently of the vehicle. Both the Main Character and the vehicle start the trip together, move through the same space and time together, and arrive at the end of the trip together. Then the Main Character exits the vehicle and goes on with the rest of their life. The road trip ends, and the Main Character leaves the vehicle behind because it is not their car.

In this analogy, the *A-Story* is the *vehicle*.

But *why* did the Main Character get into the car? And just whose car is it anyway?

In this analogy, let's suppose that someone else *caused* the Main Character to take the road trip. Someone called the Main Character on the phone and interrupted the Main Character's day (their ongoing B-Story). That person calling the Main Character has a need, that person has a goal. They hand the Main Character the keys to *their car*, and the Main Character goes on a road trip in that *other person's* car.

These ideas are covered in detail in Chapter 10, but we can't have a meaningful discussion about the A-Story and the Primary Situation without understanding one of the most important and misunderstood ideas of storytelling: The A-Story Is *not* the *Main Character's story*!

The *call* that put the Main Character behind the wheel and caused the trip is the "inciting incident." It is the moment the Main Character is brought into someone else's story—not the Main Character's. The *Reason* the car owner needs the Main Character to take the trip is what we call the *Proximate Cause*. And the person who calls the Main Character to go take the trip is the *Proximate Cause Character*.

There is more to say about Proximate Cause Characters—exactly who they are and why they cause the A-Story to happen—but, for now, the thing to understand is taking the road trip (aka, getting involved in the A-Story's Primary Situation) is *not* the Main Character's idea.

And once the Main Character is engaged in that road trip, while the Main Character is driving the borrowed car (the A-Story), the Main Character's destiny and the vehicle's destiny are intertwined for the duration of the trip. The Main Character existed before the road trip, and the Main Character will go on after the road trip ends. The Main Character's B-Story and the car owner's A-Story are linked temporarily. The road trip is a brief episode in the grander story of Main Character's life. The Main Character's decisions as the driver affect the road trip and the outcomes of the A-Story and the current episode of the B-Story simultaneously. If the Main Character is distracted by other people or events outside the vehicle, this affects the trip. If the vehicle experiences a malfunction or hits a pothole in the road or strikes another object, it affects the trip. In fact, any interaction between the Main Character and the vehicle determines the outcome of the trip.

Hopefully, the analogy is clear. In all great stories, one story belongs to the Main Character, namely the B-Story. And one story, the A-Story, belongs to another Character, the Proximate Cause Character. (See Chapter 10 for a much more in-depth exploration of these concepts.)

Of course, every road trip needs a roadmap, and with that in mind, here is our Character Wave roadmap for the A-Story and the B-Story that shows the **STRUCTURAL CONNECTION POINTS** along the route:

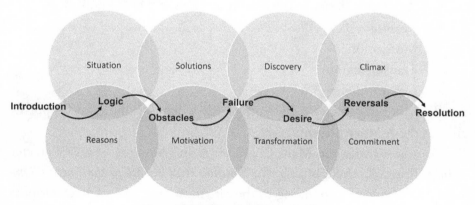

Figure 57: The Complete Character Wave

The Primary Situation Movements

It should be easy to understand the Primary Situation Movements are the practically ordered progression of dealing with the Problem or

Opportunity the Main Character encounters in the A-Story. The four Movements of the A-Story are:

- Situation
- Solutions
- Discovery
- Climax

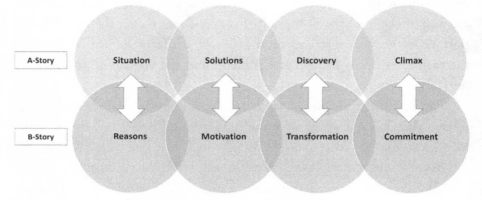

Figure 58: A-Story and B-Story Movements

Compare these to the analogous B-Story Movements:

- Reasons
- Motivation
- Transformation
- Commitment

The Main Character is living their life when a Problem or Opportunity in the A-Story presents itself.

Because of who the Main Character *is* and how the Main Character *thinks* (Reasons), there is a *Logical Solution* that occurs *to the Main Character* as a means of responding to the Situation. The Main Character puts the plan into action (Motivation), but it *fails* to resolve the Situation. The Main Character finds that the Situation tests their inner Personal Goal. The Main Character is forced to reevaluate their Values and/or approach to the Situation. A new solution is not readily apparent. This leads to *Despair*.

The Main Character begins to shift their approach and consider alternatives (Transformation). In the course of finding a new way of handling the Situation, the Main Character makes an important *Discovery*—maybe something factual they did not know about the Situation, maybe a reappraisal of their Values, maybe it's an assessment of the Proximate Cause Character introducing the A-Story. Typically, there are *multiple* discoveries in the Discovery phase. Whatever the Discovery, it sheds light on how the Situation must be dealt with. This results in a moment of *Clarity*.

Armed with the new perspective, the Main Character takes action—the Resolution Goal—to address the Primary Situation, bringing about the *Climax* of the A-Story and completion to the Transformation process that will carry on into their personal life once the Revealed Story is concluded (Commitment and Revealed Potential).

Structural Connection Points

Let's turn our attention to the Main Character's path in our roadmap. As the Main Character moves through the Movement progression of the A and B stories, there are *seven* essential Connection Points along the way. This Journey's route forms each *wave* of the Complete Character Wave.

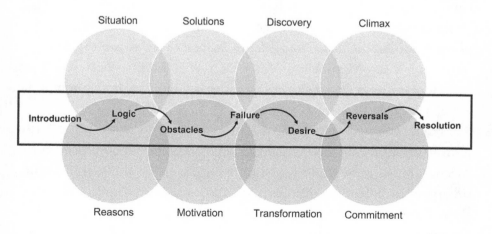

Figure 59: Waves in the Complete Character Wave

- Introduction
- Logic
- Obstacles
- Failure
- Desire
- Reversals
- Resolution

At this point in the book, the overlap in explanations probably makes these points fairly self-evident. Some of this we have already discussed in the last chapter as part of our Underlying Cause Movements description. Nonetheless, let's take a quick look at each of these points along the path for maximum Clarity.

Introduction

In this method, we take care to use the most precise language we can find. The traditional term used for the beginning of a story is either *Beginning* or *setup*. Neither of these terms is accurate in describing what actually happens as a story gets underway.

By now it should be clear that both the B-Story and A-Story are already happening in the Hidden Past by the time you start writing the first page. In this method, we emphasize the importance of thinking of a story as existing outside the *Now*. Your Main Character comes into the Revealed Story with a *lot* of Momentum from the rich B-Story already *in progress*. Therefore the term *Introduction* is far more accurate as a description of the events taking place at the Beginning.

There is another important reason to not use the term "setup." This term has traditionally been taught to emphasize the establishment of the A-Story. But as we've seen from most of our examples, the A-Story is subsidiary to the B-Story at the outset, only as a story picks up its steam does the A-Story take center stage.

Another concern with using the term "setup" is that this term carries with it the connotation of something *new* taking place. Yes, there is a new Situation impacting the life of the Main Character, but *nothing* is new.

The A-Story itself has its own Hidden Past, its own Proximate Cause and Proximate Cause Character, and all of that is well underway by the time a story *begins*.

This is why we use the term *Introduction* to start a story as opposed to *setup* or *Beginning*.

Your *Introduction* needs to bring us into the ongoing life of the Main Character. It frames the *relevant* B-storylines this Main Character needs to deal with in their life. It needs to introduce the Primary Situation (the A-Story). And hopefully, it should at least begin to establish *why* the Main Character is a Uniquely Extraordinary Main Character for *this* story (their Reasons). Establish *Relevance* as early as possible and do not waste an opportunity to make every element practically and thematically relevant.

Logic

The Underlying Cause Reasons (remember: the Main Character's *Personal Goal* and *Characterization*) converge with the Primary Situation and lead to a Logical Solution in the mind of the Main Character. When that happens, there is Motivation on the B-Story side and **SOLUTIONS** on the A-Story side. Every decision made and action taken in **ACT I** by *any* Character is based on *Logic*.

Obstacles

Of course, it's not much of a story if it's all smooth sailing for the Main Character. There is an age-old storytelling aphorism that says, "Drama *is* conflict." This does not mean that every scene in a story must involve Characters beating each other's brains in, but in some capacity, there are always Obstacles preventing success. And whatever the Main Character tries as a means to address the Primary Situation, it *does not work*. In great storytelling, both the A-Story *and* the B-Story should contribute forces that stand in the way of the Logical Solution's success.

The Primary Situation itself can be complex or formidable. Most stories (but not all) will have an *Antagonist* in one form or another with perhaps many agents working for the Antagonist. In such a story, the Antagonist along with their cronies stands in the way of success.

Perhaps confronting the Primary Situation necessitates taking a daunting Journey, because the solution is not readily available. Imagine an asteroid is on a collision course with the Earth (as in the movie *Armageddon*), and the only way to stop it is to Journey into space in order to use a specialized bomb to alter its course.

The Main Character is not only dealing with Obstacles from the A-Story, but also from the B-Story as well. In great stories, the Underlying Cause presents the Main Character with a Problem or Opportunity at the very same time. This can be an obstacle for handling the Primary Situation, such as in *Liar Liar* when Fletcher's son's wish comes from the B-Story and is the very reason he can't lie in the A-Story. Of course, if the Primary Situation offers a direct challenge to the Main Character's deeply held convictions—directly conflicts with their Personal Goal—internal conflict can be an obstacle.

The A-Story challenges to the Logical Solution are rooted in the **PRIMARY OBSTACLE:**

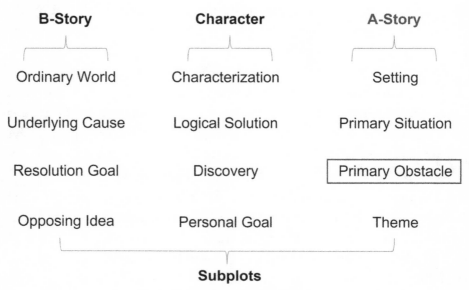

B-Story	Character	A-Story
Ordinary World	Characterization	Setting
Underlying Cause	Logical Solution	Primary Situation
Resolution Goal	Discovery	Primary Obstacle
Opposing Idea	Personal Goal	Theme

Subplots

Figure 60: The Primary Obstacle Element

The Primary Obstacle presents itself as a *Complication* or a *Journey* that is introduced at the end of Act 1 and gives Act 2 most of its energy. The *Primary Obstacle* stands in direct opposition to the Main Character's easy success. (More on Primary Obstacle when we get to the deeper dive into the Core Elements.)

The possibilities are endless, but the key takeaway about Obstacles is that the Introduction leads to a Logical Solution that runs up against a *Complication* or a *Journey.*

Failure

At the end of the last section on Obstacles, we said the Main Character's Logical Solution runs into a Complication or a Journey.

Think about it this way: a Main Character needs to get into a building. Their initial attempt is to simply walk up to the front door and turn the doorknob (their *Logical Solution*). The very first easy thing the Main Character tries does not work. The Main Character discovers the Primary Obstacle: the building is locked (a *Complication*). So now the Main Character tries other various strategies for getting into the building. They go around to the back door. They climb up on fire escapes. They try opening windows. They look for a cellar door. They finally try to break out a window and discover the building has ultra-strong security glass. Nothing works, so now the Main Character is at *the Midpoint.* Their Logical Solution has failed.

What we talk about with this fourth connection point is the ultimate Failure of the Logical Solution when the Main Character realizes that their approach will not work. As we said in the Transitional doorways discussion in the previous chapter, the Midpoint is *always* a Failure. Even if the Main Character succeeds in their initial Personal Goal, it turns out that this *success* does not resolve the Primary Situation (remember in *Die Hard*: McClane succeeds in alerting the authorities, but the authorities are ineffective, so he needs a new strategy). Hence their *Despair.* The initial Personal Goal has to change.

Again, the Midpoint is the end of *Logic*. To get into the building, this Main Character will need to try something radically different.

The Failure/Despair moment should *lead to* the A-Story Discovery movement *and* the B-Story Transformation movement. The Main Character must experience the exhaustion of their Logical options before they open themselves up to outside-the-box or counterintuitive modes of thought. In *Liar Liar*, it takes Fletcher running out of ways to circumvent Max's wish so he can win the case with a lie before he is open to the Discovery that begins his Transformation—in the legal case, as in his life, he discovers that he should tell the truth!

Desire

The Main Character moves from Failure to Despair to Discovery to Transformation and Clarity. And with Transformation, a Desire is born. The Main Character now *truly wants* the *opposite* of what they wanted at the outset. The Personal Goal shifts in the Thematic Conflict (unless we are dealing with a Steadfast Character, in which case it is a close Relationship Character—or *all* supporting Characters, i.e., *society*—whose Values have been challenged and who experiences the Transformation.)

Reversals

The transformed Main Character's new goal—the *Resolution Goal*—drives them toward new strategic action. Where they had once attempted to resolve the Primary Situation one way, they are now trying to resolve it by doing the opposite thing. This new point-of-view informs their actions and approach in *every* storyline within a given story, meaning that they apply the new approach to each individual Plot/Subplot at both the A Story and B Story levels.

In *Liar Liar*, Fletcher tells the truth to:
- Win the case
- Win his son back
- Win his ex-wife back
- Win his alienated secretary back

If the Transformation process that the Main Character experiences does not change their approach to resolving each A and B storyline Plot thread, then perhaps that Plot thread does not belong in that story.

Resolution

The Climax resolves the A-Story. The Resolution structural connection point resolves the B-Storylines. Once the Main Character has finally handled the Primary Situation, the Resolution demonstrates the Commitment to the Transformation is *cemented*. The lesson is learned. Change carries over to the Main Character's personal life relationships in the B-Story. There is a glimpse of the Revealed Potential into the Unknown Future.

The Resolution also is the end of the Revealed Story.

The Complete Character Wave: Full Case Study: *Liar Liar*

Now we want to illustrate the Character Wave Journey by walking through each step. There is no point in repeating this step-by-step through each example IP we have been examining, but we will present the Character Wave for each of them in summary later.

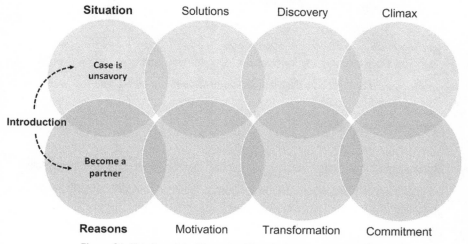

Figure 61: The Complete Character Wave in *Liar Liar* - Introduction

Reasons: Fletcher is a liar, which affects his relationship with his son and his ex-wife. It causes his son to make the wish that he can't lie for one day. Lying is how he approaches his work as an attorney. He wants to make partner and will employ ethically bent tactics to win cases.

Situation: His firm recognizes him as "ethically flexible" and therefore perfect to handle an unsavory case that everyone believes cannot be won on the merits of the facts.

Fletcher's Logic feeds *both* stories.

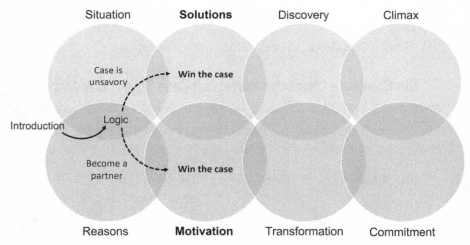

Figure 62: The Complete Character Wave in *Liar Liar* - Logic

Solution: Win the case by lying.

Motivation: Win the case by lying. Remember: Fletcher's Personal Goal is to make partner. What Fletcher Values is leaving a legacy, which for him means being the best provider and achieving status. And he expects others to share his Values. He is a good father when he is there. The Problem is that he places work above his relationships, so he is rarely there.

Fletcher does not know it at first, but Max has made a birthday wish that his father *cannot lie* for one day.

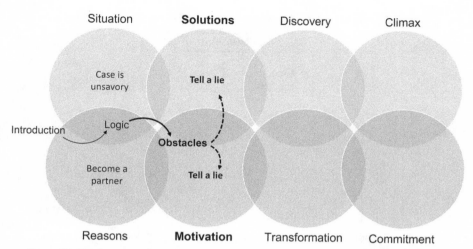

Figure 63: The Complete Character Wave in *Liar Liar* - Obstacles (Complication or Journey)

Secondary to that, the case is being heard on the same day this wish is in effect. Ideally, Fletcher would like to be able to lie and easily win the case. He would achieve his Personal Goal (become a partner) by simply weaving a false story—which he can skillfully do—and by suborning perjury—which he has no moral qualms doing. Unable to lie on the day of the trial, Fletcher tries to postpone the case to a day when he could lie, but he is unable to find a legitimate reason to ask for a continuance and cannot lie to invent one.

As a corollary to his inability to lie, Fletcher also discovers that he is unable to carry off the smallest socially tactful evasions of the truth, which leads him to multiple faux pas and openly bizarre, awkward behaviors. It's wonderful fodder for comedy, but it has effects beyond the case. It ends up delaying him in travel, having his car impounded, and eventually landing him in jail for contempt of court. And his truth-telling exposes previous falsehoods he told to his secretary. Unvarnished truth bruises numerous relationships outside the court and in his immediate family.

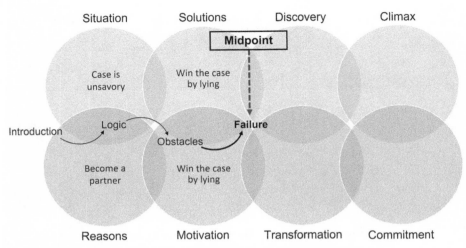

Figure 64: The Complete Character Wave in *Liar Liar* - Failure

One of the iconic pieces of physical comedy in *Liar Liar* features Jim Carrey *beating himself up* in the courthouse restroom. In his bid to win a continuance, Fletcher physically roughs himself up. When he's brought back into court with the assistance of a bailiff, the judge demands to know who did this to him. Without lying, Fletcher tells the judge: "A madman, your honor! A desperate fool at the end of his pitiful rope!"

Even this evasion of truth does not work. The judge, who is prepared to grant a continuance, asks if Fletcher feels he could continue despite his injuries. And of course, Fletcher cannot lie. The Midpoint Failure results in *Despair*.

There must be another way...

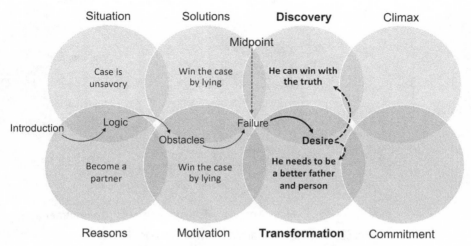

Figure 65: The Complete Character Wave in *Liar Liar* - Desire

Transformation is almost always a *process*. From the beginning, Max's wish confronts Fletcher with realizations about his Character. The truth continually holds up a mirror, and he doesn't like what he sees. We noted earlier that ex-wife Audrey helps Fletcher get his car out of impound, they argue and Fletcher blurts out, "Let me tell you something... *I'm not a good father*." This hits him hard. Every ugly utterance he hears coming from his own mouth is an accusation.

By the time his client drags her kids into court as a move for *sympathy*, Fletcher already has reached the point where he's displaying open contempt for her low character: "I feel sorry for them already," he tells her.

A-Story Discovery: He can win the case with the truth!

B-Story Discovery: He really wants a better relationship with his son.

B-Story Discovery: He can tell the truth and succeed.

Transformation: He sums it up, "And the truth will set you free!" He has tasted the power of *honesty*.

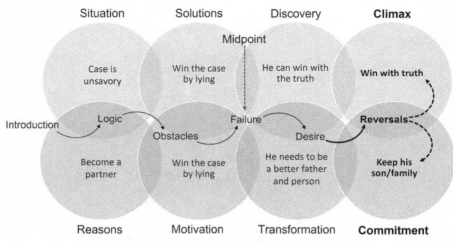

Figure 66: The Complete Character Wave in *Liar Liar* - Reversals

We listed the things Fletcher wants in the general discussion at the beginning of the chapter. Again:

- Win the case
- Win his son back
- Win his ex-wife back
- Win his alienated secretary back

How? By telling the truth. The Thematic Conflict played out.

The Climax of the Primary Situation is winning the case.

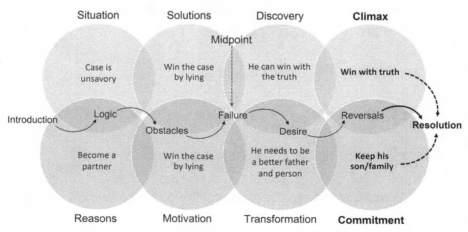

Figure 67: The Complete Character Wave in *Liar Liar* - Resolution

The Commitment to honesty is *lasting*. It's part of Fletcher's Character from this point forward, even after the time limit on his son's wish expires. It is now his Revealed Potential, and it moves on into the Unknown Future of his B-Story. His B-Story relationships are healed by it. We understand that his priorities are forever changed because of it. He won't continue at that dishonest law firm, having vowed to start his own firm helping the less fortunate.

Character Wave Summaries Four Example IPs

Star Wars

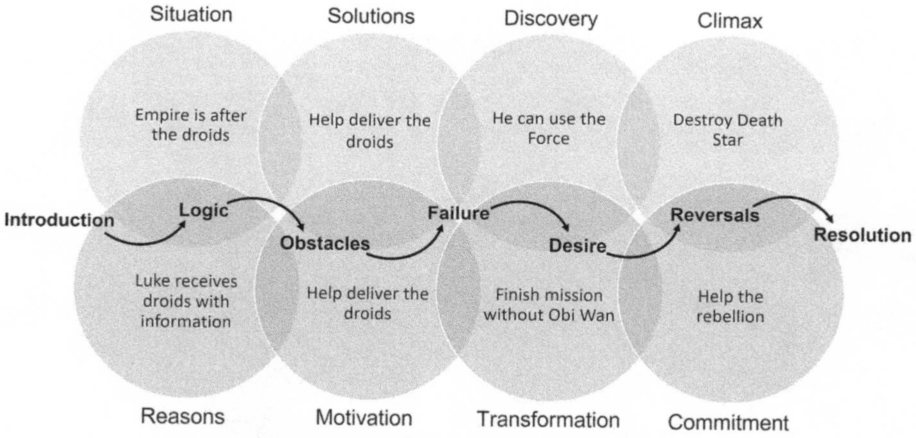

Figure 68: The Complete Character Wave in *Star Wars*

The Character Wave Journey for Luke Skywalker is a move from unremarkable farm hand longing to join the Rebellion against the evil Galactic Empire as a rank-and-file pilot to

- Receiving droids who possess valuable information
- Agreeing to join old Obi Wan Kenobi on a mission to deliver the droids to the Rebel leadership and learn about the ways of The Force as his long-gone father once did
- Being captured by the Empire, learning the Rebel leaders to whom they were taking the droids are dead, rescuing the captive Princess Leia who sent the droids, and witnessing the death of Obi Wan

- Feeling the Despair of losing his mentor
- Joining up with the remaining Rebels at their hidden base
- Joining the Rebels' long shot gambit to attack and destroy the Empire's Death Star
- Discovering he can still communicate with Kenobi through The Force and use his growing connection with The Force to guide him
- Using The Force to strike the fatal blow against the Death Star, thus saving the entire Rebellion
- Becoming a central figure in the Rebellion, it's New Hope, and the last of the Jedi

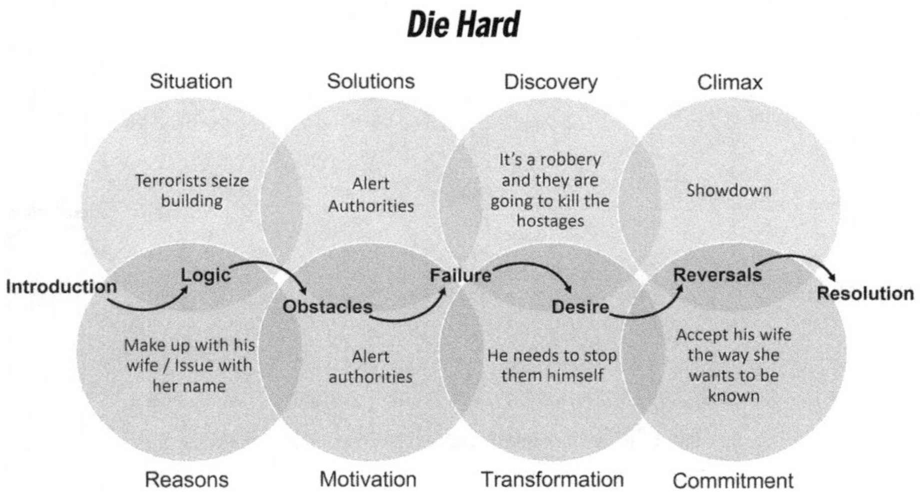

Die Hard

Figure 69: The Complete Character Wave in *Die Hard*

The Character Wave Journey for John McClane moves from a New York cop traveling to LA to try to reconcile with his estranged wife Holly and get her to renounce her West Coast life and maiden name to

- Narrowly escaping the apparent gang of terrorists seizing the building during Holly's company's Christmas Party
- Making every effort to stay hidden as he spies on the terrorists to gather intel
- Making a committed effort to alert the authorities to the Situation

- Participating in a cat-and-mouse guerilla combat where he obtains some crucial equipment, including a CB radio and the "terrorist's" explosive detonators
- Successfully alerting the authorities, who send a lone squad car before McClane dumps a dead body on it and the "terrorists" open fire
- Struggling with Despair as he observes the LA cops and FBI agents sent to the scene employ ineffective tactics that only complicate matters and fail to resolve the Situation
- Taking matters into his own hands to save some of his brothers-in-blue by exploding what seems to be all of the "terrorist's" C4 explosives
- Making the Discovery that leader Hans still wants the detonators because there is more C4 set to blow up the building roof during a helicopter rescue of the hostages, killing the hostages and covering for a getaway, and he discovers they are not terrorists at all but thieves, and thwarting this plan means taking on Hans and the remaining crew by himself from inside the building—at the same time, Hans discovers the identity of McClane and Holly because of a television reporter
- Brought into a direct confrontation between McClane and Hans with Holly used as a pawn
- Defeating Hans and accepting Holly's right to her choices and identity, leading to a reconciliation between the couple

Rocky

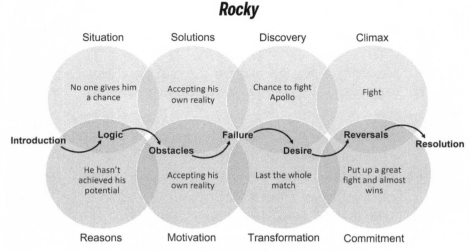

Figure 70: The Complete Character Wave in *Rocky*

The Character Wave Journey for Rocky Balboa is a move from a down-and-out boxer who has never lived up to his potential and makes his living roughing up money borrowers for a criminal loan shark, and whose entire life affirms he has no shots, no breaks to

- Confronting himself as an aging going-nowhere loser, losing his boxing gym locker, which is a sign of the end of the road for the one thing he clings to as his core identity
- Accepting the amazing break of being offered the chance to fight the heavyweight champ for the title belt, though he sees it as little more than a payday and chance for humiliation
- Beginning to believe in himself thanks to his trainer's efforts and Adrian's love
- Experiencing a crisis of confidence as he realizes he cannot beat the great fighter
- Embracing a new Personal Goal of just surviving the bout, something no other boxer has done against Apollo, to prove to himself that he is somebody
- Putting up a tremendous, gritty performance exhibiting incredible heart and stamina
- Lasting the entire match and nearly defeating the champ

The *Harry Potter* Series

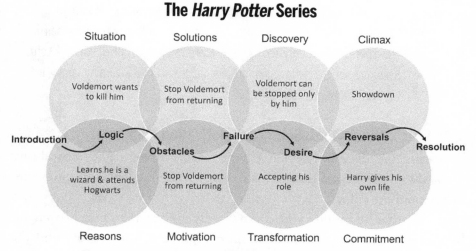

Figure 71: The Complete Character Wave in The *Harry Potter* Series

The Character Wave for Harry Potter over the course of the seven-book series is a move from a neglected orphan living under the stairs in his relatives' house to

- Learning about his heritage as a wizard, that he is special among wizards for surviving the evil wizard's attack that killed his parents, and receiving the invitation to attend wizarding school
- Accepting the invitation and entering the wizarding world
- Dealing with the expectations of many wizards that he must confront the Dark Lord Voldemort, which means preventing the evil wizard from returning to bodily form
- Having a series of adventures surrounding the effort of keeping Voldemort away and weathering the attacks of his minions
- Experiencing the Despair over failing to prevent Voldemort's return
- Assuming a lower profile, defensive posture as he solidifies his alliances and seeks the keys to the dark wizard's destruction
- Discovering the existence of Horcruxes and the mission to destroy these soul-storing talismans
- Learning he himself is a Horcrux, joined with Voldemort since the attack when he was an infant
- Enduring the sacrifices of his guardian-protectors, Dumbledore and Snape

- Accepting that vanquishing Voldemort once and for all is up to him
- Having the final showdown with Voldemort, including putting himself in grave personal jeopardy and using several strategies to outwit the Dark Lord
- Assuming an "ever after" comfortable life as part of a wizarding family, living a not-too-remarkable life

Quick Word: Solutions/Motivation Alignment

Repeating the disclaimer from Chapter One: Always does not always *mean* always. There are exceptions to every rule. The key is to know and understand the rules.

With that in mind, you undoubtedly notice that our Movement breakdown descriptions for the Solutions phase of the A-Story and the Motivation phase of the B-Story (the second Movement of each side of the story) are all identical:

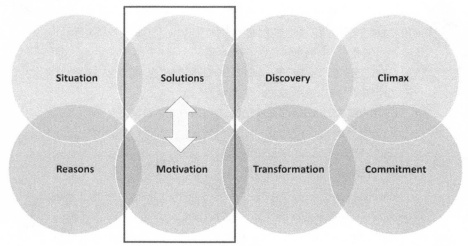

Figure 72: Solutions/Motivation Movement

What this illustrates is the A and B stories colliding and coming into alignment at this juncture of the narrative for your Main Character. And it's *not* merely a mirror image here. What we're saying is the Main Character applies Logic to the new Problem or Opportunity that has been introduced into their life and takes actions that make sense in addressing *both* the Primary Situation *and* the Underlying Cause storylines.

Let's go through them:

In *Liar Liar*, Fletcher wants to *win the case by lying* in the A-Story because, well—heck, he needs to win the case! Pretty simple. He's a lawyer. It's his job. And he needs to win the case *by lying* in the B-Story because:

- He wants to become a partner.
- He wants to leave a legacy for his son and be a great provider.
- He competes in life with his wife's new boyfriend for Max's affection and ultimately hers. He cares about the status that a great career brings him in their eyes (or so he believes).

In *Star Wars*, Luke decides to *help Obi-Wan deliver the droids* in the A-Story because the Rebels need the information in R2D2, and Obi-Wan confesses he's too old to do it alone. And Luke decides to *help Obi-Wan deliver the droids* in the B-Story because he has a longing for adventure and a true Desire to contribute in some way to the Rebellion against the Empire. Additionally, he learns about his father's identity as a Jedi Knight and now has the Opportunity to learn the ways of The Force from Obi-Wan.

In *Die Hard*, John McClane needs to *alert the authorities* in the A-Story because this is a crime scenario and handling crimes is the job of the cops and the FBI. Plus, he's outnumbered. He also wants to *alert the authorities* in the B-Story because his wife is one of the hostages. Of course, as a decent person and as a cop, he is motivated to stop the "terrorists" anyway. But, specifically, taking the most prudent approach to keeping the hostages safe is paramount, as is staying as hidden as possible because his wife can be used as leverage against him. He has a particular interest in protecting her. This is the more sane route for John's B-Story rather than rushing in guns blasting away.

In *Rocky*, Rocky Balboa's A/B story split comes as a *boxer versus life in general*. So, on the A-Story side, *accepting his own reality* means coming to terms with the looming end of his once-promising but unfulfilled boxing career. On the B-Story side, *accepting his own reality* refers to the deeper self-awareness of what a post-boxing life as a financially unsuccessful low-level criminal muscle living in decaying conditions entails. Who is he as a man?

In the *Harry Potter* series, Harry has little choice but to *prevent Voldemort from returning* in the A-Story because otherwise, Voldemort wants to kill him and execute his chilling plot to purify the wizarding race by slaughtering so many half-bloods. On the B-Story side, Harry must *prevent Voldemort from returning* because he is growing into himself as a wizard. He has the Opportunity to attend Hogwarts and take his place in wizard society. He has a prophesied destiny. Every relationship he forms as a wizard is predicated on this identity as "The Boy Who Lived."

Our examination of the Complete Character Wave is complete. You should now better understand the four Movements of the A-Story and how the interplay between the forces of the A-Story Movements against the analogous B-Story Movements creates the Main Character's Transformation we think of as the *Character Wave* in this system. We described the seven Structural Connection Points that define the Character Wave pathway. Hopefully, you now see why we choose the term *Character Wave* over the traditional Character Arc to describe this Journey.

In the next chapter, we delve into the Twelve Core Concepts of the Your Storytelling Potential Method. Master these twelve elements, and you will have the building blocks necessary for constructing solid, amazing stories.

CHAPTER 7:

Twelve Core Elements

Consider our effort to build your understanding of the Your Story-telling Potential Method analogous to road construction. We started by surveying the geography with the two-story model. The Movements of the A and B stories are like the rolling hills of a landscape. The foundational ideas of the Three Branches and Thematic Conflict are your engineering and architecture study. The Complete Character Wave is the planned roadway across the region. And the seven connection points are signposts while the three Transitional doorways are planned bridges.

In this metaphor, the *Core Elements* are the *pavers*. These twelve blocks are the necessary building materials you use. In our future discussion on Story Structure, we will see that the conceptual plan we have laid out dictates the distribution of these Core Elements across the timeline of the Revealed Story. If you have come this far, then perhaps you are already seeing that skillful application of these principles maximizes your potential for producing richly Layered, thematically relevant narratives. A solid road for your Main Characters and audience to experience a satisfying transformative Journey together.

And for the same reasons you would not build a road without planning, the seventh universal storytelling truth is: Constructing a great story requires *thorough planning* before attempting the first draft.

We have already given you a few peeks at the Twelve Core Elements because we needed to talk about most of these Elements as they related to other topics in previous chapters. But the time has come to focus on the Elements themselves and clarify any gaps in your understanding.

Once again, here are the Twelve Core Elements of the Your Storytelling Potential Method:

B-Story	Character	A-Story
Ordinary World	Characterization	Setting
Underlying Cause	Logical Solution	Primary Situation
Resolution Goal	Discovery	Primary Obstacle
Opposing Idea	Personal Goal	Theme

Subplots

Figure 73: The Twelve Core Elements

How to think about the Twelve Core Elements

There is an old aphorism about writing that goes, "Writing is Rewriting."

We are not precisely taking issue with that time-tested wisdom, but we do believe the preparation available to students of this method sets them up for striking closer to the center of the target on the initial pass. We have said continually throughout this book that creating great stories is a creative *iterative* process of discovery. That's not terribly different from saying "writing is rewriting." It is only a question of when you do the creative *discovery,* before or after you've invested the time in writing a first draft—you'll need to do it either way.

Our contention is that most traditional methods leave student-writers unclear about *how* and ultimately leave them operating in the blind hoping to stumble upon the answers by accident. They sort of tell student-writers what the finished product looks like and maybe offer some structural rules for what type of things should happen and when, but provide no clear understanding of why. And it is knowing *why* that empowers your creativity.

What makes the Core Elements unique is that they let you think *dynamically* and *relationally* about your story. This is the biggest difference you need to understand if you are going to *get* this method. Plot is not a string of beads but the system of interrelationships among related Elements, like the inside of a watch.

Instead of thinking *linearly* about the story—Event #1, then Event #2, then the First Act Turning Point, then Events #4, 5, and 6, and on to the Midpoint, etc.—you can have the *full picture* of the puzzle, like the box top to a jigsaw puzzle, before you ever start assembling it. You can understand the foundational conceptual relationships *before* sorting out temporal cause and effect actions.

Details, event order, and dialogue become extensions *implied by* the Core Elements. These are foundational creative guideposts. Knowing these essential ingredients to your story enables you to whip up the recipe. They spark inspiration for scenes. It becomes easier to find the connective tissue that holds the major story points together.

When you take an original concept and flesh out the Core Elements, it clarifies how much you know about your story. There is no shame if an exciting new idea only allows you to complete details for just a couple of the Core Elements. It simply shows you what else you need before you're ready to write the story.

Layers: Brick-by-Brick

The Twelve Core Elements are organized into three columns, each corresponding to one of the Three Branches: B-Story, Main Character, and A-Story.

In case it does not leap off the page at you, they are also organized into four relevant *rows*. Each row represents a *story Layer*. The Main Character sits between the A and B Stories. First, the Main Character is a practical participant in each story. And, second, the Main Character Core Element in each Layer relates conceptually to the other two Elements in the same Layer.

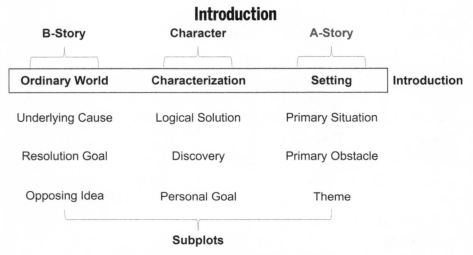

Figure 74:Core Elements - The Introduction Layer

The **INTRODUCTION LAYER** reveals information and story Elements that *already exist* prior to the Beginning of your Revealed Story. The Introduction orients the audience to the *Setting*—which is the place and time or *arena* in which the A-Story takes place, and also the source of the Proximate Cause and Proximate Cause Character, a very deep and important concept that we will explore more in Chapter 10. The Introduction also introduces the Main Character (*Characterization*), familiarizing the audience with relevant information about the life they have led to this point (*Ordinary World*) and establishes their *Personal Goal*.

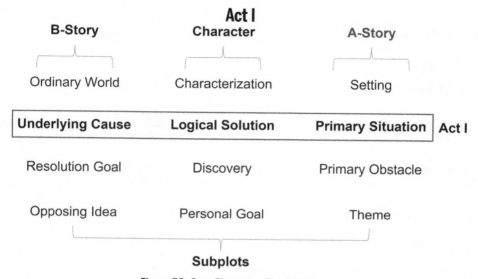

Figure 75: Core Elements - The Act I Layer

The **ACT I LAYER** begins the Revealed Story and contains the Convergence of the A-Story and the B-Story.

A Main Character living an already complex life suddenly faces a new Problem or Opportunity (*Primary Situation*) and makes their first decision about what action to take in response to it (*Logical Solution*). At the same time, there is something else going on in the Main Character's life, an *Underlying Cause* that also offers a Problem or Opportunity and complicates matters for handling the Primary Situation. Usually, the Logical Solution for the Primary Situation and for the Underlying Cause is the same thing.

Author-Storytellers rarely have much difficulty with Act I, except perhaps having to edit it down. The temptation is to underestimate the audience and feel like an extensive background needs to be established all at once, so it can easily become overstuffed. Generally, though, this is a good problem to have when the goal is to have a compelling tale that moves along with purpose.

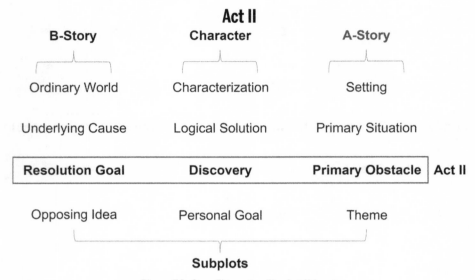

Figure 76: Core Elements - The Act II Layer

The **ACT II LAYER** begins with the Introduction of the Primary Obstacle.

Act 2 has two distinct parts, or *tiers*, separated by the Midpoint.

The Main Character's *Logical Solution* runs into difficulty in the form of the *Primary Obstacle*. The Main Character remains committed to their Logical Solution and makes several attempts to overcome the Primary Obstacle to reach it. There is a Midpoint Failure. This leads to Despair. In their Despair, the Main Character questions their *Personal Goal*, and, as they seek a better solution, they make a *Discovery* about why their Logical Solution is not working. The Discovery inspires a Desire to apply a new solution, called the *Resolution Goal*.

Act 2 is usually the most challenging part of a story to get right. It is the largest of the three acts and contains the hardest objectives to pin down. Middles can often get muddy.

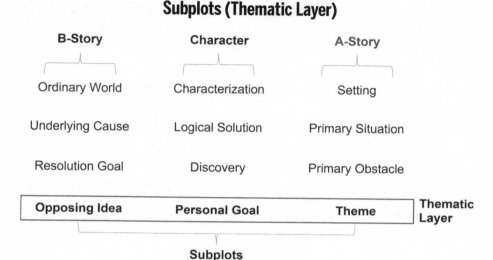

Figure 77: Core Elements–The Thematic Layer

The **THEMATIC LAYER** functions as the glue holding all of the storylines together, most notably the A and B stories.

In the organization of the Core Elements, the Main Character sits between the B-Story column and the A-Story column. Both sides exert force, pushing and pulling on the Main Character. In the Thematic Layer, the Personal Goal defines the Thematic Conflict between the *Theme* and the *Opposing Idea*. Additionally, the Theme finds expression through the *Subplots* which center on all of the key relationships that the Main Character has or establishes in the course of the entire story.

It goes without saying that Theme informs the entire story and is not relegated to any one part of it. (Review Chapter Three for a thorough examination of Theme dynamics.)

What about Act III?

Act III has no Core Elements or story information of its own. It's too late to introduce new information in the third act.

Act III is the culmination of the Revealed Story. Everything needed for Act III is already in place from Act I and II. Act III is for resolving all of the storylines that have been opened.

Closer Look: The B-Story Elements

B-Story

Ordinary World

Underlying Cause

Resolution Goal

Opposing Idea

- The world of the B-Story
- Frames the Introduction
- Frames the Main Character's Personal Goal
- Frames the Subplots
- The Main Character's reality before the story begins
- The Hidden Past
- There is *no* going back

Figure 78: The B-Story Elements - Ordinary World

Emphasis here on the last point: In this method of thinking about stories, we do not use the term *Ordinary World* in precisely the same way you might have encountered it when you learned about other systems.

Traditionally, *ordinary world* is a literal place and/or the lived experience of a Protagonist's mundane life that they *leave* to enter a new world of the story. The Protagonist experiences an adventure and *wins* something of great value at the conclusion that they *bring back* to their *ordinary world*. This thing is often called the *elixir*. It may be something tangible, but more often it is a lesson the Protagonist has learned. Virtually all systems attempt to quantify the process of Transformation over the course of a narrative. We simply disagree that the model where a Protagonist departs from their ordinary life and then returns to it is the most accurate.

In the Your Storytelling Potential Method, the Ordinary World is the Main Character's life as it has been lived from the Hidden Past into the Now. There truly is no *leaving* this world. The essence of the Ordinary World is woven into their being. It's *who they are*. Physical location is irrelevant. A person can have a grand adventure without leaving their bedroom, just as traveling from one planet to another might be just a mundane day in the life of another Main Character.

Of course, we understand that the traditional concept of departing from the ordinary world does not simply mean *the Protagonist takes a physical trip away from home*. What we want to clarify is that just because the Main Character experiences significant events in the Revealed Story, it does not mean they are doing anything more than continuing to live the life they have always been living. From the Main Character's point of view, they are just dealing with something that is *new*. The key difference is the amount of baggage they bring into the Now. They haven't packed away all their troubles into storage in some faraway locker that puts their *backstory* on hold while they go do something else for a period.

And the Ordinary World is *never the same* after the *Transformation* of the Main Character. Their Outer World reflects the Inner World. As we have pondered the existential question about how to consider a person absent from the life they live, we believe accuracy dictates thinking of the two as necessarily entangled relative to the Transformation. The Revealed Story is a period of Transition for the Main Character, and this Transition must also change their Ordinary World as well.

The adventure of the story may leave the Main Character in a different physical space. Or it may see them back to familiar environs. Either way, that Transformation alters their relationship so profoundly that it simply is not accurate to see them as having come back to the same place.

- The Problem/Opportunity from the B-Story
- B-Story Problem/Opportunity derives from Underlying Cause Character
- In great stories, the cause of the A-Story's potential
- The Reason why the Main Character is Uniquely Extraordinary

Figure 79: The B-Story Elements - Underlying Cause

Early in the book, we said that *B-Story* and *Underlying Cause* are virtually synonymous. Yet, now we show Underlying Cause as one of the four B-Story Core Elements.

It should be clear that Underlying Cause is the major Now aspect of the B-Story. It is a *current* and *relevant* Problem or Opportunity stemming directly from the B-Story. And it is generally not directly related to the Primary Situation of the A-Story. For all intents and purposes, the two are the same when viewed through the lens of the Revealed Story.

In *Liar Liar*, the Underlying Cause is Max's wish—and telling that aspect of the story necessarily encompasses the relevant details and relationships of the B-Story.

In *Star Wars*, the Underlying Cause is the hand of fate (The Force) bringing the droids into Luke's life—which speaks to his Personal Goal of joining the Rebellion and puts him in touch with his familial lineage and destiny as a Jedi.

In *Die Hard*, the Underlying Cause is McClane's Opportunity to reconcile with Holly, who is using her maiden name at work—which puts him in the building as a wildcard and creates a sizzling dynamic of cat and mouse enhanced by hidden identities.

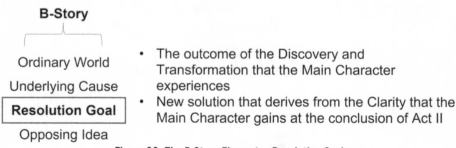

Figure 80: The B-Story Elements - Resolution Goal

The Resolution Goal is straightforward.

The Main Character's efforts to resolve the Primary Situation Problem or Opportunity have crashed on the rocks by the Midpoint of the story. This leads to Despair, which leads to soul searching and a reappraisal of mindset and Values. The reappraisal leads to a Discovery (or many Discoveries). The Discovery facilitates the completion of Transformation. With the complete picture and a renewed mindset, a *new* approach to the Primary Situation emerges. That *Clarity* informs the Resolution Goal.

One of the great ironies revealed by the Resolution Goal is that typically the actions that are required to resolve the story and bring about the final Climax and Resolution are the opposite of the actions attempted with the Logical Solution.

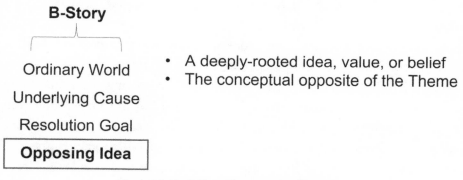

B-Story

Ordinary World
Underlying Cause
Resolution Goal
Opposing Idea

- A deeply-rooted idea, value, or belief
- The conceptual opposite of the Theme

Figure 81: The B-Story Elements - Opposing Idea

We have talked extensively about the Thematic Conflict between Theme and the Opposing Idea. It's important to understand that our concept of Theme is *not* a preachy message for the audience. It's also critical to understand that a properly integrated Theme requires an Opposing Idea dynamic playing against it.

Closer Look: The Character Elements

Character

Characterization
Logical Solution
Discovery
Personal Goal

- Relevant and specific information about the Main Character that defines who they are and why they are Uniquely Extraordinary
- Not a biography

Figure 82: The Character Elements - Characterization

172 | **YOUR STORYTELLING POTENTIAL**

This description pertains to the Main Character alone. All other significant characters are defined by their relationship to the Main Character—the main subject of the Revealed Story. In this method, we think of every character other than *the* Main Character as a *Subplot*. The portrayed relationships between the Main Character and the main Relationship Character, the Antagonist, and any mentors, lovers, friends, and enemies are Subplots.

When we say that Characterization is *not a biography*, what do we mean?

Every writer has their own process. Many writers and many creative writing teachers espouse a practice of writing extensive *backstory* biographies for their major Characters as a prelude to writing the actual body of their story. It is not unheard of for some Author-Storytellers to crank out dozens of pages detailing their Characters' every life moment since birth. And if you feel devoted to this level of detail to gain a grasp of your Characters, there is likely nothing we can say to dissuade you from it. As preparation-centered as the Your Storytelling Potential Method is, we nonetheless counsel that spending an inordinate amount of effort on backstory may be a waste of your time and energy.

It takes a *lot* of work to build a story. What we hope to give you in this method is a structure for thinking about your narrative architecture that places attention where it is needed most. For this reason, we talk about *Convergence* as the *first takeaway* of the method and continually hammer on the idea of *Relevance* as it leads to sound Structure and thematically Layered, deeper, and richer storytelling. Attention to Relevance breeds completeness. Building your stories using the Core Elements in conjunction with the concepts we explain and exercises we provide will result in well-rounded, three-dimensional, *relevant* Characters.

That process, we believe, relies on a process of beginning with your core story concept and *working back to* a relevant Main Character with a relevant Personal Goal. We talked about this in the third chapter's discussion of Theme. So a lengthy backstory has little value if it just creates an irrelevant backstory with irrelevant details that have no bearing on the story you intend to tell. It's not just a matter of time wasted thinking up life details that won't play a part in your Revealed Story—though that is also a danger here. But literally, there is a folly in beginning the story construction process with a Character history not in-service to the Theme and the Revealed Story you want to tell.

If you have thoroughly built out the Core Elements, *then* it might make some sense to spend time fleshing out the meat on those bones. Just to be armed with interesting *relevant* details. But your knowledge of the Main Character's essence should be complete once you have established all of the Core Elements.

As an example, nothing about the Revealed Story of *Liar Liar* informs the audience of Fletcher Reede's backstory that explains *why* he is so career-focused or what childhood experiences gave him a bent moral compass concerning honesty. *Maybe* those are details the writer(s) considered. There's no harm in brainstorming that kind of Main Character history in case you discover a need for it somewhere in your story.

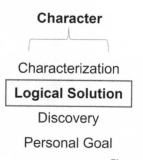

Character

Characterization
Logical Solution
Discovery
Personal Goal

- The plan or goal that frames the first series of actions that a Main Character takes in response to the current situation
- Main Character believes that this the best response to the Problem or Opportunity before them

Figure 83: The Character Elements - Logical Solution

Situation means *both* the Primary Situation *and* the Underlying Cause!

Yes, the Logical Solution is the Main Character's immediate response to the Primary Situation, *but* it also takes into account constraints placed by an Underlying Cause Problem or strategically attempting to take advantage of an Underlying Cause Opportunity.

In *LIAR LIAR*, Fletcher's Logical Solution is to *win the case by lying* despite *his son's wish that prevents him from lying.*

In *Star Wars*, Luke's Logical Solution is to *deliver the droids to defeat the Empire* while *growing into a significant part of the Rebellion by learning the ways of the Force and becoming a Jedi like his father.*

In *Die Hard*, McClane's Logical Solution is to *alert the authorities* without *placing the woman the terrorists don't know is his wife in jeopardy.*

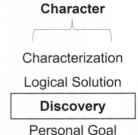

Character

Characterization

Logical Solution

Discovery

Personal Goal

- Experienced by the Main Character towards the end of Act II
- New information about the A-Story compels the Main Character to reconsider their Logical Solution
- Discovery is primarily an experience for the Main Character, not for the audience (although it can be for the audience as well)
- Can be multiple Discoveries
- Associated with the Theme and Personal Goal

Figure 84: The Character Elements - Discovery

Discovery provides one or more keys to unlocking a new solution for resolving the Primary Situation. It occurs in the wake of the Midpoint Failure and subsequent Despair. And it acts as something of a catalyst that completes the Transformation.

Not all of the discoveries in the Discovery phase must necessarily *help* the Main Character. One of the important discoveries toward the end of *Die Hard*, for example, is seen when Hans Gruber learns that Holly Gennaro is McClane's wife. This Discovery is obviously linked to the *identity* Theme, and it also factors into McClane's realization that he must confront Gruber and save the day by himself. Other discoveries in *Die Hard* include McClane's learning that this is a robbery, not a terrorist takeover, and finding explosives intended to blow up the roof during the hostage rescue.

Character

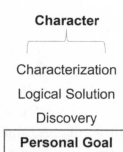

Characterization

Logical Solution

Discovery

Personal Goal

- The fundamental desire of the Main Character in the context of the story
- Associated with the Theme and the Opposing Idea

Figure 85: The Character Elements - Personal Goal

The Personal Goal is *independent* of the B-Story's Underlying Cause.

Differentiating between the Personal Goal and the Underlying Cause's Opposing Idea may present a challenge. It might not be clear how there are two Thematic Layer Core Elements coming from the Main Character and from their B-Story personal life. The Personal Goal tends to be *specific* to the Main Character whereas the Opposing Idea is a broader Value that supports it. The Personal Goal should be in-alignment with the Opposing Idea, but they are not precisely the same thing.

Obviously, the Personal Goal is separate from the A-Story. The A-Story is new and the Theme stemming from it should *challenge* the Main Character's Personal Goal.

Closer Look: The A-Story Elements

A-Story

Setting

Primary Situation

Primary Obstacle

Theme

- The world where the story takes place in the Now
- The source of the Proximate Cause
- Different from the Ordinary World even if the location is the same
- The source of the Problem or Opportunity presented to the Main Character that ultimately transforms the Main Character and their Ordinary World

Figure 86: The A-Story Elements - Setting

The Setting is primarily defined by the Proximate Cause.

As we've explained, the A-Story is not the story of the Main Character, rather the A-Story belongs to the Proximate Cause Character, and the Proximate Cause Character is motivated by the Proximate Cause itself.

The Proximate Cause is rooted within the Setting of the A-Story. In fact, the Proximate Cause is the *reason* for a specific Setting. All this goes back to Relevance in storytelling: nothing is arbitrary. If the A-Story takes place within a certain domain or arena, it is because the very reason for the A-Story is linked to that domain or arena, and that link is the Proximate Cause.

The Setting can also have a unique duplicity to it. Even though the Setting can be the same *place* as the Ordinary World, the Situation is different.

By this point, it should be clear that a story's *worlds* are more than the physical setting. It's about how the Main Character relates to their environment. Great Journeys of mind are possible for one lone individual locked in a 6-foot-by-6-foot prison cell whereas a futuristic worker with a dull job whose daily commute takes them from planet-to-planet can feel like their life is going nowhere.

In *Liar Liar*, none of Fletcher Reede's physical world changes in the story. He moves through a *world* of home, law office, familiar city streets, elevators, and courtrooms. The *challenges* he faces in the Now of the story change his *world* radically. He does not know how to navigate it. Unable to get by without deceptions, he is lost. He might as well be on Mars.

On a *practical level*, yes, Setting does involve factual data like physical location and time period. But you also must understand that the Main Character's *relationship* to time and place makes the Setting the arena for the unfolding events of the story.

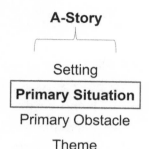

A-Story

Setting

Primary Situation

Primary Obstacle

Theme

- The Problem or Opportunity presented to the Main Character by the A-Story
- Associated with the Proximate Cause and the Proximate Cause Character

Figure 87: The A-Story Elements - Primary Situation

As we've already explained, the Primary Situation is the A-Story based *Problem* or *Opportunity* that represents the *new* Situation or circumstance introduced into the Main Character's Life.

The Primary Situation is directly related to the Proximate Cause Character. The Primary Cause Character's interest in the A-Story's outcome is based on the Proximate Cause itself, which creates the main reason for the A-Story to take place.

The Primary Situation is what links the Main Character to the Proximate Cause. The Problem or Opportunity that is presented to the Main Character by way of the A-Story comes from the Proximate Cause Character.

These ideas are fully explored in Chapter 10, but at the heart of any A-Story is another Character whose actions present themselves to the Main Character as a *Problem* or *Opportunity* we call the Primary Situation.

Back in the first chapter's breakdown of the Your Storytelling Potential Method, we presented a case study of *Liar Liar*. Recall that we asked what you think the Primary Situation of the movie is. Do you agree that most people would answer that question mentioning the magic wish and/or a lawyer who cannot lie?

Place yourself in the shoes of the writers of *Liar Liar* brainstorming to capitalize on the *high concept: a lawyer who cannot tell a lie*. Most writers would start off thinking that *a lawyer who cannot tell a lie* would be the Primary Situation, but it's not. Rather the *Opportunity* to become a partner if Fletcher wins a specific case is the actual Primary Situation, that is the A-Story. And that A-Story stems from the firm's Desire to win the case, not Fletcher's.

What we are driving at here is the power of the Core Elements. It cannot be overstated: story construction is a creative *iterative* process. As you work through your ideas and flesh out the Core Elements before writing your story, very often you will discover that what you have been thinking about your story is all wrong. Elements will get moved. Now you see the *magic wish* is actually just part of your B-Story, and you truly don't know what your A-Story is.

Better to find out now before you've written half a screenplay or hundreds of pages of a novel!

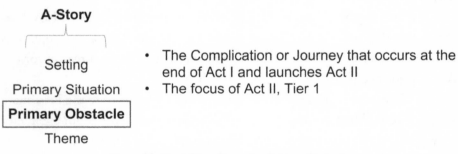

A-Story

Setting

Primary Situation

Primary Obstacle

Theme

- The Complication or Journey that occurs at the end of Act I and launches Act II
- The focus of Act II, Tier 1

Figure 88: The A-Story Elements - Primary Obstacle

We resist saying that the presence of a Primary Obstacle is merely a storytelling device. Arguably it is.

However, if you think about the hundreds of problems you solve and opportunities you take advantage of *each day*, you probably wouldn't consider many of them to be compelling stories worth telling. It's a modern-day cliche criticism about social media; for example, that people get tired of posts detailing the mundane events of life such as a picture of what you ate for lunch.

Like, oh, you made a sandwich. And it was yummy? Wow. (yawn)

A key ingredient to the fuel that feeds the fire of interesting storytelling is a formidable Primary Obstacle. It's a big reason why the Main Character's Logical Solution to the Primary Situation Problem fails at the

Midpoint. It's the wrinkle to the plan that provides the challenging catalyst for Transformation.

Why does the Main Character's Logical Solution prove to be inadequate?

The Main Character has a Primary Obstacle to overcome before they can directly address the Primary Situation head-on. The Primary Obstacle comes in many forms. Often it's an Antagonist or one of their agents. It can be a magic wish or a legal hassle that prevents the Main Character from moving forward. Sometimes the goal is far away, requiring a (perilous) Journey to get there. There's a piece of the puzzle missing, and it has to be located first. The Primary Obstacle could be an internal fear or something that conflicts with a deeply held conviction. Endless possibilities.

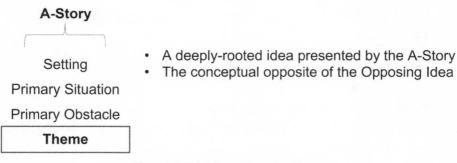

Figure 89: The A-Story Elements - Theme

In previous chapters, we've explored the concept of Theme as it applies to this method of storytelling. We explained that Theme is not some message for an audience, nor should it be confused with the subject matter. The Theme is a Value or idea.

Theme, and its counterpart, the Opposing Idea, are conflicting Values or ideas that form the Thematic Layer that contains the Thematic Conflict found in great stories. The Thematic Layer presents opposing viewpoints to the Main Character, whose Personal Goal is based on the Opposing Idea, which is challenged by the Theme.

Theme is a tangible **PHILOSOPHICAL IDEA** that is challenging the Main Character at a deeply rooted core Layer, namely their Personal Goal, and that Thematic Conflict gets developed in the Subplots:

Subplots

- All the relationship-based storylines from both the A-Story and the B-Story
- The Subplots are always rooted in the conflict between the Theme and the Opposing Idea
- The Main Character represents the Opposing Idea while other Subplot characters represent the Theme

Figure 90: Subplots

Basically, every interaction and dialogue the Main Character has with supporting Characters that get time on the playing field is a *Subplot*. That excludes bit players like cab drivers and sales clerks who appear as a blip on the radar. It also excludes the aunt the Main Character is supposed to pick up at the airport but we never meet or hear about again.

We will talk about Subplots and what you need to know about them later. For now, what's important is that Subplots are not arbitrary scenes to flesh out the story's world and give your Main Character the appearance of a full life. They play a functional role in moving the story forward, at least at the thematic level. What we will see in the broader discussion is that Subplots drive the story forward—they *cause* Complications, they *cause* the Problems, they *cause* the Opportunities, and they *cause* the Journeys.

These interactions should always be rooted in the Thematic Conflict. For this reason, it's helpful to think of Subplots as **THEME PLOTS**. Relationship Characters who do not drive the story forward nor develop the

Theme simply do not belong in your story, no matter how fun and quirky or interesting they might otherwise be.

Case Studies: The Core Elements of the Example IPs

Let's take a look at the Core Element breakdowns for each of the five major IPs we have been examining throughout *Your Storytelling Potential*. With these IPs, we have the advantage of analyzing produced work by discussing the concept material. As Author-Storytellers building up new narratives, we need to have this level of complete relational understanding of our Core Elements before there is enough foundation to build upon. This precedes any outline, timeline, or serious construction of individual scenes.

Use the exercise tools from Chapter 4—the Reasons and Thematic Connections exercise and the "What is it about?" exercise. These should focus your creative process as you work to complete the Core Elements grid.

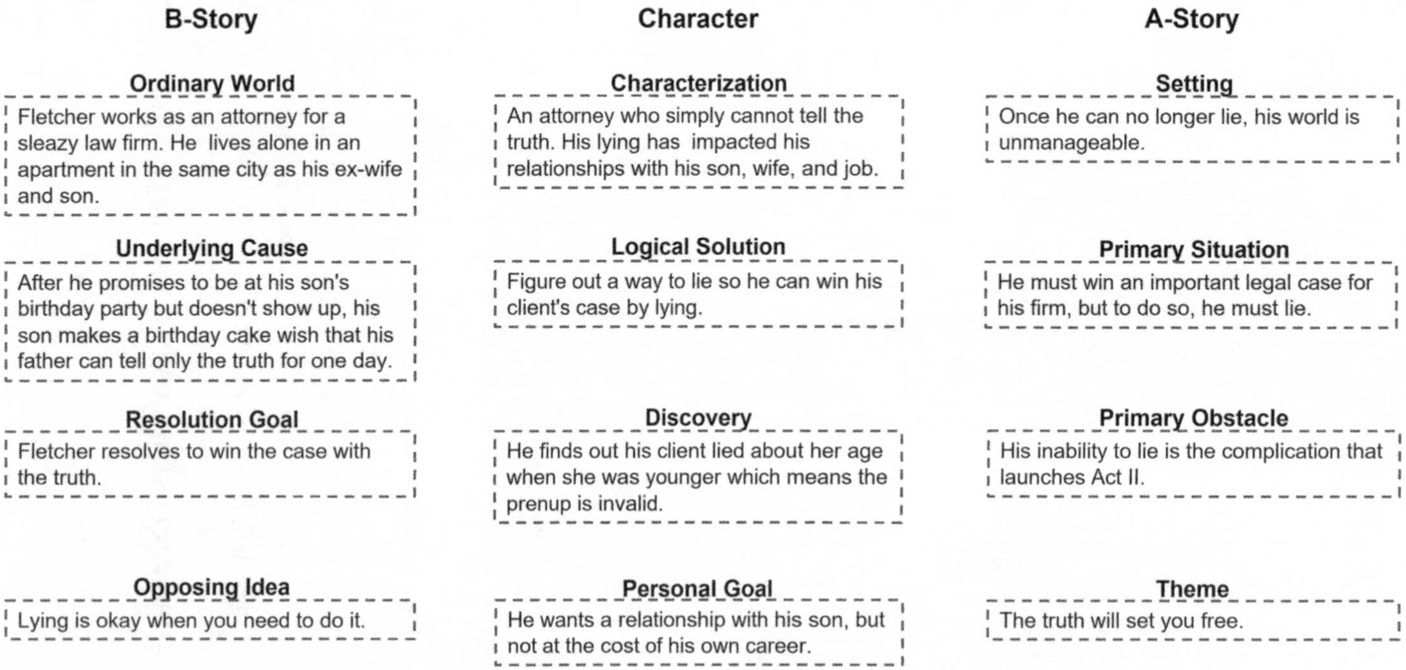

B-Story

Ordinary World

Fletcher works as an attorney for a sleazy law firm. He lives alone in an apartment in the same city as his ex-wife and son.

Underlying Cause

After he promises to be at his son's birthday party but doesn't show up, his son makes a birthday cake wish that his father can tell only the truth for one day.

Resolution Goal

Fletcher resolves to win the case with the truth.

Opposing Idea

Lying is okay when you need to do it.

Character

Characterization

An attorney who simply cannot tell the truth. His lying has impacted his relationships with his son, wife, and job.

Logical Solution

Figure out a way to lie so he can win his client's case by lying.

Discovery

He finds out his client lied about her age when she was younger which means the prenup is invalid.

Personal Goal

He wants a relationship with his son, but not at the cost of his own career.

A-Story

Setting

Once he can no longer lie, his world is unmanageable.

Primary Situation

He must win an important legal case for his firm, but to do so, he must lie.

Primary Obstacle

His inability to lie is the complication that launches Act II.

Theme

The truth will set you free.

Figure 91: Core Elements for *Liar Liar*

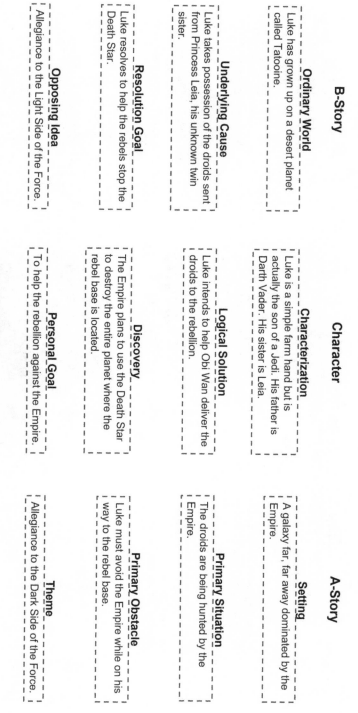

B-Story

Ordinary World
Luke has grown up on a desert planet called Tatooine.

Underlying Cause
Luke takes possession of the droids sent from Princess Leia, his unknown twin sister.

Resolution Goal
Luke resolves to help the rebels stop the Death Star.

Opposing Idea
Allegiance to the Light Side of the Force.

Character

Characterization
Luke is a simple farm hand but is actually the son of a Jedi. His father is Darth Vader. His sister is Leia.

Logical Solution
Luke intends to help Obi Wan deliver the droids to the rebellion.

Discovery
The Empire plans to use the Death Star to destroy the entire planet where the rebel base is located.

Personal Goal
To help the rebellion against the Empire.

A-Story

Setting
A galaxy far, far away dominated by the Empire.

Primary Situation
The droids are being hunted by the Empire.

Primary Obstacle
Luke must avoid the Empire while on his way to the rebel base.

Theme
Allegiance to the Dark Side of the Force.

Figure 92: Core Elements for *Star Wars*

B-Story

Ordinary World
McClane's world is 1980s New York City.

Underlying Cause
McClane wants to reconcile with his wife who has moved to LA to pursue an independent life in the corporate world.

Resolution Goal
McClane resolves to stop the terrorists himself.

Opposing Idea
Hidden identity.

Character

Characterization
John McClane is a tough NY City police detective who has traditional views of marriage but is estranged from his wife who has left to seek an independent life.

Logical Solution
McClane thinks that the best response to the terrorists is to alert the authorities.

Discovery
McClane discovers the terrorists are going to kill all the hostages. The terrorists discover the identity of McClane and his wife.

Personal Goal
McClane wants to reconcile with his wife and have things return to the way they were.

A-Story

Setting
McClane's wife works at the Nakatomi headquarters, a high-rise in LA.

Primary Situation
Terrorists seize the building where McClane's wife works and take all the employees as hostages.

Primary Obstacle
Terrorists know someone is trying to alert the police, and they need to stop him from spoiling their plans.

Theme
Revealed Identity.

Figure 93: Core Elements for *Die Hard*

B-Story

Ordinary World
A shabby section of Philadelphia, filled with folks who are working at dead-end jobs. The only place that offers a way out is a run-down boxing school.

Underlying Cause
He aspires to be a professional boxer, the Italian Stallion, but because he really does not believe someone like him can succeed, he does not give it his all.

Resolution Goal
To prove he is not just another bum by going the distance against Apollo.

Opposing Idea
You just can't win.

Character

Characterization
Rocky has not had a chance to succeed. He has a big heart but considers himself to be just a nobody.

Logical Solution
Rocky is going to take his best shot all on his own knowing that he will be defeated.

Discovery
Rocky realizes he doesn't have to win to be a success; he just needs to last the whole match.

Personal Goal
To be somebody in the eyes of others.

A-Story

Setting
Once Rocky is given the opportunity to fight Apollo, everyone suddenly supports him and wants to help him succeed.

Primary Situation
Rocky gets a chance to fight Apollo.

Primary Obstacle
Rocky believes Apollo is superior and that he cannot defeat him.

Theme
"It's when you know you're licked before you begin, but you begin anyway and see it through no matter what."
-Harper Lee

Figure 94: Core Elements for *Rocky*

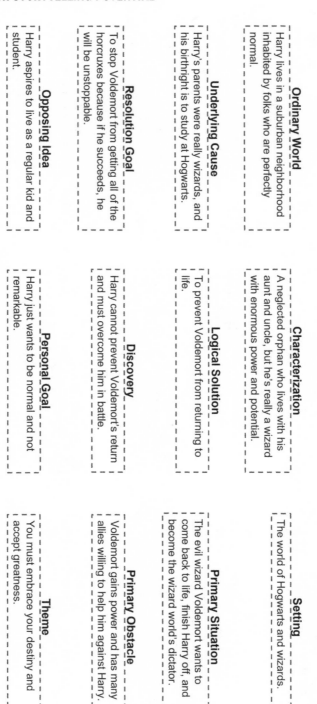

B-Story	Character	A-Story
Ordinary World Harry lives in a suburban neighborhood inhabited by folks who are perfectly normal.	**Characterization** A neglected orphan who lives with his aunt and uncle, but he's really a wizard with enormous power and potential.	**Setting** The world of Hogwarts and wizards.
Underlying Cause Harry's parents were really wizards, and his birthright is to study at Hogwarts.	**Logical Solution** To prevent Voldemort from returning to life.	**Primary Situation** The evil wizard Voldemort wants to come back to life, finish Harry off, and become the wizard world's dictator.
Resolution Goal To stop Voldemort from getting all of the horcruxes because if he succeeds, he will be unstoppable.	**Discovery** Harry cannot prevent Voldemort's return and must overcome him in battle.	**Primary Obstacle** Voldemort gains power and has many allies willing to help him against Harry.
Opposing Idea Harry aspires to live as a regular kid and student.	**Personal Goal** Harry just wants to be normal and not remarkable.	**Theme** You must embrace your destiny and accept greatness.

Figure 95: Core Elements for the *Harry Potter* Series

Although we have discussed most of these Core Elements in relation to topics in the previous chapters, you should now have a fuller understanding of them. More importantly, you should see their relationships with one another and have a strong sense of how to use them.

A strong command of the Core Elements in conjunction with the brainstorming guidance tools supplied throughout this book will not make building a story easy work. The tools will, however, sharpen your preparation and focus your thinking about your story where it belongs. (See Chapter 11 for a complete discussion of these tools.)

In the next chapter, we return to Theme. We cannot place too much emphasis on Theme. As we just covered in *this* chapter, the Thematic Layer of a story—the Thematic Conflict expressing the Personal Goal as Theme vs Opposing Idea—comes from *Subplots*. Our next discussion centers on how to think about Subplots and how to integrate them into your story.

CHAPTER 8:

The Theory of Subplot Relativity

L et's talk a bit about the misery whip.

Whoa, that's a strange place to start a discussion about story Subplots… (Just hang in there a second!)

No, the misery whip is not trying to get the second act of your story right. It's a two-person saw:

Figure 96: A Misery Whip

Here comes one of the *worst* stories you can imagine (although it's all too common):

One day, a Protagonist came along and noticed a misery whip leaning up against the trunk of a fallen giant oak. Next to the oak is a sign that reads, "Free Oak Table Top! Just find a second person to use this saw and slice a piece of oak off this trunk! Whichever one of you cuts off the piece of oak with the last sawing motion gets to claim the wood!" This was an exciting prospect for the Protagonist because they were in desperate need of a new tabletop for a meeting of the Do-Good Society. Then along came antagonist. Antagonist read the sign and said, "Dang! I need an oak table-top to lay out my plans for world conquest!" So the Protagonist and antagonist each grabbed one end of the saw and started sawing. The Protagonist pulled the saw in one direction. The antagonist yanked it back in the other direction. And so on and so forth. Each committed to their Goal. They sawed…back and forth…non-stop…for over two hours of screen time or three hundred plus pages of a novel. Just…sawing away.

Wow… talk about your misery whips. (No lie!)

There is a point here about *wrong think*.

Although that absurd story is awful and ridiculous, it's pretty much the way storytelling is taught. A Protagonist with a goal comes up against an obstacle, usually an Antagonist. And it's focused on the story Plotline, as though that were the thing taking up most of the story's time.

Consider our eighth universal storytelling truth: Subplots are not sub-ordinate to the main *Plot*.

We do not assume that you have a background in story construction. But, as we have acknowledged before, very likely you do. Most people with an interest in storytelling have at least taken a high school level litera-ture course, and they have a growing library of how-to books and a history of taking expensive adult learning courses.

Presentations vary, but the essence of *plot* theory remains rooted in the ideas found in Aristotle's *Poetics* and 19th-century German playwright Gustav Freytag. Freytag devised a graph called "Freytag's pyramid," which breaks down a plot into 5 essential elements:

- Exposition
- Rising Action

- Climax
- Falling Action
- Resolution

Sometimes this is presented as 7 essential steps, which include the *inciting incident* (or *catalyst*) and the *denouement*. Doubtless, if you have had instruction in story analysis, you have seen at least one of the many versions of a Freytag pyramid. It looks like a peaked mountain or perhaps a lopsided circus tent:

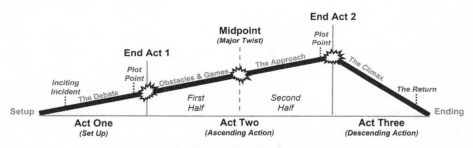

Figure 97: Freytag Pyramid Showing Three-Act Structure

Of course, there are other giants in the field of narrative theory (or *narratology*). One example would be Joseph Campbell's influential work, *The Hero with a Thousand Faces*. Campbell was a literature professor who specialized in comparative mythology and comparative religion. His focus was on mythological Archetypes. He popularized a central plot pattern called the hero's journey. That one uses a circular pattern to trace the steps of the Protagonist's journey.

Before the literary intelligentsia break out the pitchforks and torches to come to finish us off at the Your Storytelling Potential Method, understand that the goal here is not to take down the time-honored observations of others. We don't aim to bury their legacies.

What we are challenging is the efficacy of *teaching story construction* based on their observations. Those ideas have tremendous value for *story analysis*. But not necessarily for story construction.

We said from the get-go that this is not just another *how-to* book so much as a how to *think about* book.

Getting back to the Misery Whip story, the point is that there is a flaw to thinking about building your story with a hyper-focus on the Plot. Plots are more like an undersea cable that contains a bundle of wires or optical fibers rather than a single strand. Plots give an *illusion* of being a strong single throughline of logically ordered events. And they give an *illusion* of being focused on a single central story. The fact is most story *Plotlines* are an intricately woven series of related parallel threads wound together by Theme and Relevance.

We don't shy away from employing original terminology for the concepts in this method. Sometimes, however, you must defer to convention. Honestly, we don't love the term *Subplot* because of the *lesser than* denotation. Most dictionary definitions of Subplot will talk about it as a *secondary or subordinate* Plot running alongside the *main Plot*.

But even main Plots are composed of many parallel threads. Then what are Subplots, really?

We are going to talk about "Subplots" just so we're all speaking the same language. Just understand it's something of a flawed word.

Types and Functions of Subplots: The Theory of Subplot Relativity

If a story's Plot has a "line" to it, that line merely represents the forward Momentum of time. It is not appropriate to graph Plotlines in a single directional Movement to represent the *action* of the story. To say that the action is *rising* for this predictable ratio of the story, *peaking* somehow in the middle, and *falling* for another quantifiable duration before reaching the resolution neither accurately portrays what is actually occurring nor what is observed in far too many stories. It's not so universal. Looking at the plot from the perspective of the Your Storytelling Potential Method, the action of the A-Story reaches certain junctures simultaneously with the B-Story action. But we also find plenty of examples of stories where the two sides of the story are out-of-sync and everything realigns by the true Climax and resolution (which is not necessarily in the middle).

Here is what we see as a more accurate overview representation of the Momentum of a story's Subplots:

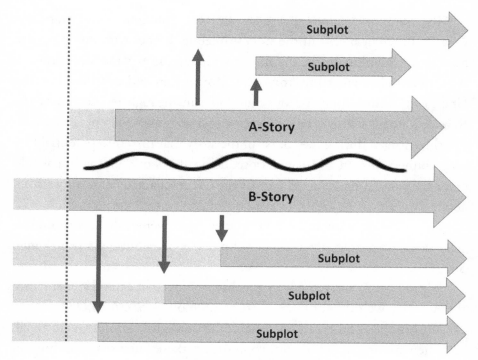

Figure 98: Subplot Momentum

The Subplot diagram probably does not need explanation, but it should be understood that the first vertical dashed line represents the Beginning of the Revealed Story in the Now. As we have discussed previously, the B-Story is presented through Subplots. The Subplots reveal the preexisting relationships from the Main Character's life prior to the Introduction of the new Primary Situation, which initiates the Revealed Story.

A-Stories/Primary Situations tend to feel a bit more concrete. There is a clear order of business for the Main Character to pursue in order to address the major new Problem or Opportunity presented to them. It's possible that your story may have no A-Story relationships—say, a Main Character stranded alone on a desert island or remote planet kind of Situation where the Primary Situation is survival itself. But the vast majority of narratives involve the Main Character encountering a cast of new people related to the A-Story, friends and foes alike.

The Subplot diagram illustrates different Subplots "swimming into view" at different points in the story's timeline. It goes without saying the number of Subplots in the graphic is arbitrary for explanation purposes. B-Story Subplots enter the story with Momentum and continue into the Unknown Future. *Most* A-Story Subplots run through to the end of the Revealed Story's Climax, but the vector that goes on represents those relationships forged during the course of the story that turn into potential lifelong connections. In an imaginary sequel to this story, that vector would enter the subsequent story as part of the Main Character's B-Story (think about Sergeant Al Powell in *Die Hard* and *Die Hard 2*, for example).

Given the diagram and everything we just covered, then, it should be clear that stories have *two kinds* of Subplots: *A-Story* Subplots and *B-Story* Subplots.

Within the A-Story, there are breakaway Plots that extend and enhance the A-Story. We think of these A-Story Subplots as **SIDE PLOTS**.

Within the B-Story, all potential for meaningful, genuine, emotional, and thematic impact of a story comes from these Subplots. We think of B-Story Subplots as *Theme Plots*.

All Subplots are *relationship Plots*. A Subplot shows the Main Character's relationship with every other major or prominent Character within the story. All meaningful Subplots need to be considered as *independent* Plots.

This includes the *Antagonist* if there is one. Much like we consider the Character Branch separate from the B-Story Branch, the Antagonist may be driving the A-Story as the Proximate Cause Character who has a life and motivations of their own. It may be the Antagonist's plan is what forms the Primary Situation. But the *relationship* between the Main Character and the Antagonist is a Subplot.

For example:

Terrorists take over the building is the Primary Situation. John McClane's relationship with Hans Gruber is a Subplot.

Defeating the Dark Lord's plan to come back and take over the wizarding world is the Primary Situation. Harry's relationship with Voldemort is a Subplot.

Helping the rebellion to destroy the Death Star is the Primary Situation. Luke's relationship with Darth Vader is a Subplot.

While they are closely entwined, these are distinctively different Elements.

Subplots often feature these relationships:

- Love Interest Character
- Main Relationship Character
- Other Relationship Characters

The advantage of viewing every meaningful relationship to the Main Character through the *individual Subplot* lens keeps us mindful of each Character's essential humanity, that every Character is experiencing a B-Story life of their own, and that each of them moving through the story has a Journey they are on as well. It allows us to imbue every thread of the Plot with depth, richness, and **THEMATIC RELEVANCE**.

Another thing this Subplot diagram moves us towards is *Story Structure*. We believe that mastering the internal logic and Thematic Relevance that comes from the Core Elements and the Three-Branch, 2-Story Model already lends your stories a great deal of natural structure. Everything we have presented has been about building, Layer-by-Layer, and that produces a certain amount of natural structure. It also should place your stories on firmer ground if you choose to experiment with structure because your stories will retain the internal logic of consciously applied Relevance. But there is much more to come on the topic of Structure in a later chapter.

Implementing Subplots

Let's review what we have said about *Subplots*:

- Theme is expressed through Subplots
- Theme is the connective glue between the A and B stories
- B-Story is entirely expressed through Subplots
- Every meaningful Character in the story has a relationship with the Main Character
- Every meaningful relationship is a Subplot
- A-Story Subplots move the A-Story forward

The conclusion you are forced to draw is that the *majority* of a Revealed Story consists of *Subplots*!

You might recoil at that assertion.

You mean to say that *all* of the B-Story and *most* of the A-Story are just *Subplots*?

This is an idea that has to take into account *scale*. Going back to the very beginning where the goals for this book were laid out, we said these essential principles are applicable to all manner of storytelling. So it is to be expected that things vary based on format and genre concerns. Is this absolutely true for an anecdote, a short story, or a 5-minute film? Obviously, the briefer the content, the more focused on the Primary Situation it necessarily has to be.

The larger and more complex your story, however, the more we find that A-Story Plot focus takes a backseat to human relationships and Thematic concerns. This is definitely true for most long-form fiction. Novels, screenplays, stage plays, episodic television, serialized comics and graphic novels, and so forth.

This is something you can prove to yourself through an analytical thought experiment. Take your favorite work and scrupulously identify how much page or screen time is devoted to the A-Story Problem or Opportunity. It can be shocking to go through a movie and identify the scenes that address the Primary Situation head-on. Not just how *few* scenes are devoted to it, but just how *short* those scenes can be.

The simplest illustration of this principle is the action movie where the A-Story *moves* via the action sequences. There are examples of action movies that are essentially non-stop action. By and large, these are not well received but by the most ardent action junkies. General audiences looking for richer storytelling gravitate toward action movies with great human stories to justify the action. These are the films that stand the test of time. The genre demands action sequences at regular intervals and a certain amount of straightforward Plot development and strategic discussion dialogue—such as the agency commander briefing the agent about the mission. But the *majority* of a great action movie deals with the human drama so that the audience becomes invested in the outcome of the physical conflicts. In other words, A and B story Subplots.

Good Will Hunting

We have discussed Academy Award winner *Rocky* at length throughout this book. And we have repeatedly noted that it's a story that is almost all B-Story.

Decades later comes another Academy Award winner for best original screenplay. And it is almost the same story. We are now talking about the 1997 film *Good Will Hunting*. Matt Damon's Character, Will Hunting, is a uniquely talented genius. He is a lower-middle-class working guy holding down a janitorial job at MIT who gets caught expressing his hidden aptitude when he solves a challenging publicly posted mathematical problem that would take most elite mathematicians months, even years, to solve. At the same time, Will is a street brawler who finds himself behind the 8-ball legally when he strikes a police officer. Lambeau, the professor who posted the math problem, persuades the judge to remand Will to his supervision provided he agrees to work on advanced math under his guidance and to attend psychological counseling. Over the course of the story, Will finds romance with a Harvard undergrad, Skyler. And ultimately, he has to confront the emotional damage inflicted on him through the foster care system before he is ready to take on life and love.

The A-Story—the new Primary Situation in his life—is the Opportunity to develop his math genius under Lambeau's supervision. A major A-Story Subplot (the *side Plot*) is a relationship he forges with Robin Williams' counselor Character, Sean. It's fair to say that Will spends much more screen time with Sean than he does with Lambeau. And of course, the very nature of counseling means they relate on a very personal (and therefore *thematic*) level. They're *not* discussing math. The math-related material is a handful of short scenes, most less than a minute, scattered over the two-hour runtime. Perhaps a total of 5 minutes or so.

Even the scenes between Lambeau and Sean do not, strictly speaking, *move* the A-Story forward. In the most perfunctory sense, Sean has to report Will's progress as part of the court order, but that is not what the content of those scenes is predominantly about. Lambeau and Sean have a relationship history, and Sean's story parallels Will's on the thematic level—hence the connection they make. Both Lambeau and Sean have significant Character Wave Journeys in their own right, all related back to the same central Theme.

Meanwhile, a large part of the story is Will's B-Story. Much like Rocky Balboa, Will Hunting is a guy from the grimy streets who hasn't realized his potential. They both have settled into being products of a lesser environment. Both have been beaten down by life: Rocky in the tough Philadelphia neighborhoods and Will at the hands of abusive foster parents. Rocky maintains a relatively positive outlook on life but harbors low self-esteem. Will is a bit of the opposite—confident in his abilities but absolutely guarded against an outside world that he mistrusts. The movie spends a lot of time with Will hanging out with his lifelong gang of blue-collar, going nowhere drinking buddies. And although Skyler enters his life during the course of the Revealed Story, they meet during one of these hangouts at a bar. She has nothing to do with MIT or his Opportunity with Lambeau. Their relationship reveals Will's inability to open up, trust, and connect.

You could unravel *Good Will Hunting* into a series of parallel short story plots: Will and his best friend Chuckie (Ben Affleck), Will and Lambeau, Will and Sean, Will and Skyler, Sean and Lambeau. The amount of time spent *directly* on the Primary Situation (the mathematics) and the Underlying Cause (legal troubles) is negligible. They're there. They frame the story. But the time is rightly devoted to Subplots of human relationships.

One of the most powerful throughlines in the film involves a recurring motif between Chuckie and Will. These Main Characters are introduced in a seemingly throwaway dialogue-less mini-scene cut into the opening credits. Chuckie and their pals, Billy and Morgan, roll up the alleyway in Chuckie's old beater to the back door of the rundown building where Will rents his basic one-room apartment. Chuckie gets out, walks across the littered backyard to Will's porch, and knocks. Will comes out. They walk together back to the car. The car drives off for the group to go waste time hanging out and getting into the day's trouble. This visual motif repeats itself, again seemingly establishing not much more than a mundane routine.

But near the Climax of the film, Will and Chuckie are sweating the day away at a construction job and taking a break for lunch. Will has let Skyler go off to California without him, and he's making it clear that nothing is going to come of the math work he's been doing with Lambeau. He's satisfied with continuing to remain underemployed and a forever member of their buddy crew. Chuckie slams Will's satisfaction with this projected future. He tells Will that for him to waste his opportunities in life—opportunities the rest of his friends will never see—would be an insult *to them*. And he confesses the best part of his day is walking up to Will's door to collect him for these hangouts, hoping that one day Will won't be there, having skipped town without a goodbye to go take hold of the life he could have. Of course, that is precisely what happens in the film's final moments.

As that final visit to Will's door happens on-screen, the film also cuts to Sean, who has been so incredibly instrumental in Will Hunting's transformative Journey. Will has left Sean a personal note on his door. The note echoes something Sean said when he relayed a story about meeting his now-deceased wife while passing up the Opportunity to attend a legendary Boston Red Sox playoff game. It was a story about pursuing chances with no regrets. And the note declares Will's intention of chasing Skyler to California, having finally reached the place where he can be vulnerable, trusting, and willing to go after a better life for himself.

Great examples of the weaving of Plotlines—aka *Subplots*.

Subplot Case Studies: The Thematic Conflict Arena

Theme is the glue that binds stories together. Remaining mindful of Theme presents the possibility of infusing relevant depth into every aspect of your story, leading to a richer, more coherent tale. But, as we have detailed previously, the Thematic Layer of your Core Elements—wherein the Thematic Conflict of Theme-vs-Opposing Idea plays out—primarily comes by way of Subplots.

Think back to this conceptual image from the fourth chapter on Thematic Connections:

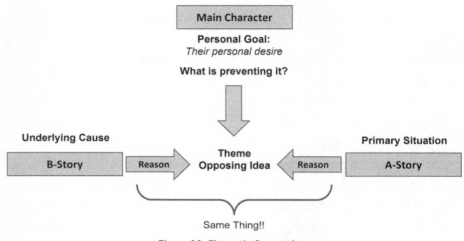

Figure 99: Thematic Connections

As we isolate Theme and Subplots in this dynamic, we see the Thematic Conflict at work:

Figure 100: Thematic Conflict

This essential duality provides the framework for the Thematic Conflict present in every meaningful relationship to the Main Character in the story. And, as we know, this back-and-forth of opposing forces creates the Character Wave.

Rarely does anything in life operate in simplistic cut-and-dried terms. We consistently caution against black-and-white absolute thinking. It's far too oversimplified to say that *every* relationship presents a polarized opposite conflict of ideas. This is a limited and general observation, but the more strongly drawn the moral sides—as with most good-versus-evil conflicts in action stories, for instance—the more apt we are to see *good guy* Characters in opposition to *bad guy* Characters. Therefore, *some* of the thematic influence arguments present in certain relationship Character Subplots pull more in one direction than the other. It's a zero-sum game, and it should be only as complex as necessary to serve the needs of a given story.

Now we return to our five major example IPs and explore the Thematic Conflict within the important Subplot relationships. We acknowledge that there are almost always multiple thematic ideas at work in stories, so disagreeing with our perspective on the specifics of any one story's major Theme does not automatically discount the validity of the Subplot-Theme dynamic. These are stories with complexity, so these ideas are open for debate. But the conversation itself should be enough to make the point and empower you to infuse your own tales with amazing, relevant, thematically-rooted Subplots.

Liar Liar

Major Thematic Conflict: Ethical Honesty vs Necessary Lying to Achieve Ends

Subplot 1: Fletcher's Son vs the Case

The B-Story Subplot is the story of Max making his wish that his father *cannot lie* for one day. Opposing that, the A-Story counters with the *needs* of *the case*.

Subplot 2: Fletcher's *strained relationship* with his ex-wife vs Fletcher's Desire to have the *best relationship he* can envision with his son

This one may be harder to see as a struggle at first. Fletcher's ex, Audrey, feels compelled to take any opportunity to *put distance between* Max and his father who continually *hurts him* with his lies, to the point that she is prepared to move to Boston to pursue a relationship with a man she isn't that crazy about. On the other side of the coin, Fletcher's Desire to be a provider with a legacy of achievement is a crucial element of being his best version of a dad to Max he can be, thus justifying his *unscrupulous behavior* to get ahead at work. He fears losing his son. The Characterization of Fletcher is hugely important because it reveals a man whose dishonest behavior is in service to his (misguided) idea of what it takes to be a good father.

Subplot 3: The Job vs the Wish

On the B-Story side, the job reinforces the idea that lying is *okay* and sometimes *required* in order to succeed. Fletcher stands to be rewarded handsomely for being a liar. From the other side, the wish *prevents* him from *lying,* which jeopardizes his ability to perform in the case he must win, and sets him down the path of confronting his ethics. Subplot 3 mirrors Subplot 1 as both sides of this coin are woven into the two sides of the story.

Subplot 4: Secretary Greta vs Fletcher's Inability to Lie

Fletcher relies on the support of his loyal secretary, who swallows her own sense of ethics to follow her boss's directives and back up his plays. But she fails to realize how much of *their* relationship is predicated on deceptions as well. Suddenly when he cannot lie, Fletcher experiences the pain of losing his support system because when people learn the truth, there are *consequences* to lying. His desperate attempts to circumvent the inability to lie cause him to seek Greta's help carrying out deceptions on his behalf, thus exposing the lies he has told her.

Star Wars

Major Thematic Conflict: Light Side of the Force vs Dark Side of the Force

Subplot 1: Leia's Example of Leadership.

There are additional Layers of complexity to the Theme in *Star Wars*, as certain relationships become revealed in subsequent episodes. In Episode IV, the audience is unaware that Leia is Luke Skywalker's sister. But she is part of the Rebellion—a *family* of sorts bound together by a common cause. All Luke learns in the first on-screen adventure is that his father *was* a Jedi who fought for the same principles represented by the Rebels today. He knows his would-be mentor, Kenobi, has an alliance with Leia's people. His Personal Goal relative to the galactic conflict is to oppose the Empire, though he does not understand his actual role.

    Without getting hypercritical about defining the B-Story aspects of the Leia Subplot versus the A-Story aspects, suffice to say between the Underlying Cause familial relationships involved and the Primary Situation causation, Leia straddles both stories. In addition to the personal connection, Leia clearly inspires Luke with her strong example of *selfless* leadership and *commitment* to cause. She plows forward like a force of nature, razor-focused on the business at hand. Obi-Wan offers Luke a spiritual view of life where his problems can be solved by letting go and trusting in mystical powers that guide things. Leia offers Luke a down-to-earth approach where decisive action and picking up a blaster gives you a chance against very real enemies.

Subplot 2: Obi-Wan and the Jedi
This one could just as well be *Obi-Wan vs The Dark Side of The Force*. Each of the three *Star Wars* trilogies details a three-episode Character Wave where the Dark Side battles the Light Side for the soul of one principle novice in the ways of The Force. And each saga supplies both a mentor and a tempter representing the dual sides. In *Episode IV*, it's the older Obi-Wan *embodying* the Light Side and the *lure* of becoming a Jedi that appeals to Luke's better nature.

Subplot 3: Darth Vader and the Empire
Vader is less of a tempter in *Episode IV* than he is in its two sequels. Luke does not learn the truth of their relationship until after this installment. But he does learn from Obi-Wan that Vader was once a Jedi *like* his father and that he was *seduced* to join the Dark Side. If nothing else, Luke is aware of the danger the Dark Side presents. Though the series gives us little reason to doubt Luke's goodness and resolve, the later revelation that Obi-Wan needed to lie about Vader's true identity to shield Luke from the danger of falling prey to the Dark Side makes us appreciate its attractive power.

Subplot 4: Han Solo and Personal Preservation
Like Leia in *Episode IV*, Han Solo represents a skeptical perspective. He does not even believe in the Force. It's all a lot of *simple tricks and nonsense*. And nothing beats having a good blaster at your side. Unlike Leia, Han does not want to be involved. He is just in it for the *money*. He's an outlaw with a bounty on his head, and anything he does has a price tag on it because he needs to pay off some heavy debts to sinister Characters. If the chips are down, Han believes in gathering up what you have and getting out while the getting is good. It's not that he has no backbone, he's down for

a fight if the situation calls. He's just about taking the calculated risk and looking out for *number one*. A rogue space pirate.

Lest it should ever sound as though the Your Storytelling Potential Method champions a viewpoint that stories have just one theme—the *Theme*—here is a case that demonstrates that is not what we're saying at all. The *major* Theme of *Star Wars* is the two sides of The Force. With the Leia and Han Subplots, we see a secondary but related thematic idea: *selfless devotion* to principle and leadership versus *self-interest*. It is easy to see how the Light Side of the Force relates to selfless leadership for a young Jedi-in-Training. Just as it stands to reason that if Luke were to adopt Han's philosophy, the easier it might have been for him to turn to the Dark Side.

Die Hard

Major Thematic Conflict: True Identity vs Hidden Identity

Die Hard demonstrates that Theme need not be something transcendent and profound. Theme is frequently a simple idea. A motif. Often it is the variations on a Theme that enrich the work.

Subplot 1: Holly *McClane* vs Holly *Gennaro*

This is the dynamic of the marriage identity versus self-identity: *wife* vs *career*. Things are rocky in the McClane household. John has an old-fashioned patriarchal view of family life. Holly made a decision at some point to assert her identity and took an opportunity that pulled her away geographically *and* gave her independence, as she decided using her *maiden name* best served her interests for advancement in a company where a married woman is seen as having different priorities than those of the business. *Gennaro* is a statement about both the marriage and her sense of self. Then, of course, it also becomes a shield of sorts when it keeps Hans from connecting her with McClane.

Subplot 2: Hans Gruber vs "Mr. Cowboy"

For a large part of the film, Hans does not *know* who John McClane is or exactly why he is in the building. This is a Problem. One of the very first advantages McClane claims is by learning the names of Hans and most of his crew thanks to the CB radio he steals from one of the team. Hans tries to get the mystery man to divulge his name by taunting him with a guess that he might be a rogue security guard who's seen one too many cowboy movies, and is trying to emulate the classic western movie star Roy Rogers. Failing to elicit any actual information, he dubs McClane "Mr. Cowboy." It's not only vexing—which can be an advantage itself, playing on the man's psychology—but also offers a real tactical advantage because Hans cannot accurately predict his strategies.

On the flip side, McClane has not seen Hans because he's staying hidden. And no one knows Hans and his team are really thieves and not terrorists. So Hans is playing the *hidden identity* game as well.

Subplot 3: LA Cop Al Powell and "Roy"

McClane has no private mode of communication with the outside world. It's all open CB signal. McClane and Powell know the *terrorists* are listening in. Drawing on Hans's earlier goading comparison to Roy Rogers, McClane initially introduces himself to Powell as "Roy." And he feeds Powell as much information about the "terrorists" and their plan as he can without overtly stating that he's a New York cop or involved in law enforcement. Powell makes guesses that "Roy" may be a *cop* based on inference, though his less sharp superior remains suspicious about the possibility that this faceless nobody on the radio could be one of the terrorists feeding them false intel. They forge a genuine bond by reading between the lines to protect McClane's identity. McClane's communications with Powell constitute an A-Story Subplot or *Side Plot*.

Subplot 4: TV Reporter Richard Thornburg and *His Own* Identity

Thornburg represents the unscrupulous ratings-hungry modern media. Even by the late 1980s, there was a growing sense that journalistic ethics were beginning to take a backseat to sensationalism and a drive to *be first* with salacious news, even if it sometimes means being factually wrong. Thornburg is shown to be a slimy opportunist who does not care who he hurts—stooping so low as to threaten Holly's immigrant housekeeper-nanny about revealing her legal status if she does not grant him access to the McClane children for his report. He's all about *his own identity* and shining as a *rising star*. As a result, he puts lives in jeopardy by revealing John and Holly's *identity* on public airwaves, thus arming Hans with information about who he is up against, and most significantly, who Holly really is.

Rocky

Major Thematic Conflict: INNER vs OUTER—Belief in Yourself/Self Worth vs Outward Achievements/Validation

Subplot 1: Adrian's Lack of Self Confidence

Adrian is truly Rocky's complement. He is *outgoing*; she is *shy*. Neither has any sense of self-worth. Adrian works in a pet shop and at some point, sold Rocky a pair of turtles. Metaphorically, she is almost like a small pet turtle—timid and ready to withdraw into her shell at the slightest provocation. Rocky has a big heart. Rocky loves his turtles, and it's understandable that he would be drawn to Adrian, who could benefit from his protective nature. In an earlier discussion of *Rocky*, we detailed the reciprocal advice received from their parents: he needs to develop his body because he doesn't have much of a brain, and she should develop her brain because she doesn't have much of a body. As Rocky notes, "She's got gaps, I've got gaps, together we fill gaps."

Subplot 2: Paulie and Failure

There is not a lot to help us understand the friendship Rocky has with Paulie. Paulie demonstrates few likable characteristics beyond his loyalty. He's a grousing, heavy drinking, slovenly, abusive, loudmouth. We believe that Rocky's kinship with Paulie has been forged in the fires of tough neighborhood life and familiarity. Paulie represents their childhood and their environment. Rocky accepts Paulie as he does the rest of the urban decay and filth of the blue-collar Philadelphia streets. In short, Paulie reflects the *acceptance* of the lack of opportunity. Nothing is ever likely to change in their lives. It's the same old corners, with the same neighborhood bums, hanging out at the same bar, and grinding it out at the same punch-the-clock jobs. Over the course of the films, Rocky and Paulie trade the same low-level jobs: alternating between collecting for loan shark Gazzo and hauling sides of beef at the meatpacking plant. All that prevents Rocky from becoming Paulie is boxing.

Subplot 3: Mickey and the Need to Want It

Here we're talking about *genuine commitment*. There's a key scene after Rocky learns that his boxing gym locker has been given to a younger prospect where Mickey angrily barks his true feelings about the Italian Stallion. He says Rocky had the talent to become a good fighter but wasted his talent becoming "a leg breaker for a two-bit loan shark." Mickey genuinely believes in Rocky and laments that he never made the most of his gifts, opting instead to accept the life of low expectations he was born into. He *gave up* on Rocky because Rocky failed to go all-in. But Mickey has also learned some very hard lessons about making the most of chances and wasted potential in his own boxing career. So when Rocky's Opportunity shows up, Mickey sees an opening for himself to genuinely help Rocky and achieve something together.

Subplot 4: Apollo and Overconfidence

The counterpoint to Mickey would have to be Apollo Creed. Mickey thinks Rocky has the goods to be a good fighter but has lost faith in Rocky and takes away Rocky's chances of continuing his training. Apollo is prepared to offer Rocky a chance, specifically because he is a nobody-unknown underdog. No respect. He doesn't take Rocky *seriously*. He brushes off any warnings about the challenger's boxing style and isn't interested in watching the hard-hitting bruiser cracking frozen beef ribs while training on television. For Apollo, this boxing match is a gimmick. He's only interested in putting on a *show* for cash.

Harry Potter Series

Major Thematic Confidence: Greatness vs Normalcy

Subplot 1: Hagrid and the Call to Be Special

"Yer a wizard, Harry." A *call to adventure* doesn't get more overt and specific than that. Up to this point, Harry Potter believes himself to be the orphaned son of two people killed in an auto accident. Of course, the flurry of letters that Harry is not permitted to look at arriving by the bushel via owls begins to raise suspicions that something extraordinary is going on. But the arrival and friendship of a legitimate magic-wielding giant, Hagrid, opens Harry's eyes to his true nature. More than that, Hagrid fills Harry in on his elevated status in the wizarding world through the legend of thwarting Voldemort as "The Boy Who Lived." And he guides Harry through the initial introduction to the passageways accessing the hidden world, the bank where his parents have left him a fortune, the shops where he equips himself, and the special train that transports him to his new school and life. Hagrid is also the one to inform Harry that he is considered a *half-blood*—part wizard, part regular human—which is a significant central class conflict in wizard society.

Subplot 2: Hermione and Muggle Bloods

Harry's two best friends throughout his Hogwarts adventures offer an interesting thematic dichotomy. Hermione is a *muggle blood*. "Muggle" is the wizards' word for non-magical, ordinary human beings. But Hermione *excels* in the wizarding world disciplines nonetheless, casting spells like an expert and mastering potions with precision. She demonstrates the wizarding arts are available to anyone committed to them. Yet there is a social price to pay in a community as sadly preoccupied with status, inheritance, and purity as the rest of humanity often is.

Subplot 3: Ron and Pure Bloods

Balancing Hermione is Harry's try-hard underachiever buddy, Ron Weasley. Ron is Hermione's opposite—so perhaps it's little wonder they are destined for one another. The Weasley Family are almost literally the *red-headed stepchildren* of the wizarding world. Ironically, they are "purebloods"—100% wizard blood. They are notoriously rough around the edges, a bit eccentric, materially not well-off, and looked down upon by wizard high society. In particular, Ron struggles with his studies. His spells usually go a bit off the tracks and his potions are more likely to produce toxic results. He's trying to get by with secondhand equipment and isn't able to replace a broken wand if he has one. He *struggles* in the wizarding world, despite his pureblood status.

Subplot 4: Dumbledore and Acceptance

Hermione and Ron might be Harry's immediate allies in the trials he faces, but on the larger stage, they are reliant on the wisdom, support, and experience of Hogwarts headmaster Professor Dumbledore and several of the major faculty. Dumbledore represents the *good* side of wizarding. A lot of what he has to teach Harry is acceptance—specifically about *accepting one's role*. There are a good many difficult realities that must be faced and hardships to overcome. Wizarding ain't all rainbows and ponies. More than anyone, Dumbledore shepherds Harry to grow comfortable with his true calling and step up to the challenge of being the one who must ultimately confront "He Who Must Not Be Named."

Subplot 5: Voldemort and the Demand of Purity

J.K. Rowling leveraged a bit of history's greatest 20th-century real-world villain, Adolf Hitler, in crafting Harry's arch-nemesis, Voldemort. Part of Hitler's legacy that gets debated is what role his own appearance may or may not have played in his views of pure German ancestry, as he lacked the blond hair and blue eyes emblematic of *pure* Germans. There may be nothing to that in actuality, but it is interesting that Voldemort's ultimate goal is the purification of the wizard race while he himself is only a half-blood. Voldemort and his followers, the "Death Eaters," obviously represent the *evil* side of wizardry. The ideal wizard family by these standards are the snotty pure blood Malfoys, all of whom sport flowing golden locks.

Once again we must acknowledge this *Harry Potter* analysis focuses on the broadest aspects of the entire series arc. Each novel in the series offers its own cast of secondary-level allies and foes with relevant Thematic Conflicts.

In these last two chapters, we have immersed ourselves in the Core Elements and Subplots. This represents something of a conceptual capstone to the Your Storytelling Potential Method. We began by introducing the 2-Story Model and have shown how the Thematic Conflict reveals an ongoing conceptual war for a Main Character's soul that is expressed in the conflict between the Theme and the Opposing Idea. This dynamic produces what we think of as the Character Wave—the Main Character's Journey towards Transformation. And now you should see the Core Elements as the pavers for that Journey's path and Subplots as the vehicles for Thematic Conflict.

Taken all together, this awareness should already provide the Author-Storyteller with an amazing internal narrative Structure born of Thematic Relevance.

Moving into our next chapter, we turn to a practical discussion about *Story Structure* itself.

CHAPTER 9:

The Simple Story Timeline

This chapter will necessarily be a little bit different.

In fact, let's start with our ninth universal storytelling truth: You cannot build a great story by thinking in terms of *a single* Plotline. Great stories consist of *many interwoven parallel Plots*.

In the first section of the previous chapter, we touched on some of the traditional concepts of *plot theory* from authorities such as Aristotle, Freytag, Campbell, and hosts of others in the storytelling marketplace, most of whom are deriving their ideas from these seminal thinkers. We acknowledged the power and truth behind most of these systems, while also questioning if these ideas best serve creators constructing stories as well as they do academics analyzing already completed works.

It's not so much that the majority of finished stories don't end up operating as you have been taught in these schools. It's more that post-game analysis offers little explanation of *how and why* Structure functions as it does. These ideas are often mainly predicated on vague concepts like *rising action*, hitting specified *beats* at certain times, and thinking about the plot in terms of a single line—focused on the actions of the Protagonist as they would have you understand it. Oftentimes, these models are peppered with dense, arcane language that seems to make things murkier rather than easier to comprehend.

211

By now you understand well that these traditional concepts do not translate to the Your Storytelling Potential Method for thinking about constructing a narrative. We maintain that to the extent these models hold water (and not all do), these *truths* are the result of conscious application of Thematic Relevance.

An *inciting incident* is not something to be whipped up out of thin air in service to a story you want to tell, only to hopefully flesh out a Character interesting enough for an audience to follow while events unfold in regular beats. All of this starts with a Main Character, and the *inciting incident* is the Convergence point of a flowing B-Story life *merging with* the Momentum of an A-Story Problem or Opportunity.

Our view is that *Story Structure* is not something to be considered until *after* the internal Thematic Relevance has been established by building out the Core Elements. It should be a naturally flowing progression from the grasp on the story you gained through the work completed using the visioning tools you now have at your disposal. You know your story so well, its *Story Structure* is inevitable. It's logical. The clear next step progression.

Very likely many of you will view this chapter's discussion of Structure as practically obvious.

The major difference for this chapter compared to the previous chapters is a greater reliance on graphic imagery to convey the content. Throughout this book, we have endeavored to explain each idea as thoroughly as possible and then supplement them with key graphics that best illustrate points. This content, however, is better delivered through graphic representation than text. Expect the words to support the graphic representations.

With Structure, our primary concern is the Conceptual Timeline. *Conceptual Timeline* means *showing* the relationship of the Core Elements and Thematic Connections to one another as the story progresses.

Another critique we have of traditional Plotline Graph thinking for building a story is that Plotlines tend to conflate *what* and *when*. They ask the Author-Storyteller to think about *what* happens as a function of *when* it happens. As you have seen, we have discussed *what* happens at length before we arrived at this exploration of *when* events should happen.

That *what/when unit* thinking holds a dangerous potential for very flat, two-dimensional storytelling. The *when* should follow the *what*. And *what* happens should follow logically based on Thematic Relevance, not timelines.

Think about it this way: *if* you were to get your first draft's Story Structure *wrong* (whatever that means), would you rather have all the right things happening in terms of Thematic richness and Relevance but somehow happening according to the *wrong* timeline, *or* would you prefer to hit all the structural timeline beats according to the formula, but have a flat, two-dimensional story filled with irrelevant material?

When should follow *what*, not the other way around.

We reiterate that this is *not* a screenwriting book. It's important to remind readers of this here because, if you have ever studied screenwriting, you are aware of how much the form demands Structure. Moreso, perhaps, than any other form of storytelling. More to the point, the movie industry demands a certain standard of structure. Executives primarily speak in terms of "three acts."

In a typical 100-page screenplay, it becomes important for the objectives described for each segment to be achieved in a roughly set number of pages. Traditionally, a screenplay is broken into three acts, with approximately 25-30 pages available for Act I, 40-60 or so devoted to Act II, and the remaining 15-25 pages for Act III.

A comic book has about 24 pages to tell its complete story, and structure must work within those boundaries. Graphic novels, on the other hand, can run 80 to 120 pages on the low end, with major works that can run several hundreds of pages.

And of course, the most widely distributed novels are at least 250-300 pages and can run over a thousand. The boundaries are less firm for the novel writer, whose material is less costly to produce and who has the most direct control over their content.

In all of these cases, the novice Author-Storyteller is well-advised to bring sparkling examples of work that is tightly written and well within their industry's standards for length. Those expansive epics are usually reserved for top professionals with a stellar track record. But that is as much career advice as we're prepared to give in this book.

Our point about Structure as we present it for this method is the focus is less on set page numbers or exacting percentages of story length to hit certain story beats. Rather it's about *accomplishing* the described *objectives*. Again, many forms will dictate how much space you have to accomplish what you need to do.

Formulaic adherence to a preset structure can feel as though it handcuffs creativity. That comes from being boxed into a rigid program *and* not having a clear understanding of *why* things must be arranged as you are told beyond the admonition that "those are the rules."

Structure flows naturally from the internal logic stemming from a well-integrated, thematically relevant story. Things that do not contribute to this internal logic, irrelevant things, are off-topic and do not belong. Cut the fat—that which does not belong—off and what you are left with is a tight story that keeps your audience engaged. But knowing what belongs and what does not starts with understanding the deeply rooted *why* of every aspect of your story. You are either progressing the A-Story, or you're progressing the B-Story, or you're building and exploring the Thematic Conflict—and doing all three at the same time as much as possible. The key is understanding the Core Elements give you a clear roadmap to follow if your Main Character is going to Journey through a satisfying Character Wave.

- Structure ensures the *progression* of a story.
- Structure ensures *Convergence* of the A and B stories.
- Structure dictates *what is taking place* at intervals within a story.

Here is the master structural graph showing the **THREE-ACT STRUCTURE** of a well-told story in the Your Storytelling Potential Method, which we call the *Simple Story Timeline*:

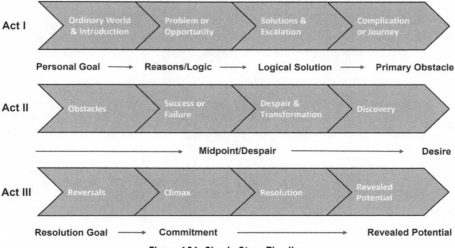

Figure 101: Simple Story Timeline

If you have read this entire book up to here, this graphic should be understandable. Every label in it references an idea we have previously explained. You should probably see that the Core Elements and the Character Wave essentially fill in the timeline naturally.

A key difference between the Your Storytelling Potential Method timeline and other plot graphs—which we will see as we examine each act separately—is that these objective-based phase Movements operate in parallel for both story tracks. Broadly speaking, whatever is going on in the A-Story is what is going on in the B-Story, even when the two stories are unfolding independently of each other.

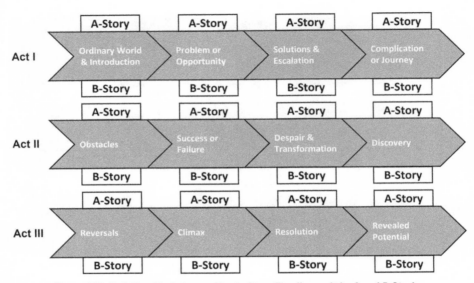

Figure 102: Relationship Between Simple Story Timeline and the A and B Stories

This will be made clearer as we go through each phase segment of the three acts and reference *Liar Liar* examples along the way. We will visit other IPs at the end of the chapter and look at those in their entirety.

Be attentive to the two-story track development. In our view, the proper understanding of a Revealed Story as two essentially separate-but-converging A and B Stories is highly problematic for the traditional notion of a *Plotline* in most any graph you have encountered. Often, these phase Movements are *not perfectly aligned* in the unfolding of the Revealed Story. The A-Story's Midpoint Failure can present the Obstacles or the Complication for the B-Story, for example. Things are not so cut and dried as a single *line* suggests. Different stories have different structural needs in varying proportions. Focus on the Core Elements and the achievement of objectives in a logical progression.

As you study these graphic structural breakdowns, notice there is often a shift in perspective that defines the action in A-Stories as opposed to B-Stories. B-Story action rarely cuts away from the Main Character. A-Story action often gets told from the Main Character's perspective but is just as likely to center around A-Story Subplot characters, such as the

Antagonist (if there is one) or what we call the Proximate Cause Character. These are not hard *rules*, but are generally true.

"Writing is rewriting," so the old maxim goes. Nothing we present in this book will change the necessity of completing a draft, gaining distance from it, analyzing it, and then improving it on subsequent passes.

But… our sincerest belief is that *if* you have a *thorough understanding* of your story before you begin—that comes from the preparation work of identifying the Core Elements, the Thematic Connections and "What is it About?" exercises, and plotting out the Character Wave—that first draft will be *far closer* to a complete work than striking out blindly with a vague idea and a beat-sheet model of plot structure hoping to *find* the story along the way.

Act I Structural Phases Breakdown

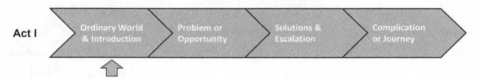

Figure 103: Act I - Ordinary World & Introduction

- Introduces the Underlying Cause and Proximate Cause
- Reveals Relevant information about the Ordinary World and Setting
- Introduces the B-Story (Underlying Cause)
- Introduces the Main Character's Personal Goal
- Introduces the A-Story (Proximate Cause)

In the strictest *literal* sense, the Revealed Story start is the *Beginning* of the story from your audience's point of view. But our understanding of story as a peek in on an already flowing series of life events means a better way of thinking about the start of the Revealed Story as an *Introduction* to the Main Character, their life, and the events broiling in the A-Story preparing to collide with the B-Story. Again, very few stories begin with the Main Character's birth, and even in the ones that do, there are things in motion that have Relevance to the tale (otherwise it's starting too early at an irrelevant point).

The Theme and Opposing Idea are introduced with the B-Story. And of course, Theme touches everything!

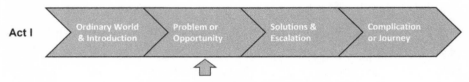

Figure 104: Act I - Problem or Opportunity

- Presents the collision point of A and B Stories
- Introduces the A-Story Problem/Opportunity
- Reveals Primary Situation to the Main Character
- Initiates the Main Character's pursuit of the Logical Solution

Many systems refer to this collision of A and B stories as the *inciting incident*. There's no problem with that term, but it's not quite as clear as recognizing that what the story *does* here is to introduce a *new* Problem or Opportunity into a Main Character's life. Other systems label this *the catalyst*. Again, though, ask yourself if it's fruitful to get bogged down in terminology or whether you would rather focus on *accomplishing goals* in your storytelling.

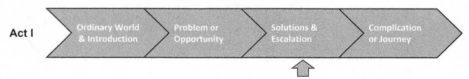

Figure 105: Act I - Solutions & Escalation

- Main Character moves toward resolution using the Logical Solution.
- Main Focus is placed on the A-Story Situation.

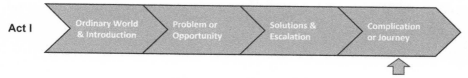

Figure 106: Act I - Complication or Journey

- Ends Act I
- Introduces the Primary Obstacle
- Presents a Complication or Journey to Main Character while they are trying to apply their Logical Solution
- Does not cancel the Logical Solution
- Could be the full manifestation of the B-Story Problem or Opportunity (cf. Fletcher in *Liar Liar* forced to tell the truth on the day of the trial)

Another point where we choose clearer language over tradition: the *Complication* or *Journey* says what actually happens here in a way that *Act I turning point* or *big twist* just does not convey.

The Complication or Journey that sends the action from Act I into Act II is a storytelling convention. At this point, the story follows these essential Movements:

- Main Character encounters a *Problem* or *Opportunity.*
- Main Character decides how to *respond.*
- Main Character *responds* to the Problem or Opportunity.
- The story *ends.*

This is often a problem for writers. They have a strong sense of their setup. They know how the story ends. What they lack are sufficient Complications to the Main Character's Logical Solution that create a satisfying Character Wave Journey through Act II. This leads to stuffing the Act II landscape with a lot of irrelevant filler, bloated dialogue, and tangential asides that go nowhere.

At the same time, this is *not* the Midpoint Failure. At this stage, the Main Character remains committed to their Logical Solution. It's not the end of the road for the Logical Solution; it's about hitting potholes and bumps in the road.

Act I in Action

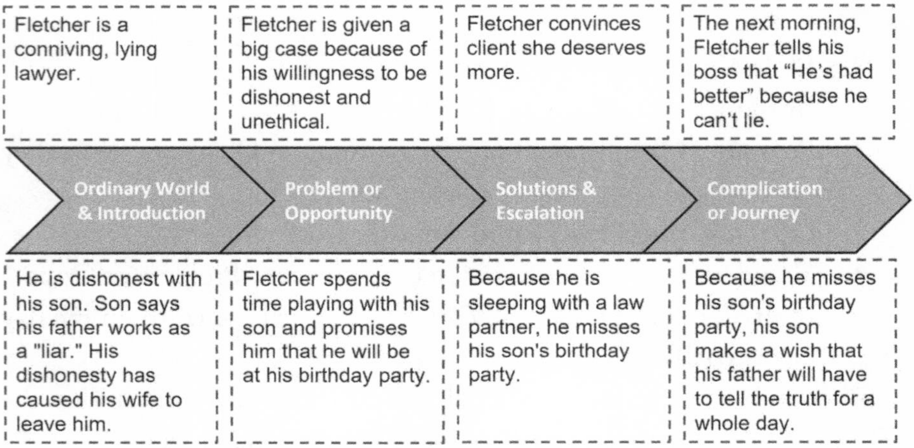

Fletcher is a conniving, lying lawyer.	Fletcher is given a big case because of his willingness to be dishonest and unethical.	Fletcher convinces client she deserves more.	The next morning, Fletcher tells his boss that "He's had better" because he can't lie.
Ordinary World & Introduction	**Problem or Opportunity**	**Solutions & Escalation**	**Complication or Journey**
He is dishonest with his son. Son says his father works as a "liar." His dishonesty has caused his wife to leave him.	Fletcher spends time playing with his son and promises him that he will be at his birthday party.	Because he is sleeping with a law partner, he misses his son's birthday party.	Because he misses his son's birthday party, his son makes a wish that his father will have to tell the truth for a whole day.

Figure 107: Act I Case Study - *Liar Liar*

Notice how the two stories impact one another! The progression of the B-Story has ramifications for what's going on in the A-Story, and vice-versa. Sometimes one side is slightly ahead of the other, and then they switch a bit. Ebb and flow, the action is always connected even though the A and B Stories never directly interact—two story tracks impacting one Main Character.

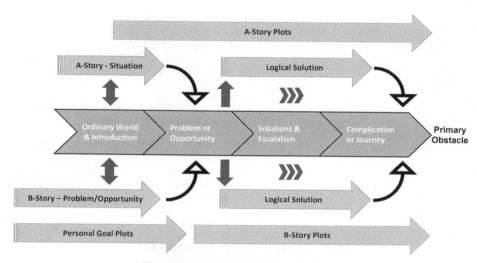

Figure 108: Act I Full Plot Dynamics Graph

While this is a *common* Act I Structure dynamic, it is not fixed in stone. These Elements can be adjusted to fit the needs of a particular story.

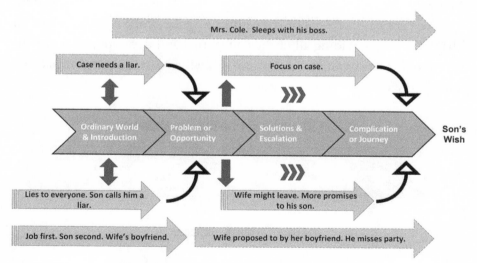

Figure 109: Full Act I Plot Dynamics Graph for Liar Liar

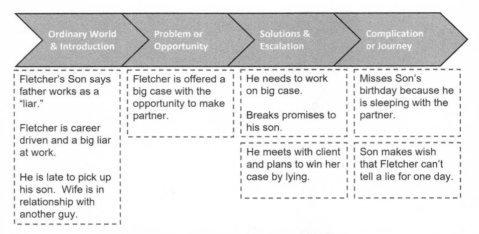

Figure 110: Act I Integrated Timeline for *Liar Liar*

This represents the process of fashioning the totality of what you have built from the Core Elements to the Simple Story Timeline to, now, a fully-integrated Outline. Once the Simple Story Timeline is built for all three Acts, we merge the A and B Stories into a single *Plotline* progression.

The strength of this approach (and using the worksheets provided in Chapter 11) is providing all of the conceptual and developmental organization tools to arrive at an outline like this which can then sit alongside an editing program as you write your draft.

ACT II Structural Phases Breakdown

Figure 111: Act II - Obstacles

- Focus of story shifts to the Primary Obstacle.
- Main Character encounters the Primary Obstacle, which will prevent an easy application of the Logical Solution.

Act I ends with the introduction of the Primary Obstacle. The first *half* of Act II is the Main Character's attempts to execute their Logical Solution to the Primary Situation, and that effort is now hampered by the Primary Obstacle.

As Primary Obstacles come in many forms, so do the challenges they represent. Might be a direct conflict with an Antagonist or one of their agents (an Enforcer-type for the Boss Bad Guy who does the dirty work of pulling the triggers and throwing punches). If the Primary Obstacle is a Journey, it can be the sheer physical distance involved, it can be the logistics of obtaining transportation, running out of fuel, getting a ticket or plane fare stolen, the car breaking down, getting arrested while speeding, etc. With an Opportunity for the Primary Situation, maybe the Main Character's struggle is internal—such as overcoming insecurity about trying to ask the person out, so instead of being direct, they invent some convoluted scenarios where they would run into one another and have to interact, and those attempts repeatedly backfire. Always serve the story and the Theme!

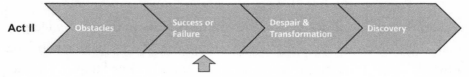

Figure 112: Act II - Success or Failure

- Midpoint of a story
- Midpoint either a Success or a Failure
- Midpoint Success does not resolve the ongoing Problem or Opportunity
- Midpoint ends the Logical Solution
- Structure hinges on midpoint

Remember: whether the Midpoint is a *success* or a *Failure*, ultimately the outcome is always *inadequate*. Even when the Main Character succeeds with their Logical Solution, the *solution* fails to resolve the Primary Situation. As with *Die Hard*, McClane successfully alerts the authorities, but ultimately they do no good, and he ends up having to save the day by himself from inside the building.

The other thing to note here is this Midpoint success or Failure moment is not a *twist*. It's not about some major reveal, although a major reveal could be presented in the Midpoint. Fundamentally, the Midpoint is the moment where the Main Character is forced to accept that their Logical Solution has not worked. Oftentimes, the audience can see that this solution was going to fail all along.

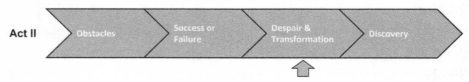

Figure 113: Act II - Despair & Transformation

- Low point for the Main Character
- Focus moves to the Thematic Elements
- Focus on the Personal Goal

Stories tend to shift *emphasis* toward the B-Story in this phase. Despair and Transformation naturally tend to cause the Main Character to look inward. To some degree, this usually holds for all major Subplot Characters in both the A and B Stories. In this phase, most Main Characters are questioning their personal beliefs (Personal Goal), assumptions (Logical Solution), what it is they thought they knew, and what options there are for moving forward.

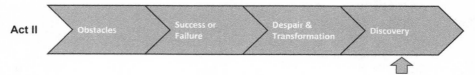

Figure 114: Act II - Discovery

- Discoveries change the direction of the outcome of *all* the storylines.
- Discovery(s) occur at the A-Story level.
- Discovery(s) occur at the B-Story level.

There can be and usually are multiple discoveries. These set up the Resolutions for both A and B Stories.

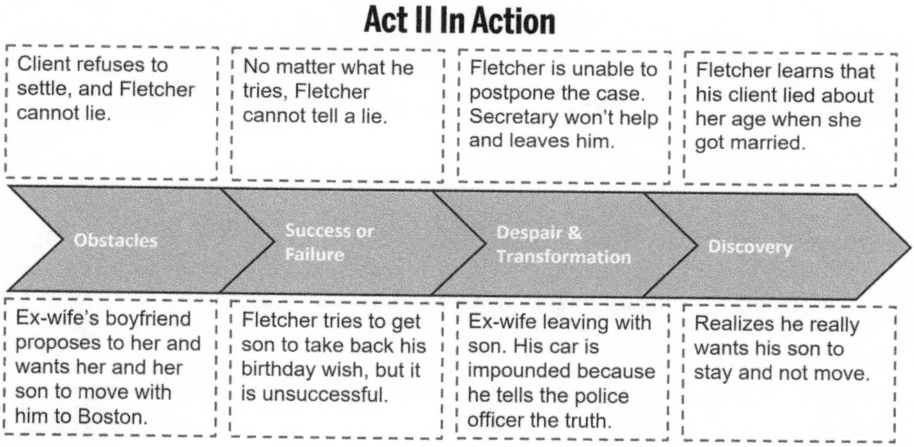

Act II In Action

Obstacles	Success or Failure	Despair & Transformation	Discovery
Client refuses to settle, and Fletcher cannot lie.	No matter what he tries, Fletcher cannot tell a lie.	Fletcher is unable to postpone the case. Secretary won't help and leaves him.	Fletcher learns that his client lied about her age when she got married.
Ex-wife's boyfriend proposes to her and wants her and her son to move with him to Boston.	Fletcher tries to get son to take back his birthday wish, but it is unsuccessful.	Ex-wife leaving with son. His car is impounded because he tells the police officer the truth.	Realizes he really wants his son to stay and not move.

Figure 115: Act II Case Study - *Liar Liar*

If you have never seen *Liar Liar*, we hope that the process of reading this material inspires you to seek it out so you can witness these principles playing out for yourself. Assuming you are familiar with the movie, think about how Fletcher's A-Story and B-Story impact the entire narrative while never actually intermingling. Fletcher's ex-wife and son never once set foot in the courtroom or his law offices. His secretary never has a conversation with anyone in his private life. But *all* of these events have a bearing on Fletcher's Character Wave and push on one after another through him.

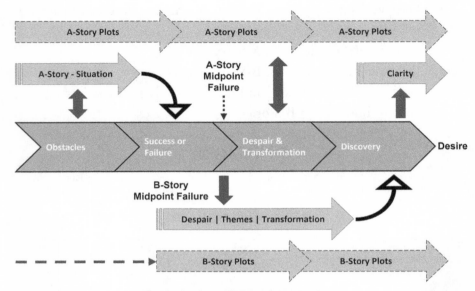

Figure 116: Act II Full Plot Dynamics Graph

Notice the dashed throughline of the B-Story at the beginning of Act II suggest a first-part/second-part shift in emphasis between A-Story and B-Story. **ACT II-PART 1** *tends* to be a bit more A-Story focused, while the second half *tends* toward the B-Story. And when you think about it, this makes perfect sense. The first half naturally deals with the practical matters of handling the Primary Situation. **ACT II-PART 2**, the post-Midpoint Despair-into-Transformation phase, naturally requires inward reflection.

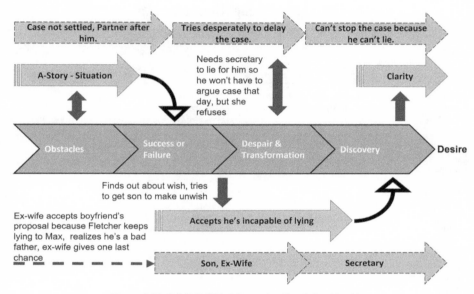

Figure 117: Act II Full Plot Dynamics Graph for *Liar Liar*

Notice here that the *Clarity* relates to the central Theme: *Win with the Truth*. And this applies to both stories. He can win the case with the truth in the A-Story, and he repairs his relationships with truth in the B-Story. Look for this in other examples, and strive for it in your own work!

Putting Act II Together: *Liar Liar*

Obstacles	Success or Failure	Despair & Transformation	Discovery
Fletcher tries to settle case, but it proceeds.	He tries to get son to make unwish but fails.	Fletcher interacts with senior partners, stakes are rising.	During testimony, Fletcher learns his client lied about her age when she got married.
He finds out ex-wife plans to move to Boston.	Secretary finds out truth about Fletcher and leaves.	Fletcher beats himself up.	
He plans to meet with his ex-wife, but his car is impounded.	Case proceeds.	Case still proceeds because judge asks Fletcher if he can continue, and he says "Yes" because he can't lie.	
He finally meets his ex-wife and tries to convince her to stay.		Once again, Fletcher promises to play with son that night.	
He promises to play with his son that night.			
He finds out about son's wish.			

Figure 118: Act II Integrated Timeline for *Liar Liar*

Another seamless merge of Plot Elements organized into scene progression through time.

ACT III Structural Phases Breakdown

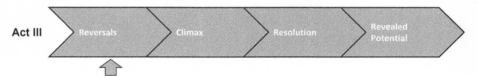

Figure 119: Act III - Reversals

- The Discovery(s) lead to a Reversal in the story's outcome.
- Reversals occur in *every* storyline.

- Resolution Goal is introduced.

Resolution Goal is a Core Element. We have worked hard to sort out these concepts to present them in an order where everything builds through the principle of *Relevance*. If you let Theme be your guide in building out your Core Elements to understand your story, then you should now see how you are working toward a *target*: a Resolution Goal that stems right from the Clarity gained through Discovery and Transformation. Transformation is the end product of the Character Wave. **REVERSALS** take place at all levels of the story. Every Reversal is fed by *Theme*.

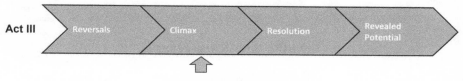

Figure 120: Act III - Climax

- The outcome of the A-Story
- The outcomes of most of the A-Story plots

The Climax marks the end of the A-Story.

The second bullet point here acknowledges this is the end of *most* A-Story Subplots because it's very likely that one or more A-Story relationships the Main Character establishes along the way continues on into their greater B-Story life. Review Chapter Eight for more on A and B Story Subplots.

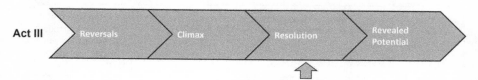

Figure 121: Act III - Resolution

- The outcomes of the B-Story plots
- The outcome(s) of any carryover A-Story plots

- Completion of Main Character's Transformation

Another way of thinking about this is to say the Resolution is the *Climax* of the B-Story. And for these ongoing Plotlines, the *outcomes* are a bit less final. Those relationships will go on after the end of the Revealed Story.

The Transformation was crucial to resolving the Primary Situation. Now the story demonstrates that the Main Character is not just going to discard Clarity and return to their old way of thinking (unless the story concludes as a tragic tale, like Stephen King's *Pet Sematary*).

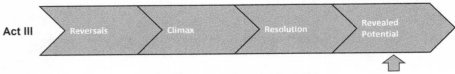

Figure 122: Act III - Revealed Potential

- A short look into the future life of the Main Character after their Transformation

And they lived happily(?) ever after. Life goes on.

ACT III In Action

Fletcher badgers his own witness with the truth.	Fletcher wins the case with the truth.	Client refuses to settle on custody. Fletcher realizes that he did the wrong thing helping her win.	Fletcher holds himself in contempt and gets arrested.
Reversals	**Climax**	**Resolution**	**Revealed Potential**
Secretary bails him out. Ex-wife doesn't love her boyfriend.	Fletcher chases down his son at the airport.	Fletcher tells his son that he really loves him. Ex-wife's boyfriend to leave without her.	Fletcher celebrates son's next birthday with wife and son. He reconnects with his wife.

Figure 123: Act III Case Study - *Liar Liar*

Here again, the A-B Story phases are not 100% in-sync in the real-time of the movie. "Holds himself in contempt and gets arrested" happens before "Secretary bails him out," of course. But the speed of Act III means these events all happen in rapid short order.

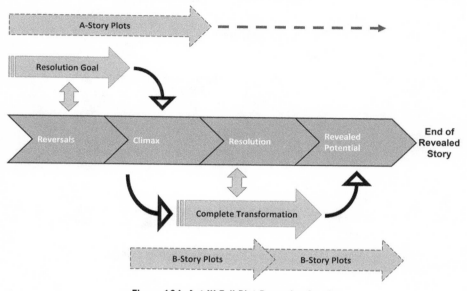

Figure 124: Act III Full Plot Dynamics Graph

Act III tends to be fast and furious by comparison to the first two acts. It's too late to introduce new Characters, new information, and new thematic ideas. It's a race to the finish line and this graph captures the more streamlined, straightforward energy of Act III.

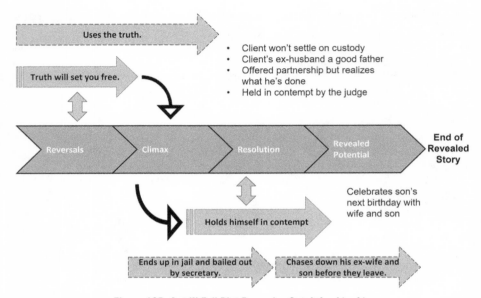

Figure 125: Act III Full Plot Dynamics Graph for *Liar Liar*

When you go back and look at the Full Plot Dynamics Graphs for all three acts, pay attention to the final piece of text for the *Revealed Potential*. The pattern emerges, and you see that each act builds toward a single moment of *significance*.

- Everything in Act I builds toward making an already difficult Situation *much more difficult* in the form of a *Primary Obstacle*.
- Everything in Act II builds toward making a profoundly unclear Situation *suddenly clear through Discovery* leading to *Clarity*, which produces a Desire that shapes the Resolution Goal.
- Everything in Act III builds toward understanding how things are going to be by way of the *Revealed Potential*.

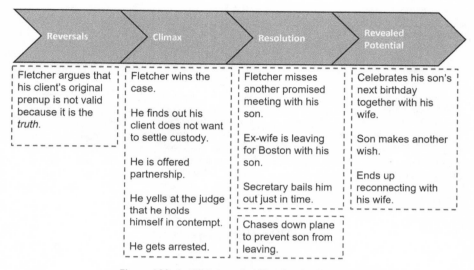

Figure 126: Act III Integrated Timeline for *Liar Liar*

This completes the structural breakdown example for all three acts of *Liar Liar*. To round out this discussion of Story Structure, we finish with breakdowns of our other IPs.

Structural Phases of the Simple Story Timeline And Full Plot Dynamics Graphs

Case Study II: *Star Wars*

Let's take a look at the Simple Story Timeline (A and B Stories) and Plot Dynamics Graphs for all three acts of *Star Wars, Episode IV*.

Act I

| Empire chases down rebel ship in search of plans for Death Star. | Droids escape with the plans. | Empire follows droids down to the planet. | Luke, Obi Wan escape with droids. |

| Ordinary World & Introduction | Problem or Opportunity | Solutions & Escalation | Complication or Journey |

| Luke is working on the farm, dealing with life on a desert planet. | Luke receives the droids with the Death Star plans. | Empire follows R2-D2 to Obi Wan. Luke's aunt and uncle are murdered. | Luke and Obi Wan hire Han to help them escape. |

Figure 127: Act I Case Study - *Star Wars*

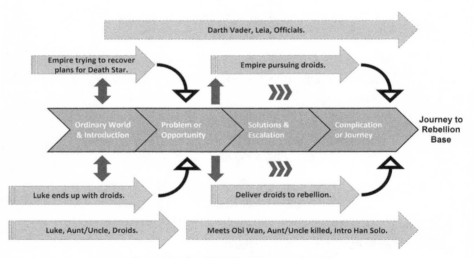

Figure 128: Act I Full Plot Graph for *Star Wars*

Act II

| Empire wants to know the location of the secret rebel base, but Leia won't speak. | Death Star apprehends the Falcon and droids. | Darth Vader kills Obi Wan. Tracking beacon placed on Falcon. | Vader learns the location of the secret rebel base. |

| **Obstacles** | **Success or Failure** | **Despair & Transformation** | **Discovery** |

| When they arrive at Alderaan, the planet has been destroyed, and they are caught by Death Star. | They fail to get to their destination because the planet has been destroyed. | Obi Wan is killed by Darth Vader. Luke escapes with Leia. | Using info from R2-D2 rebels learn how to destroy the Death Star. |

Figure 129: Act II Case Study - *Star Wars*

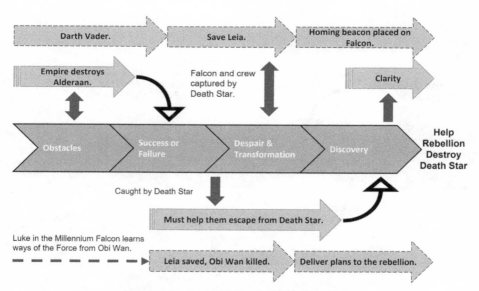

Figure 130: Act II Full Plot Graph for *Star Wars*

Act III

Darth Vader is finally going to destroy rebellion.	Rebels attack to destroy the Death Star.	Death Star is destroyed.	Darth Vader escapes.

Reversals ▶ **Climax** ▶ **Resolution** ▶ **Revealed Potential**

Luke enlists to help rebellion destroy the Death Star.	Luke uses the Force to destroy the Death Star.	Celebration takes place after the victory, and medals are presented to Han and Luke by Leia.	Luke is now a part of the rebellion and on his way to becoming a Jedi Knight.

Figure 131: Act III Case Study - *Star Wars*

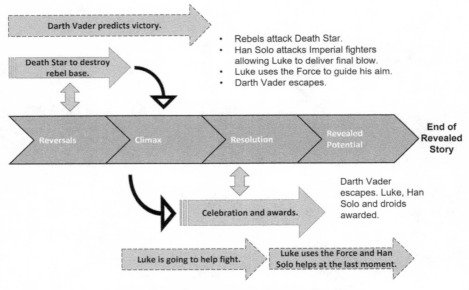

Figure 132: Full Act III Full Plot Graph for *Star Wars*

Case Study III: *Die Hard*

Our third Structure example covers *Die Hard*.

Act I

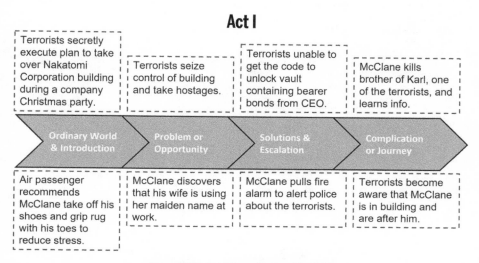

Figure 133: Act I Case Study - *Die Hard*

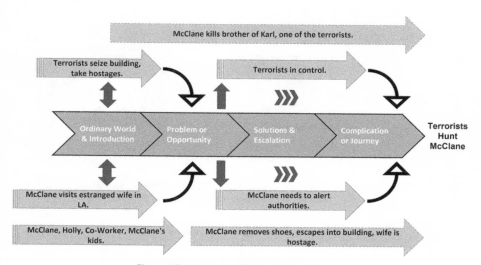

Figure 134: Act I Full Plot Graph for *Die Hard*

Act II

Terrorist Karl wants to revenge his brother's death. Hans stops him saying Theo needs to work on vault.

McClane obtains the Heinrich's C4 explosive and detonators.

McClane kills more terrorists. Hans retrieves Heinrich's C4 explosive and detonators.

Terrorists discover Holly's real identity.

| Obstacles | Success or Failure | Despair & Transformation | Discovery |

Terrorists Marco and Heinrich confront McClane, but he kills them.

McClane alerts the police who think it is a prank but send one cop. He throws Marco's body on cop's car.

Alone in building, McClane talks to cop Al Powell via radio. Asks Al to give message to wife and kids.

McClane discovers that Hans has set explosives to kill all the hostages.

Figure 135: Act II Case Study - *Die Hard*

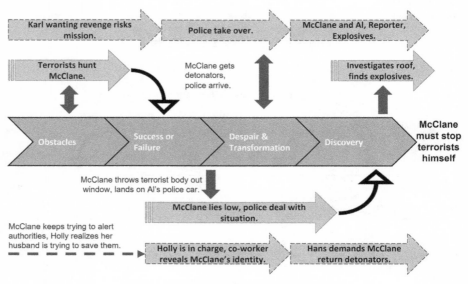

Figure 136: Act II Full Plot Graph for *Die Hard*

Act III

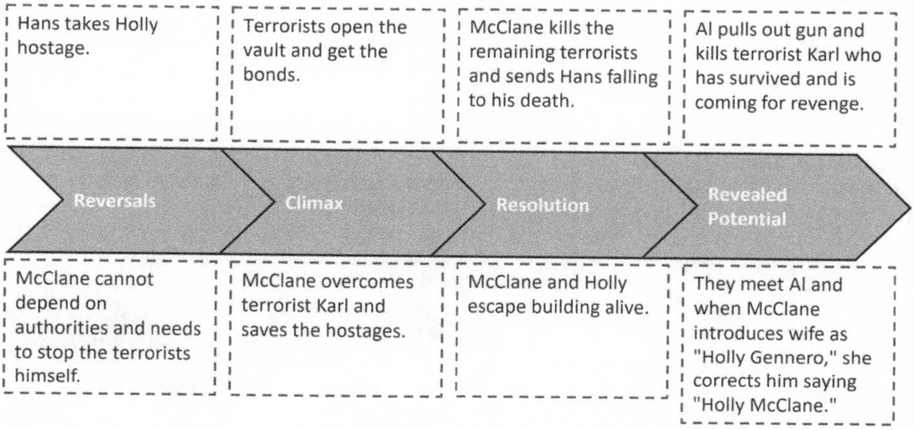

Hans takes Holly hostage.

Terrorists open the vault and get the bonds.

McClane kills the remaining terrorists and sends Hans falling to his death.

Al pulls out gun and kills terrorist Karl who has survived and is coming for revenge.

Reversals

Climax

Resolution

Revealed Potential

McClane cannot depend on authorities and needs to stop the terrorists himself.

McClane overcomes terrorist Karl and saves the hostages.

McClane and Holly escape building alive.

They meet Al and when McClane introduces wife as "Holly Gennero," she corrects him saying "Holly McClane."

Figure 137: Act III Case Study - *Die Hard*

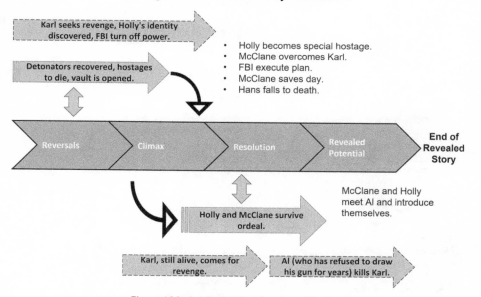

Karl seeks revenge, Holly's identity discovered, FBI turn off power.

Detonators recovered, hostages to die, vault is opened.

- Holly becomes special hostage.
- McClane overcomes Karl.
- FBI execute plan.
- McClane saves day.
- Hans falls to death.

Reversals

Climax

Resolution

Revealed Potential

End of Revealed Story

McClane and Holly meet Al and introduce themselves.

Holly and McClane survive ordeal.

Karl, still alive, comes for revenge.

Al (who has refused to draw his gun for years) kills Karl.

Figure 138: Act III Full Plot Graph for *Die Hard*

Case Study IV: *Rocky*

Our fourth IP stepping into the structural breakdown ring is *Rocky*.

Act I

| Apollo is reigning champ. | Apollo loses opponent for upcoming fight. | Apollo decides to give an unknown the opportunity to fight him. | Apollo searches for the right opponent. |

| Ordinary World & Introduction | Problem or Opportunity | Solutions & Escalation | Complication or Journey |

| Rocky is an underdog fighter and debt collector. | Rocky loses locker and what little status he had left to a new boxer, Dipper. He courts Adrian. | Rocky tries to develop a relationship with Adrian. | Adrian is very shy. |

Figure 139: Act I Case Study - *Rocky*

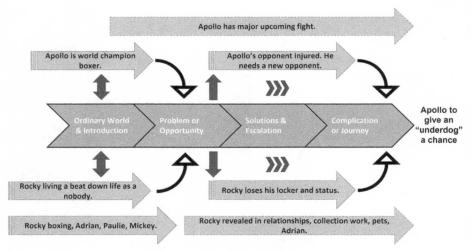

Figure 140: Act I Full Plot Graph for *Rocky*

Act II

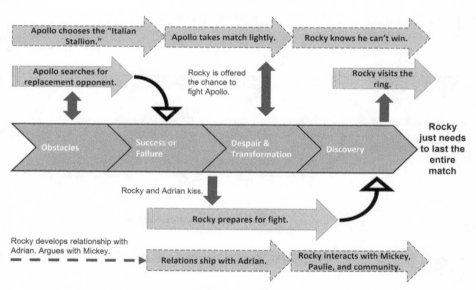

Rocky resists accepting match with Apollo.

Rocky accepts match.

Apollo takes match lightly.

Manager realizes Rocky is the real deal.

Obstacles

Success or Failure

Despair & Transformation

Discovery

Rocky argues with Mickey about his commitment as a boxer.

Rocky offered chance to box Apollo.

Rocky prepares alone for match. Mickey decides to help Rocky train.

Rocky realizes that just going the distance for the whole match will be a big accomplishment.

Figure 141: Act II Case Study - *Rocky*

Apollo chooses the "Italian Stallion."

Apollo takes match lightly.

Rocky knows he can't win.

Apollo searches for replacement opponent.

Rocky is offered the chance to fight Apollo.

Rocky visits the ring.

Obstacles

Success or Failure

Despair & Transformation

Discovery

Rocky just needs to last the entire match

Rocky and Adrian kiss.

Rocky prepares for fight.

Rocky develops relationship with Adrian. Argues with Mickey.

Relations ship with Adrian.

Rocky interacts with Mickey, Paulie, and community.

Figure 142: Full Act II Plot Graph for *Rocky*

Act III

| Apollo finds Rocky to be much tougher opponent than he thought he would be. | Fight drags on because Rocky is tough. | Rocky almost knocks Apollo out and almost wins. | Rocky is a contender. |

Reversals — **Climax** — **Resolution** — **Revealed Potential**

| Rocky shows up ready to fight. | Fight is too tough for Apollo. | Rocky goes the distance. | Adrian tells Rocky she loves him. |

Figure 143: Act III Case Study - *Rocky*

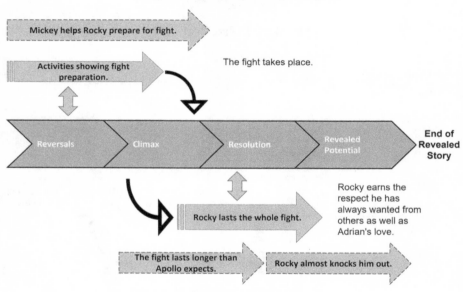

Figure 144: Act III Full Plot Graph for *Rocky*

Case Study V: The *Harry Potter* Series

Our final structural adventure explores the wizarding world of *Harry Potter*.

Act I

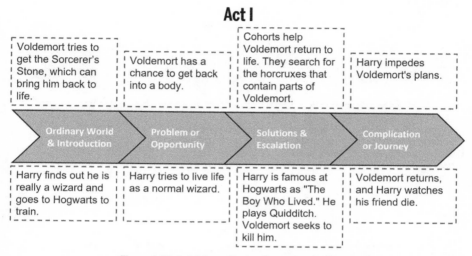

Figure 145: Act I Case Study - *Harry Potter* Series

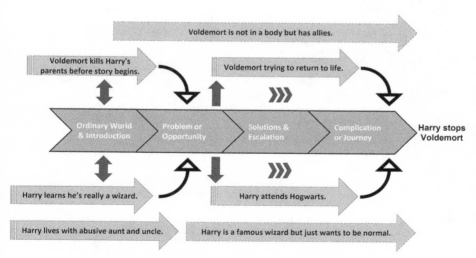

Figure 146: Act I Full Plot Graph for *Harry Potter* Series

Act II

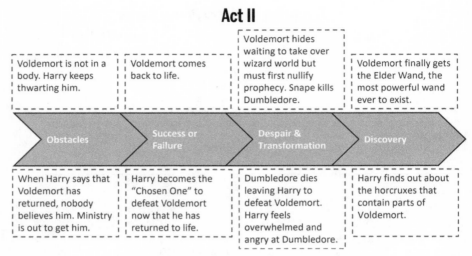

Figure 147: Act II Case Study - *Harry Potter* Series

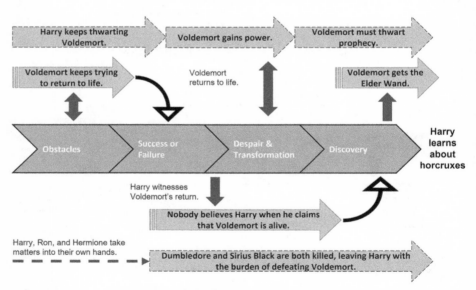

Figure 148: Act II Full Plot Graph for *Harry Potter* Series

Act III

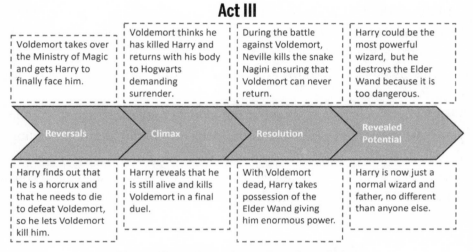

Figure 149: Act III Case Study - *Harry Potter* Series

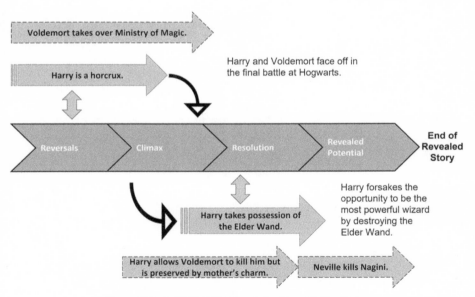

Figure 150: Act III Full Plot Graph for *Harry Potter* Series

The majority of this book laid out the conceptual construction materials for building a story. It laid out the building project proposal when we introduced the Two-Story Model and the Character Wave. It gave you the building blocks with the Core Elements. It supplied the bonding agent in our Thematic Conflict Layer concept.

This chapter provided the architect's blueprint through our discussion of Structure.

Our tenth chapter is all about populating your construction. While you have everything necessary to build stories in the Your Storytelling Potential Method, there are some important insights yet to come about Characters, actions, and dialogue. As you can guess, we are going to continue to preach the gospel of Relevance.

CHAPTER 10:

Characters as Cause

Back in Chapter 8, we mused that the Your Storytelling Potential Method attitude toward the conventional notions of *Plotlines* is so heretical, we might expect the literary intelligentsia to come after us in a lynch mob. The point there was that while thinking of a story in terms of a single *line* of progression may hold some validity for an academic analysis of completed works, it has limited utility for would-be Author-Storytellers trying to grasp the internal dynamics of storytelling for building their own tales. In other words, a Plotline provides a useful way of describing the Structure of an existing story, but is not so helpful in showing you how to tell your own story.

Now our tenth universal storytelling truth: Protagonists *don't* drive stories.

Here we may be courting similar vitriol from the entrenched schools with further blasphemous content.

We have talked quite a bit about Character dynamics, the Character Wave, the A-Story Subplots (aka *Side Plots*), and B-Story Subplots (aka *Theme Plots*). In some ways, everything in this chapter should be understood as the natural extension of everything that has preceded it.

Remember this bit from *waaay* back in Chapter 1?

One further thing this method is not: A step-by-step guide or formula. Many methods of story creation instruction teach a rigid structure born of a formulaic application of preset beats and/or a checklist of the necessary Archetypes to include. "Place Mentor A into Threshold Crossing B, secure with plot Turning Points D, G, and H, and you will have a properly structured plot.

Don't get us wrong. This is not challenging the need for solid structure. But we aren't assembling Ikea furniture here. This system is predicated on the idea that *all* Elements operating within a well-told story—structure included—mesh together organically when the author has a proper understanding of how they interrelate. Formulas don't lend insight to why things happen and what makes every part of the story *relevant*.

Rereading that section now should feel much more meaningful.

We italicized the word Archetypes in that passage because that is where we want to shift our attention. Similar to the revered position of the *Plotline* is the study of Archetypes in literature. Our feeling about Archetypes mirrors that about Plotlines: a valuable academic notion for the analysis of completed narrative works, but of limited value for the story creator.

Archetype is another area where there seems to be universal agreement about their importance while at the same time no uniformity about their definition. Very much like the varying graphs of Plotlines. There is universal agreement that plots move in a single line, even while different schools teach their own version of it.

In this method, you have seen us challenge the single-line model as the best representation of what happens in a story.

With Archetypes, we see anywhere from seven to twelve or so described. Here is one list based on the ideas of psychologist Carl Jung:

- Ruler
- Creator/Artist
- Sage
- Innocent/Childlike Optimist
- Explorer
- Rebel
- Hero
- Magician/Wizard
- Jester
- Everyman
- Lovers
- Caregivers

And another list derived from the Joseph Campbell school:
- Hero
- Mentor
- Threshold Guardian
- Herald
- Shapeshifter
- Shadow
- Trickster

Some of those labels give fairly clear indications of what they are supposed to be. *Hero* in these lists means *Main Character* as we think of them. (How did the hero end up seven on Jung's list and one on Campbell's list?!) Others require some explanation to clarify. And as we have said, there are other lists you can find if you research.

So what is the Your Storytelling Potential Method opinion of Archetypes?

So What?

Literary analysis is *not* story construction. Just as food critiquing is not cooking.

The problem with thinking about your story Characters in terms of Archetypes is that Archetypes define *Character roles* as a *function*. That is a limiting way to think about your Characters.

As we have stressed all along, *everything* in a story should be guided by the principles of Convergence and Thematic Relevance. This includes all Character actions and dialogue. Our belief is the Author-Storyteller should treat their Characters as real people, not boxed in by preconceived roles.

Characters must be unique! What they do and say must make sense according to the individual's Value system, their goals and Desires, and their knowledge and skills. A Character who acts as a mentor to your Main Character is serving a purpose, but that does not completely define who they are. More important than ensuring the funniest Character fulfills the function of a "Jester" is ensuring that their every action and dialogue is *relevant* and contributes something valuable to the Thematic Conflict needed for your Main Character's transformative Character Wave Journey.

The *Situation* and *Theme* determine specific Character *roles* and *functions,* not some *universal definition!*

If Archetypes are not the best way to think about your Characters, what is?

Characters as Cause

Our view is that the Author-Storyteller should think about their *Characters as cause*.

Cause of what?

Answer: *Problems, Opportunities,* and *Obstacles.*

- Cause of the *Situations* (A-Story/B-Story)
- Cause of the *Primary Obstacle*
- Cause of the *Midpoint*
- Cause of *Discoveries / Reversals*

Story progression is based on introducing and overcoming Obstacles. Recall our story progression graphic:

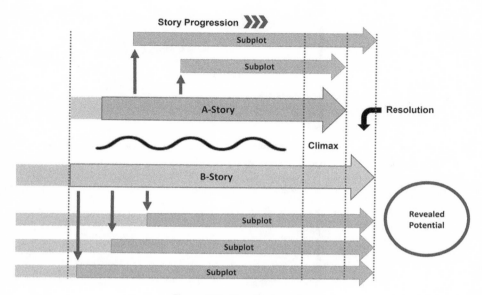

Figure 151: Story Progression

Each *Subplot* represents a significant supporting Character. The arrows running from the A and B story vector arrows out to each Subplot represent the emergent quality of these Plots becoming relevant in the Revealed Story. You now recognize the wavy line between the A and B story vector arrows as the Character Wave Journey representing the Main Character.

In a very real sense, however, those time-based arrows indicating the emergent quality of Subplots should be *reversed* to point *inward* toward the Main Character caught up in the middle. Right? Subplots are the battleground of the Thematic Conflict. Their influence on the Main Character produces the *wave*, depending on their Thematic point of view.

In terms of *events* in the story, Subplot Characters provide the *cause* of the Problems, Opportunities, and Obstacles.

Distill the story progression graphic to these *Characters-as-cause* essentials, and we have:

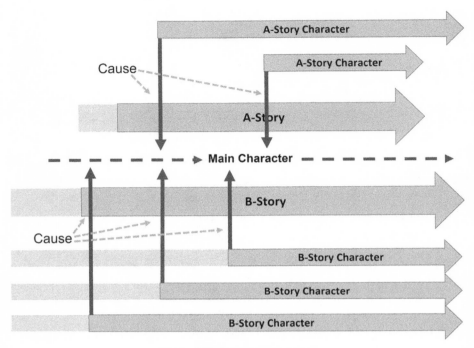

Figure 152: Characters as Cause

(Just so we remain on the same page, know that the number of A and B Story Subplot Characters depicted here is arbitrary to illustrate the point. And the timeline of the emergence of these Characters is not attempting to show scale in real-time. This merely illustrates the dynamic of significant Characters emerging to create causation throughout the story.)

In developing our own stories, we need to understand *Characters as cause* rather than as a function.

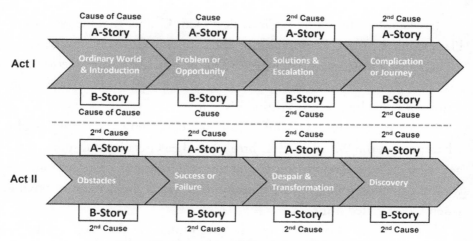

Figure 153: Characters as Cause in A and B Stories

There is one exception to this rule, and it is the most surprising of all. The Main Character is *not* a *primary causation Character*!

What?!

You read that right.

Time and again throughout this book, we have addressed the strong likelihood that our readers are people who have exposed themselves to many schools of storytelling thought. If this is you, then you have assuredly run across variations on the idea that the "*Protagonist should drive the story*."

This conventional wisdom says the Protagonist drives the story forward through their pursuit of a goal. Let's examine that.

(Forgive us for the following, but we are trying to drive home a major point here...)

In *Liar Liar*, does Fletcher Reede interfere with his future client's marriage, causing the divorce case that offers him a career opportunity? Or is he offered the case because of who he is as an unethical attorney?

In *Star Wars*, did Luke Skywalker leave his family farm to go steal the Death Star plans, hoping to get himself involved in the Rebellion against the Empire? Or did the droids with the information sort of land in his lap, calling him to an adventure he was not actively seeking?

In *Die Hard*, did John McClane alert Hans Gruber that the Nakatomi Plaza would be mostly empty during the company Christmas party, making it an ideal time to pull off a caper? Did he hear about the takeover and rush into the building to shoot some terrorists? Or was he caught in a bad Situation while he was just visiting his wife?

In *Rocky*, was Rocky Balboa training to become the Heavyweight Champion of the World? Did he break Mac Lee Green's hand so he could get the fight with Apollo Creed? Did he call Creed out on television? Or was he a nobody going nowhere, ready to accept retirement from boxing when Creed called him?

In the *Harry Potter* series, was Harry sending away for books on magic hoping to be the world's greatest wizard? Did he attack Voldemort, hoping to pick a fight? Or was he a nobody kid living under his Aunt and Uncle's stairs, completely oblivious to the wizarding world when owls started showing up delivering invites to a wizarding school?

But, wait, there's *more*!

In *Armageddon*, did Bruce Willis's Character Harry Stamper call NASA to say he could pitch in to help destroy an asteroid? Did he go and redirect the asteroid to cause it to collide with Earth? Or was he just a guy running an oil rig drilling team of roughnecks when NASA called him?

In *Sideways*, does Paul Giamatti's Character Miles suggest he take his buddy Jack on a road trip into wine country before he gets married? Or is that trip Jack's idea?

In *Home Alone*, does Kevin hide in the attic to avoid going on the trip with his family and then call up the Wet Bandits to come to rob his house? Or was he accidentally left home alone and forced to defend his house when the robbers show up?

In *Good Will Hunting*, did Will introduce himself to Professor Lambeau with a fistful of advanced mathematics proofs, hoping to get accepted into MIT? Or was he content to be a blue-collar Southie kid hiding his abilities, running with his drinking buddies from high school, and picking bar fights?

In *Field of Dreams*, was Kevin Costner's Character Ray's lifelong dream to build a baseball diamond in a cornfield, hoping to meet the ghosts of baseball legends and reconnect with his deceased father? Or was he working and struggling to maintain his farm when he received an inconvenient prompting from a disembodied voice?

In *Back to the Future*, did Marty McFly beg Doc Brown to build a time machine so he could go back and fix his parents' relationship? Or was he caught in the wrong place at the wrong time when his friend revealed he had constructed a time machine, and then accidentally ended up thirty years in the past when terrorists show up, kill Doc, and chase Marty while he's driving the DeLorean device?

Example *overload*! (We warned you.)

But we're not hoping to merely *make* a point. We really aim to obliterate the notion in your mind that the *Protagonist drives the story*. It's simply a wrong *rule* of storytelling.

Understand: the Main Character is *not* a causation Character! It's the reason we use the term *Main Character* rather than Protagonist in this method. (Using the term *Protagonist* would just confuse writers who would then think they know what we are talking about, when they really don't. In our method, a *Main Character* is fundamentally different from the misunderstood notion of a *Protagonist*.)

The Main Character is a *reactive* Character. They are *reacting* to an emergent Problem or Opportunity in their life with what we call the *Logical Solution*.

Let's consider some objections to this notion.

Well, you might counter, "when others say the 'Protagonist drives the story,' don't they mean that the Protagonist relentlessly pursues their goal? Isn't a story just about a Main Character pursuing their goal?"

As we have just seen, almost every Main Character you can think of is wrapped up in a story not of their own making. Not one of these stories begins with a Main Character lying on a couch surfing TV channels idly when they have a moment of Clarity, saying, "I need a transformative Journey!" and then goes out to encounter a bunch of formidable Obstacles.

You *could* imagine a story that begins this way, but you could probably only get away with such a Beginning once, and then you would be crafting a very unique, whimsical tale that would be starting behind the eight ball. Even if you were successful with that kind of opening, you would be hard-pressed to make a career of such stories.

You might reply, "But, what about the *Personal Goal?* Doesn't the Main Character drive the story *because* of their Personal Goal?"

The Personal Goal is a Thematic Layer concept. It certainly *informs how* your Main Character will respond, how they understand their world in arriving at their Logical Solution, and precisely what actions they will take while addressing the Primary Situation. *But,* make no mistake, their task is to *respond to* the Primary Situation—which they did not create—by implementing their Logical Solution.

You might respond, "Okay, but how about once the ball is rolling? Once they recognize their Primary Situation, surely then they are driving the story by implementing their Logical Solution, right?"

Only if there's no middle to your story. Again, we're talking about satisfying transformative Journeys in well-told stories. It is possible that we can talk about someone who encounters a Problem or Opportunity, decides what to do about it, does it, it works, and so… The End.

But that isn't what happens in a well-told story.

What happens, as we have outlined extensively, is that the Logical Solution *does not work*. It does not work because the Main Character runs up against formidable Obstacles. There is a Primary Obstacle *caused* by other Characters or the Situation itself demands a Journey.

Recall our Character Wave. The Main Character remains committed to the Logical Solution from the point of Convergence with the Primary Situation through to the Midpoint Failure. And the first half of Act II is a series of *reactions to Failures* caused by Obstacles, and the Main Character tries new variations of the Logical Solution until they have exhausted their options or come to the final realization that the Logical Solution is ineffective.

You ask, "How about the Resolution Goal? Certainly, the Main Character must take control to finally resolve the Primary Situation!"

You mean, by Act III? At the very end? With their Transformative Journey complete and things are darkest before the victorious dawn (assuming it's even a happy ending)?

You can hardly say a Main Character has *driven* a story if the only thing they get to be in the driver's seat for is how it ends.

To be clear, a Main Character is *not passive* just because they are reacting! They are rarely passive. They are usually fiercely engaged.

The point is that heroes don't run off to slay sleeping, peaceful dragons. Whether they are forced to do so to save the maiden, or they must *defend* the city against assault, the dragon attacks first.

The Main Character reacts to what is happening and implements Solutions.

What makes any story the Main Character's story?

The Main Character provides the *why* and the *Theme*! All great stories are transformative Journeys. If there is any cause coming from the Main Character, it is from the Thematic Layer.

If you follow this logic, then you are forced to conclude the A-Story is *not* the Main Character's story! If that's true, then whose is it? Who causes the Primary Situation relative to the Revealed Story?

Situation Cause Characters I: The Proximate Cause Character

Not every story has an Antagonist. Most do.

Some Primary Situations are struggles against nature for survival, inner struggles, or perhaps struggles against non-personified groups (like "a town," "the legal system," or "society")—though these stories will likely have a series of Mini-Antagonists representing certain social forces in episodic adventures.

It was the consideration of the question: "Who drives a story?" and whether that Character would always be the Antagonist, that an important insight came to light.

While we understand that the Antagonist's defining feature is that they stand in opposition to the Desires and efforts of the Main Character, it turns out that this is not the Antagonist's important function in a story! But it's not so simple as saying "the A-Story is the Antagonist's story, and the Antagonist is the one who causes the A-Story to happen." *But it's close.*

The reason, as noted just above, is that not all stories have an Antagonist. Further, we can cite cases where there *is* an Antagonist, but the Antagonist is not the cause of the A-Story (which is the case of Biff in *Back to the Future*)!

This is why we introduced a new Character *type* that we call the *Proximate Cause Character.* As we have previously explained, the Proximate Cause Character is the Character whose actions *cause* the A-Story to collide with the Main Character's B-Story.

The Proximate Cause Character has the direct link to the A-Story and its foundation called the Proximate Cause. It is the specific Character who has the greatest and most personal interest in the outcome of the A-Story itself. In a way, the A-Story is very much their own personal story that is taking place in their own life, in other words, their own *B-Story.*

The term "proximate cause" comes from the fields of law and insurance. It's the idea that an event such as an injury to body or property requiring compensation would not have happened "but for" the actions of another.

It's easy enough to understand that the majority of Proximate Cause Characters are Antagonists.

- *Hans Gruber* seizes the building, thus John McClane has to battle Hans and his crew of terrorist-thieves.
- *Darth Vader* searches for the stolen Death Star plans, thus Luke Skywalker inherits droids that motivate him to get involved with the Rebellion.
- *Voldemort* attacks and kills Harry Potter's parents and imparts some of his soul into their infant son, thus Harry is destined to fight the Dark Lord.

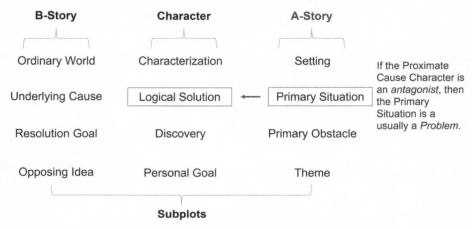

Figure 154: When the Proximate Cause Character is an Antagonist

The Antagonist is the most common type of Proximate Cause Character. The Antagonist is a *function* of the A-Story. If the story has an Antagonist, they are *usually* the *cause* of the A-Story, but there are definitely exceptions.

And not every Proximate Cause Character is an Antagonist. There are stories where there *is* an Antagonist, but they are *not* the Proximate Cause Character!

Consider Will in *Good Will Hunting*. Or Harry Stamper in *Armageddon*. There is no *Antagonist* in either of those stories. So who is *directly* responsible for bringing the Primary Situation into the lives of those Main Characters?

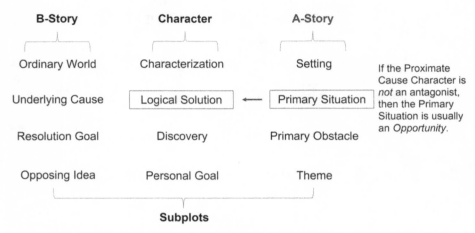

Figure 155: When the Proximate Cause Character is not an Antagonist

In *Good Will Hunting*, Will exercises his abilities in secret. And he frequently gets into legal trouble as a hardened product of the foster care system. He's just living his life. It's that *Professor Lambeau* takes notice of Will's genius and wants to be associated with it so he can take credit for discovering a great, natural talent. Lambeau cannot be rightly considered an Antagonist to Will. This is a movie about a person struggling with their inner demons if there ever was one. Lambeau is here to offer Will an Opportunity, full stop. Without Lambeau, Will goes to jail. He never develops his genius or makes contact with employers who need his gifts. And most importantly, Will never meets Sean, the catalyst for his personal transformative Journey. Without Sean, Will never seizes his Opportunity with Skyler. Lambeau is the Proximate Cause Character of the film.

In *Armageddon*, we might superficially say the meteor is the Antagonist. But that does not really satisfy the notion. The meteor is a Situation. And the Main Character, oil rig driller Harry Stamper, is not immediately in charge of doing anything to prevent the meteor from obliterating the Earth. It is *Billy Bob Thornton's role* as a NASA official whose job is to prevent the planet's destruction. He is the one to contact Stamper with a plan for how the driller's experience might be instrumental in preventing disaster. And, if Harry and his crew refuse the call or prove not to be up to the task, *Thornton's Character* is the one who will need to find Plan B, not Harry. Thornton's *Character* is the Proximate Cause Character.

We promised an example of a story with an Antagonist who is *not* the Proximate Cause Character. *Back to the Future* seems like a light, fanciful summer popcorn flick. But it is a surprisingly sophisticated, deep story. Biff Tannen is clearly the Antagonist for multiple generations of the McFly family. But he does nothing to directly cause the A-Story adventure that sends Marty through time or skew events between Marty's future parents that nearly undoes Marty's existence. The A-Story of *Back to the Future* is *Doc Brown's* time machine. It's Doc's actions, creating the device and deciding to rip off terrorists to secure the plutonium to power it, that get the ball rolling for Marty's trip. Doc Brown is the Proximate Cause Character in the first *Back to the Future* (though Biff does become the Proximate Cause Character in the sequels).

Back to the Future is also an example of the *non-Antagonist as Proximate Cause Character* where the Primary Situation is *not* an Opportunity, but rather a Problem. In our other examples, *Good Will Hunting* and *Armageddon*, the Non-Antagonist Proximate Cause Characters offer the Main Character an Opportunity. (Yes, the meteor is a Problem for Billy Bob Thornton and the world at large, but it's an Opportunity for Bruce Willis and his team to be heroes and to cash in, never paying taxes again, etc.) *Back to the Future* is the exception, rather than the rule.

Here are some other examples of Non-Antagonist Proximate Cause Character stories that illustrate the general *rule* that these stories offer the Main Character an Opportunity:

Field of Dreams. The Voice leads Ray on his mysterious soul-stirring adventure to build a baseball diamond in his corn field, which draws together spirits in need of healing—including himself.

French Kiss. (And most any romance story.) The love interest *is* the Primary Situation Opportunity in these stories. While Meg Ryan's Character perceives herself to have a Problem (her fiancé has fallen for another woman), the Journey is her coming to realize what she has found in Kevin Kline's Luc.

Sideways. Miles's wild-spirited pal, Jack, seeks to help Miles break out of his post-divorce downward spiral by offering the Opportunity of an off-the-hook blowout road trip to the Santa Ynez Valley wine country. It's the cure for what ails Miles in Jack's mind.

In all of these stories, the Main Character encounters difficulties by way of Obstacles that complicate things, but the Primary Situation is unmistakably an Opportunity.

Proximate Cause Character Characteristics

- The A-Story is their personal story. They have a personal stake in the outcome of the A-Story.
- This Character *causes* the Convergence of the A and B stories. The Character that makes the *Revealed Story* happen.
- They are the *primary* cause of the *Logical Solution* from the A-Story.
- There is only *one* Proximate Cause Character.
- The Main Character should *not* be a Proximate Cause Character because they are a reactive Character who is implementing a Logical Solution.

Secondary Cause Characters

As a story progresses, there are always new challenges, such as Complications, Failures, Journeys, and Obstacles, as well as Discoveries and Reversals, as we've discussed.

Each one of these new events helps move a story forward and keep a story interesting. And for each one of these events, there is a cause. In other words, there is a reason for anything and everything that happens in a story to happen. And behind every cause is a Character, and we call these Characters *Secondary Cause Characters.*

By *Secondary Cause* we mean causation within the B-Story and causation of the other major Movements in the story beyond the Introduction of the A-Story Primary Situation (the Obstacles, the Failures, the Discoveries, and the Reversals, etc.).

ANY Character—including the Main Character and Antagonist—can be a *Secondary Cause Character*.

Cause of a Cause

Stories are artificial.

In the most literal sense of the word "artifice," which means *cunningly inventive, a skillful or artful contrivance,* a story that *mimics* life. It takes the artful skill of the Author-Storyteller to pull the audience into their world and have them invest their interest in its artificial reality.

One of the things we have repeatedly emphasized is the idea that all of these *truths* about stories are true from the Main Character's *perspective*. The B-Story is the Main Character's life story. The A-Story, we now understand, is the relevant part of the Proximate Cause Character's story in the Revealed Story. And all of the events in the Revealed Story have a Momentum of a Hidden Past rushing through the Now toward an Unknown Future and Revealed Potential.

Bear that perspective in mind as we discuss the idea that there is *always a Cause of a Cause*.

In an ultimate sense, everything revealed in a story represents a link in an endless chain of events that began with the origins of existence itself. But it's impractical as hell to start every story at the Big Bang. So it's up to us to identify *where* our Revealed Stories *begin* (where they are *introduced*). At this stage, you understand that *nothing* in a story just springs uncaused into existence from the ether.

Antagonists are the most common variety of Proximate Cause Characters—their actions pursuing their goals *cause* the A-Story Situation to intersect with the ongoing Ordinary World of the Main Character. We should understand that no matter how twisted and morally bankrupt we wish to craft our Antagonist, there is little opportunity for satisfying narrative depth if they are motivated by committing evil for evil's sake.

More than likely, your stories will not be dealing with moral absolutes involving pure "good guy" Main Characters running up against thoroughly evil "bad guy" Antagonists. Life is complex. Issues are complex. Purity is extremely rare.

All of this goes to say that the wise Author-Storyteller knows their story's B-Story *and* knows the "cause of the cause"—the Hidden Past of the A-Story. We know the actions that cause the events that brought the A-Story into the Main Character's world.

What motivates *that* choice of action?

Let's go through some examples:

Liar Liar: *Miranda*, the partner in Fletcher's law firm, has a *big money* case that the originally assigned attorney refuses to litigate because the facts of the case make it impossible to win honestly.

Star Wars: *Darth Vader* needs to defeat the Rebellion, and they have stolen the plans for the very weapon the Empire Vader intends to use to destroy the Rebels.

Die Hard: *Hans Gruber* wants the bearer bonds in Nakatomi's vault. He's committing a robbery.

Rocky: *Apollo Creed*'s next opponent gets injured while training and the scheduled fight is too soon for another legitimate contender to step in and be ready.

Harry Potter: *Voldemort* wants to eliminate muggles and purify the wizard race.

Home Alone: *Harry* (leader of the Wet Bandits) is robbing houses on that block vacated during the holidays.

The Princess Bride: *Prince Humperdinck* wants to start a war.

The Proximate Cause Character is invested in the outcome of the A-Story in the very same way the Main Character is invested in the direction of their B-Story. We see this is also true for stories where the Proximate Cause Character is *not* an Antagonist but rather a *love interest* or other type of Main Relationship Character. Again, *usually*, these stories have an Opportunity as the Primary Situation.

Here are some examples of Cause of a Cause for non-Antagonist Proximate Cause Characters:

Armageddon: *Dan Truman*, played by Billy Bob Thornton, heads the NASA team whose responsibility it becomes to stop the runaway asteroid from devastating the planet.

Field of Dreams: *The Voice* is the subject of debate, but whether The Voice is Ray's conscience or soul or The Voice of God or another Character, the significance is that it represents an entity with a vested interest in Ray's unfinished business with his own father. The Voice's agenda includes providing soul-healing experiences for numerous people through Ray.

Good Will Hunting: *Professor Lambeau* recognizes Will's potential. Much of Lambeau's conflict with Robin Williams' therapist Character derives from unfulfilled potential and ambition. Interestingly, Lambeau's intentions for Will are somewhat unclear. Lambeau does not have a specific project he needs someone with Will's talents to realize—for example, it's not as though he's working for the government and needs Will to help them decrypt foreign codes that might save lives or program a deep-space rocket that might lead to colonization of other worlds, etc. So it seems the end game for Lambeau is simply the notoriety of *discovering* Will.

French Kiss: Kevin Kline's *Luc* wants to start a winery.

Back to the Future: *Doc Brown* needs plutonium to power his time machine device.

Sideways: Thomas Hayden Church's Character, *Jack*, wants to help his friend Miles move on from his post-divorce depression.

Situation Cause Characters II: Underlying Cause Characters

It should come as no surprise that there is an analogous Character (or Characters) to the A-Story's Proximate Cause Character present in the B-Story. Both stories present the Main Character with a Problem or Opportunity. The B-Story also has a causation Character responsible for the Underlying Cause.

We call these **UNDERLYING CAUSE CHARACTERS**.

As we think about Underlying Cause Characters, recall the first chapter distinction between the Character Branch and the B-Story Branch.

The impulse is to think that the Main Character would likely be the cause of the Problems or Opportunities they face in their personal life story.

While the Proximate Cause Character is closely associated with the A-Story and is the causation Character for the A-Story's Convergence with the Main Character's B-Story world, Underlying Cause Characters can come from any relevant area of the B-Story. Which is to say it can be the Main Character themselves. But more likely, an Underlying Cause Character is a significant B-Story Subplot Character.

The Underlying Cause Character's Cause of a Cause is related to the Theme. Proximate Cause Characters are events-focused causation Characters. Underlying Cause Characters tend to be more Theme-focused.

Not only can the Underlying Cause Character be the Main Character themselves, but another potential difference from the Proximate Cause Character is that there may, in fact, be more than one Underlying Cause Character!

Relevance and perspective are key once again. Because the Revealed Story is the Main Character's Journey, their B-Story is the one we think of as larger. A story is their transformative Journey, so the Theme relates to their B-Story and Personal Goal. This means there is more room, so to speak, within the story for Theme to be explored and therefore more room for there to be more than one causation Character in the B-Story.

Likely, if there is more than one Underlying Cause Character, they will not all be given equal weight. Especially in a screenplay where page number and screen time matter. Oftentimes Subplot Characters express nuanced differences in the Theme or lesser secondary and tertiary thematic ideas running concurrently with the Main Theme. But every significant B-Story Subplot relationships should explore the thematic conflict in some way to ensure that they all contribute to B-Story Thematic causation.

Underlying Cause Character Characteristics

- A Character who *causes* the Problem or Opportunity within the B-Story.

- A Character who *causes* the Theme to be expressed in both the A and B stories. The Character that makes the *Theme* happen.
- There can be multiple Underlying Cause Characters, each expressing the Theme and causing a unique Problem or Opportunity within the B-Story.

Some Examples of Underlying Cause Characters:

Liar Liar: Fletcher's son, *Max*, is repeatedly disappointed by his father's lies, so he makes the wish. Fletcher's ex-wife *Audrey* is a lesser Underlying Cause Character because she has had it with Fletcher's excuses for disappointing Max and decides to pursue a life with Jerry—whom she doesn't really love—by moving away to Boston.

Star Wars: *Obi-Wan Kenobi* was a Jedi and introduces Luke to the notion of The Force.

Die Hard: *Holly Gennaro*, John McClane's estranged wife, is using her maiden name professionally.

Rocky: Has several Underlying Cause Characters. *Mickey*, the trainer, thinks Rocky is a bum who never gave it his all to realize his potential as a fighter. *Adrien* is so shy that she is not willing or able to express herself, and she is Rocky's *body vs brains* complement. *Paulie* is permanently down on his luck and represents the pull to settle for less.

Harry Potter: Obviously there are many Underlying Cause Characters over the course of the entire saga. The primary example is *Dumbledore*, who sees Harry's wizarding potential, even though Harry just wants to be normal. But we can consider the roles played by Harry's closest wizard friends, many other Hogwarts professors, and invested wizards like *Sirius Black*—all of whom jump in to aid Harry at various points.

Home Alone: Kevin's *Mother* imposes the will of the annoyed family who treats him unfairly when she sends him up to the attic, which is how he gets left behind.

The Princess Bride: The princess *Buttercup* gives up on *true love* and agrees to marry Prince Humperdinck.

Armageddon: *Grace Stamper* (Harry's daughter), played by Liv Tyler, wants to marry *A.J.*, Ben Affleck's roughneck Character, but roughnecks are not good enough as marriage partners for his daughter in Harry's eyes.

Field of Dreams: *Ray* himself is the Underlying Cause Character because he has unfinished business with his father.

Good Will Hunting: *Chuckie*, the Ben Affleck Character and Will's best friend, has Will's back and will do anything to stick by a buddy, including getting into a fight.

French Kiss: Kate's fiancé, *Charlie*, falls in love with another woman in France.

Back to the Future: *Biff* has bullied Marty's father for being a loser. This is an unusual case because the story's Antagonist is *not* the Proximate Cause Character but rather an Underlying Cause Character. Time travel is *crazy*!

Sideways: *Miles* himself provides the Underlying Cause because he's so stuck in the past and still wants to reconnect with his ex-wife, who has moved on.

Timeline Movements as Causation Chains

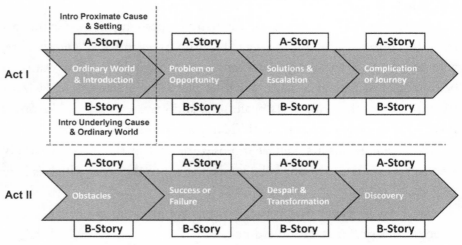

Figure 156: Proximate Cause and Underlying Cause Introduced

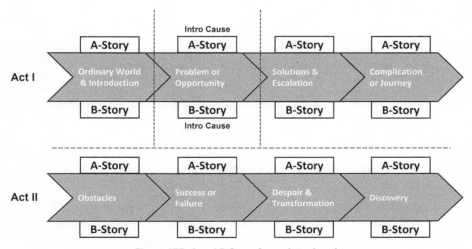

Figure 157: A and B Story Cause Introduced

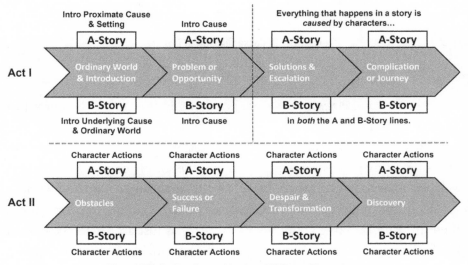

Figure 158:Action Caused by A and B Story Characters

The Final Act (Act 3) Climax and Resolution are the products of the Momentum established by this chain of causation.

Events *do not* determine the flow and progress of a story.

Character actions *cause* the flow and progress of a story.

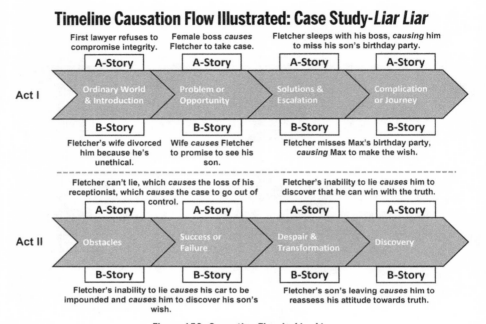

Figure 159: Causation Flow in *Liar Liar*

As we have stated elsewhere, we are not flying in the face of the norm just to be contrarian.

The study of literary Archetypes has a real value in academia. For creating and writing great stories, not so much. We simply consider Archetypes as labels placed on Characters by academics analyzing completed works.

To begin thinking about a Character in terms of an Archetype boxes them in. And thinking about your Character as just an Archetype cannot lead to Thematic Relevance - and *that* is the real goal in Character creation.

You should now have a robust understanding of the process of Character creation through considering every Character as a mechanism of *cause*, guided by the invisible hand of Theme.

Your storytelling transformative Journey has nearly run its course! In the final chapter, we bring it all together on a practical level and point the way toward *your* Unrealized Potential as an Author-Storyteller using the Your Storytelling Potential Method and tools.

CHAPTER 11:

Your Revealed Storytelling Potential

U p to this point, we have been explaining concepts. We started with the Three Branches and the Hidden and Revealed Story. We went through the Character Wave, the Core Elements, and the Simple Story Timeline.

It's now time to put it all into practice. It's time for you to truly unlock Your *own* Storytelling Potential and experience your own *Revealed Potential* as a storyteller, screenwriter, novelist, graphic artist, or writer in any form that you wish to apply these techniques.

This brings us to our eleventh and final universal storytelling truth: Creating and writing amazing screenplays, novels, and narratives with three-dimensional Characters, rich and relevant thematic ideas, well-thought-out complex A and B storylines, appropriate Structure, and meaningful and relevant Subplots doesn't have to be *unattainable*, in fact, if you follow the steps in this book and this chapter, it's downright *doable*.

Before continuing, please visit: https://www.yourstorytellingpotential. com/worksheets

On that page, you can register to download *free* copies of all the worksheets we explore in this chapter. The worksheets are fully editable and can be opened in the free Adobe PDF Reader or nearly any web browser, such as Google Chrome or Microsoft Edge.

Once loaded into Adobe PDF Reader or a web browser, you can fill out the forms and save your ongoing work. (Note: When saving your work for the first time, we recommend you use the "Save As" function to rename the document with project-specific information, so you can always go back to the blank template for each new project you plan to develop.)

Brainstorming the Core Elements

The practical application of the Your Storytelling Potential Method starts with the Core Elements Worksheet:

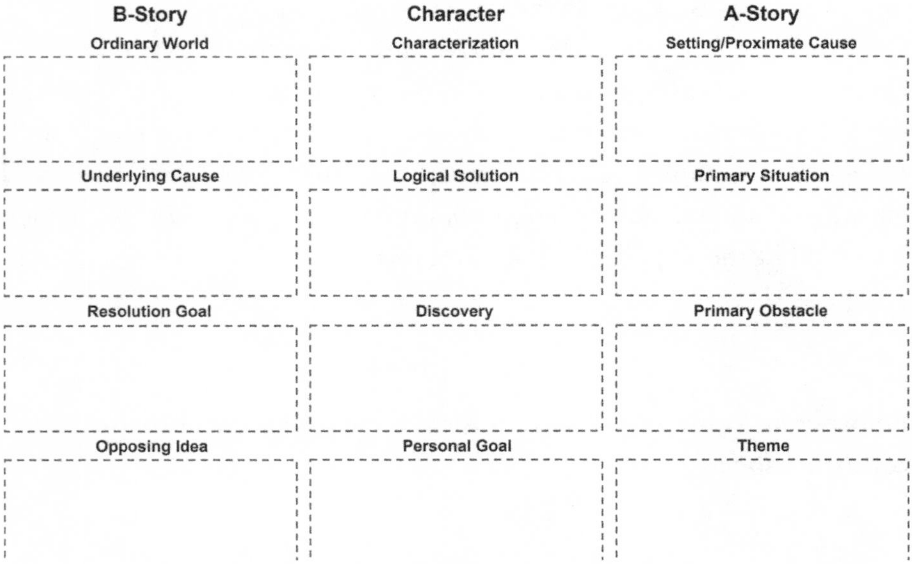

Figure 160: Core Elements Worksheet

The Core Elements allow a writer to think dynamically about a story, and we recommend that you start with this one.

Earlier in this book, we mentioned the difference between thinking about the *whats* and the *whens*. The Core Elements allow you to think about the whats. When you finish the whats, you Structure your story by thinking about the whens.

You must first figure out *what* is happening in your story; that is what the Core Elements are about.

(Review Chapter 7 for specific definitions and examples of each Core Element.)

Begin this exercise by filling in the information you know about your story and Characters.

Information specific to the Main Character goes in the *center* column.

Information about that Character's B-Story and any major B-Story Characters, such as the Underlying Cause Character, would be listed in the *left* column.

The A-Story information, such as information about the Proximate Cause and Proximate Cause Character, goes on the *right* column.

As you identify the various Core Elements, expect your understanding of your own story to evolve. You will probably find yourself moving Elements around because a Character you thought was from the A-Story proves to be more appropriate for the B-Story and vice-versa.

Don't be worried if certain Elements remain unclear for a while. Developing your story by discovering the Relevance of each part is a creative, iterative process. It will take time to get this right.

Pay special attention to the Thematic Layer. If you identify something as the *Theme* then consider possible *relevant* conceptual opposites for the Opposing Idea. Consider how your Main Character is caught between these two aspects of your story, caught between two sides of the same thing (e.g., the Dark Side and Light Side of The Force).

(Review the examples in Chapter 3 to help you identify your own relevant Thematic Layer.)

Brainstorming the Structure

As your story becomes more coherent using the Core Elements Worksheet, begin to organize your Story Structure with the Elements you have identified using the **A/B Parallel Structure** Worksheets.

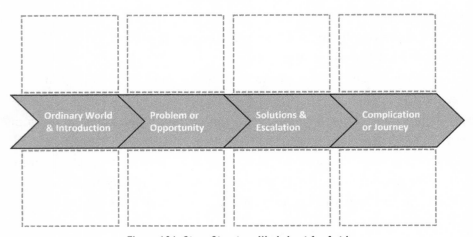

Figure 161: Story Structure Worksheet for Act I

The information you identified in the Core Elements Worksheet helps you to develop and organize your Story Structure.

Here are some tips for mapping information from the Core Elements Worksheet to the A/B Parallel Structure Worksheets:

Information from the B-Story goes on the bottom part of these worksheets.

- A-Story information goes on the top.
- Ordinary World details would be introduced in the corresponding B-Story portion on the Timeline.
- The Setting and Proximate Cause details would belong in the A-Story section.
- Characterization typically begins in the B-Story and moves to the A-Story as the story progresses.

- The Underlying Cause and Primary Situation are introduced as a corresponding Problem and/or Opportunity for each part of your story.
- Solutions and Escalations are determined by the Logical Solution. This is the benefit of using the Core Elements. Once you now know WHAT your Main Character should be doing, you can fill in more specific details.
- Act 1 ends with the introduction of the Primary Obstacle, namely the specific Complication or Journey that will frame the first half of Act II.
- You should identify at least one major Complication or Journey for both the A-Story and the B-Story. And remember they can feed off of each other, meaning that a Complication in the B-Story can cause a domino effect into the A-Story, which then causes that story's Complication or Journey.

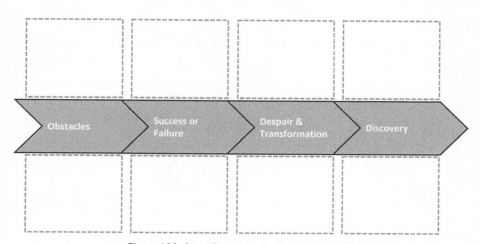

Figure 162: Story Structure Worksheet for Act II

Act II begins with the introduction of the Primary Obstacle at the end of Act I. The Primary Obstacle is typically supplied by the A-Story.

As the story progresses into Act II, the Main Character commits to their Logical Solution and is faced with at least one major Complication or Journey. Again, most stories have Obstacles specific to either the A or B Stories. These Obstacles are presented in different Subplots within each storyline.

As the story approaches the Midpoint, the Main Character faces the ultimate Failure of their Logical Solution. Everything they tried up to the Midpoint has been based on Logic, but that is about to change.

At the Midpoint, the Logical Solution either succeeds or fails, but either way both the Primary Situation and Underlying Cause remain unresolved.

It is now clear to the Main Character that Failure was the inevitable outcome all along. The Logical Solution was *never* going to work. And this ultimate Failure of the Logical Solution leaves the Main Character, and other related Characters, directionless. Their plans, hopes, and dreams smashed upon the rocks of reality.

The Failure of the Logical Solution causes the Main Character to experience Despair, which is present in both the A and B storylines. It affects all the Subplots.

Yet success and the outcome of the Revealed Story hinges on this very Failure at the Midpoint and the subsequent Despair because from this darkest moment will come a genuine, deep, thematically rich, and relevant Main Character Transformation.

The Transformation begins with an examination of the Thematic Conflict. The Main Character must face the harsh reality that their beliefs, as they pertain to the Theme, were mistaken. (In the case of a Steadfast Main Character, other Characters must face this reality.)

Through this process of self-examination, an unforeseen Discovery or Discoveries occur. These Discoveries feed new life into the story and the Characters, pushing the story into its final phase of Act III.

The Discoveries provide the Clarity that the Main Character needs to resolve the Thematic Conflict.

It now becomes clear what needs to be done to succeed, and that new plan is the Main Character's Resolution Goal. The great irony is that the solution and actions needed to achieve the Resolution Goal are usually the opposite of those proposed in the Logical Solution.

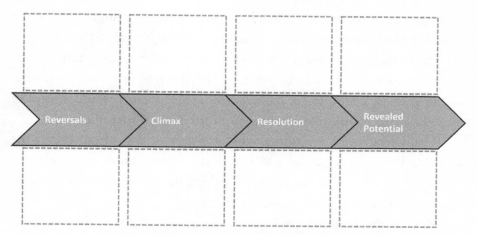

Figure 163: Story Structure Worksheet for Act III

Act III is about the *actions* necessary to resolve the multiple Situations.

Insights provided by the Discoveries lead to major Reversals in the story. And these Reversals reverberate through both the A and B Storylines, impacting every relevant Subplot.

The Reversals are action-oriented. The new information that came by way of the Discoveries at the end of Act II provides the Clarity that is necessary for the Main Character to finally resolve the Situations that were not affected by the Logical Solution.

Actions taken from this point forward as dictated by the Resolution Goal drive the story forward to the Climax and Resolution.

The Climax of a story is typically A-Story heavy, and the Resolution portion focuses on the closure of the B-Story Subplots.

Nothing new is introduced in Act III. All the necessary information about the Characters, Situations, and thematic ideas needs to be introduced before Act III begins. Act III is only about bringing the Revealed Story to its final conclusion.

The Climax of the A-Story finally resolves the ongoing Problem or Opportunity that was created by the Proximate Cause Character in Act I.

All A-Story-related Subplots (Side Plots) are closed out and finalized, although often one or two new relationships that were forged during the Revealed Story carry forward to (and beyond) the Revealed Potential.

The Resolution closes the B-Story Subplots with an emphasis on the Thematic Layer. The Main Character's Transformation is now complete. In the case of a Steadfast Character, other Characters would complete their thematic Transformation instead of the Main Character.

Finally, the story concludes with a vision of the future called the Revealed Potential. This short look into the future shows how the Main Character and all the relevant relationships have become forever transformed because of the story that has taken place.

(Review the examples in Chapter 9 to help you develop your own Story Structure components.)

Brainstorming for Relevant Characters

As you develop your story, no doubt your Characters and the relevant Themes will become more obvious. In Chapter 10 we emphasized the purpose of Characters as drivers of the forward Movement and progression of the story.

At no point have we missed the opportunity to emphasize that *Relevance* is the guiding principle for every choice that goes into planning and constructing a truly great, well-told tale. The more foundational work you do, the more Relevance directs your choices as you flesh out details.

Proceeding from our discussion of *Characters as cause*, we provide some Character worksheets to help you identify and address relevant details to consider for each of the significant Characters populating your story. These worksheet categories are central to building the relevant details that matter for their roles within the narrative than information obtained from an unfocused effort in writing out sprawling Character biography backstories.

Again, the key to all of these worksheets is to focus on *Relevance*. Relevance to the B-Story, Relevance to the A-Story, Relevance to the Theme.

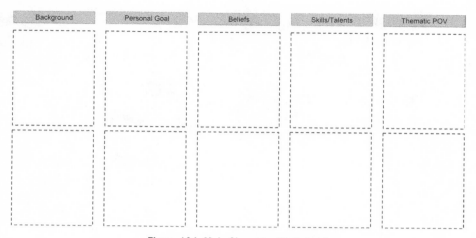

Figure 164: Main Character Worksheet

This worksheet includes:

- Background
- Personal Goal
- Beliefs
- Skills/Talents
- Thematic Point of View

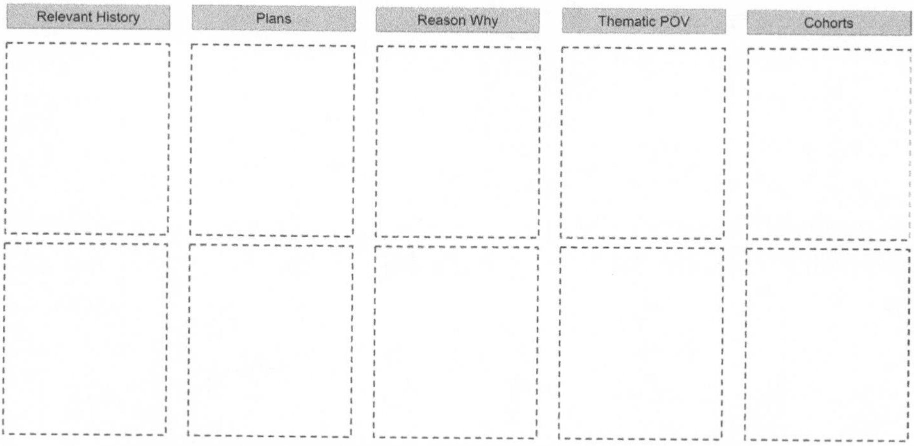

Figure 165:Proximate Cause Character/Antagonist Worksheet

This worksheet includes:
- Relevant History
- Plans
- Reasons Why
- Thematic Point of View
- Cohorts

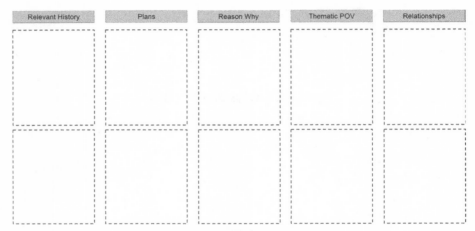

Figure 166: Underlying Cause Character Worksheet

This worksheet includes:
- Relevant History
- Plans
- Reasons Why
- Thematic Point of View
- Relationships

(Use this worksheet for each additional significant Subplot Character.)

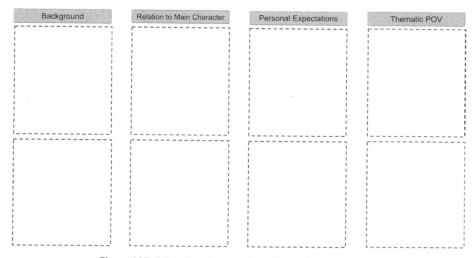

Figure 167: Other Significant Subplot Characters Worksheet

This worksheet includes:
- Background
- Relationship to Main Character
- Personal Expectations
- Thematic Point of View

Secondary Characters

Secondary Characters are functional, limited-appearance Characters such as vendors, taxi drivers, significant Characters' lawyers, etc. Secondary Characters who may have some lines of dialogue to say, but do not get developed or explored to the point where they have a Plotline of their own. The way any bit player is used *may* contribute to Theme, but not necessarily. Sometimes someone just has to bring your Main Character a cup of coffee! (But if a bartender can sell your undercover spy Main Character some Russian vodka or a passing librarian can suggest a relevant book at a key moment, so much the better!)

Build a general list of secondary Characters for your reference. For each Character, make notes about the practical function of the Character and any thematic role they might play. No additional details are necessary for these Characters.

There is some level of discovery in this exercise, but its primary value is to build out a cast list for your reference. Most of these areas of detail will have already been established through the process of building out the Core Elements and structuring the Simple Story Outline. But as you spend time completing these details for each Character, you have the opportunity to consider them in additional depth.

Consider their *motivations*, their *secrets*, their *wounds*. What might they be hiding? What might they fear? What may trigger them to have emotional responses? Never waste a chance to create meaningful Layers, so long as they remain relevant.

Charting Subplots

Let's examine in detail the forces influencing every Character's dialogue and actions.

As we explained in Chapter 8, every significant Character besides the Main Character is a relationship Character. And we know that the Main Character's actions and speech will be driven by their Personal Goal, which in turn informs their Logical Solution, their Transformation, and their Resolution Goal.

As relationship Characters, the Subplots need to relate to the Theme in some way. Some are pushing, some are pulling. Each Subplot may explore the main Theme in nuanced ways. So the place to begin breaking down these Characters is in terms of the Thematic Conflict between Theme and Opposing Idea.

In our previous exercise, we have established every Character's Thematic Point of View. Now it's time to dig a bit deeper into that.

In the Your Storytelling Potential Method *online course*, there is a worksheet that helps with this exercise, but you can begin this process by dividing a sheet of paper into three vertical columns and writing *Opposing Idea* at the top of the first column, *Characters* at the top of the middle column and *Theme* at the top at the top of the third column. List each

Subplot Character down the middle column. Your Characters will now sit between Opposing Idea and Theme. For each Character, identify how the Thematic Conflict is explored through the relationship between each Character and the Main Character.

Relevance is essential to a well-told story. If you really cannot connect a Subplot Character to the Theme in any way, consider whether this Character is necessary. Do they belong in your story at all? If not, say goodbye.

Establishing your Subplot Characters' Thematic Relevance leads to another invaluable story-building exercise. Take each Subplot Character and break down their Subplot *progression*:

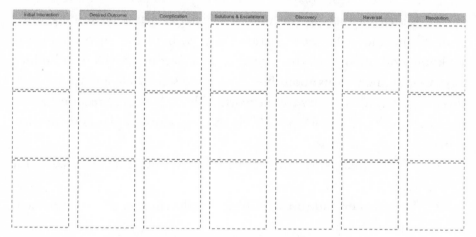

Figure 168: Subplot Character Progression

Think of this as a miniaturized version of your Simple Story Timeline where you are simply extracting the pathway of a single Subplot. This best ensures a proper and complete progression for the development of each Subplot.

This worksheet includes:
- Initial Interaction
- Desired Outcome
- Complication
- Solutions & Escalations

- Discovery
- Reversal
- Resolution

Depending on the needs of a given story, your Subplot progression work does not have to be complicated. Just because there are seven Movements described here, it does not mean every Character of significance must have seven separate scenes devoted to their Plotline. Some significant but minor Characters can complete this Mini-Journey in three beats with two or more of these objectives accomplished in very short order.

One easy example of this comes from the movie *Armageddon*:

Actor Will Patton plays one of Harry Stamper's roughneck crew named Chick Chapel. In the movie, Chick's ex has a restraining order against him, and he has no visitation rights with his son. As the audience, we know nothing of this, this information is part of Chick's own Hidden Past. Once Chick learns about NASA's plan to send them all into space on this dangerous mission to save the world, Chick decides to reconnect with his son. Chick's relationship with his son and ex then plays out in three short and simple scenes:

- Chick attempts to connect with his son but gets rebuffed at the door by his ex.
- Later, his ex and son see Chick on television as part of the rescue mission team.
- At the end of the film, his ex brings their son to greet Chick upon his return to Earth, and there is a clear reconciliation.

That entire Subplot, which explores another perspective on the *blue-collar roughnecks aren't good enough* Theme that plagues the Main Character, Harry Stamper, concerning his own daughter's choice of a fiancé, plays out in just three brief scenes. The ending is nothing more than visual shots of the ex and the boy running up and hugging Patton's Character. But every part of the Subplot progression gets expressed in those quick movements.

Creating Your Final Outline with the Simple Story Timeline

The final step in creating a truly amazing story is to create the final structural layout of your story utilizing the Simple Story Timeline.

These downloadable worksheets mirror the A/B Parallel Structure worksheets in terms of story progression and the three acts, but these sheets are designed for full story integration.

This final process is to outline the totality of your story by integrating the A and B storylines, along with Subplots and Character details into a linear form that can then be used as a guide as you write your screenplay, novel, or express your story in any other form you want.

Ordinary World & Introduction

Problem or Opportunity

Solutions & Escalation

Complication or Journey

Figure 169: Simple Story Timeline Act I

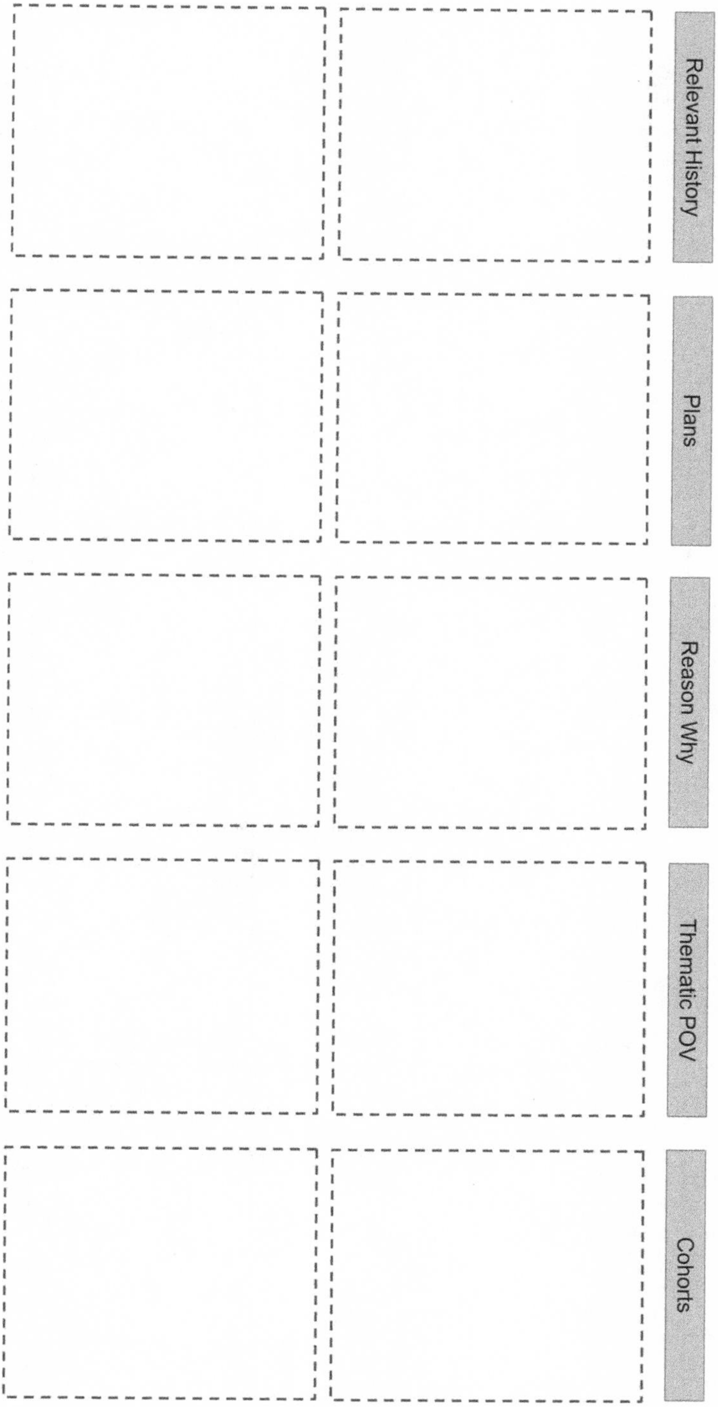

Figure 170: Simple Story Timeline Act II

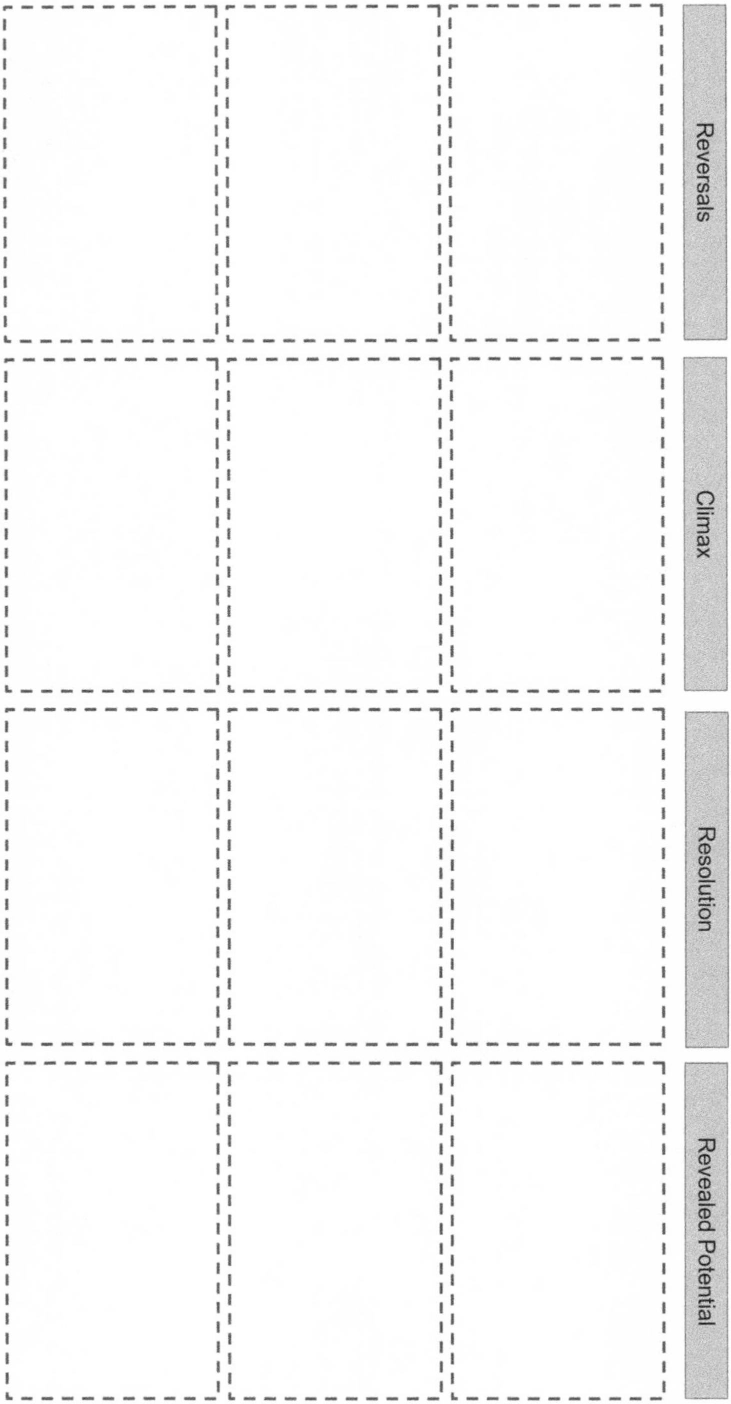

Figure 171: Simple Story Timeline Act III

Reversals

Climax

Resolution

Revealed Potential

In Chapter 1, in the very first paragraph, we promised that at some point *"you will have completed this material."* That time has now come.

Since that opening salvo you have been on your own transformative Journey as a writer. If you have absorbed the information and apply the techniques we've shared throughout this book, you should be ready to resume your life as a *transformed storyteller*, with an entirely new outlook on your own Revealed Potential as a writer.

This final chapter has provided you with worksheets and exercises that complete your transformative Journey and provide you with a truly practical and creative iterative process of discovery that you can utilize with your own stories.

Using the techniques found in this chapter will allow you to start that creative process from *any point* in the storytelling process.

You can start with an idea for a Character or an idea for a Plot. You can start with a thematic idea or Subplot. You can literally start with almost anything.

Using the Core Elements, you fill in the information you know. And then using those same Core Elements, you can discover and identify the information that you lack.

Before long you'll have Clarity about the Proximate Cause and Proximate Cause Character, as well as the Primary Situation. You'll have Clarity on the Underlying Cause and the Underlying Cause Character. And you'll understand how the Main Character is trapped between those two stories and their opposing Thematic Ideas.

You then expand your story into *time*—the Revealed Present—using the A/B Parallel Structure, while identifying both the A and B Stories and how they relate and coincide with each other.

The Character-based brainstorming exercises in this chapter should then provide you with a thorough understanding of every Character in your story. You'll know who *causes* the Primary Situation of the A-Story to happen. You'll know which Character *causes* the B-Story Problem or Opportunity with the Underlying Cause. You'll understand each Character's Thematic Role. You'll know what motivates each and every Character. From all of this, their dialogue and actions will flow effortlessly.

You then map out each individual Subplot and understand how that Subplot fits into the broader story taking place, and how each Subplot Character *causes* the story to move forward through time towards the Climax and Resolution.

Finally, you will complete the process by using the Simple Story Timeline and creating a detailed outline and breakdown of your entire story, which then serves as a detailed guide as you write your screenplay, novel, or draft your story into whatever form is needed.

We believe this book lays out a comprehensive foundation upon which a writer can craft truly amazing stories.

To learn more about the techniques found in this book or for more information about other related storytelling products, such as software, online courses, or to enquire about private consultation, please visit us at: YourStorytellingPotential.com

THE END

Actually, you are just at the *beginning* of Your *Revealed* Storytelling Potential!

ABOUT THE AUTHOR

Mitchell German, the creator of Your Storytelling Potential Method, went to college at NYU where he studied filmmaking and screenwriting. He wanted to be an exceptional storyteller in the medium of movies.

NYU is regularly recognized as one of, if not *the*, premier film studies programs in the United States. And since that includes all of the prestigious programs throughout California, the very hotbed of the movie industry, it is not unreasonable to assume that NYU has one of the very best film programs *in the world*. **Yet, what is taught in Your Storytelling Potential Method does <u>not</u> come from the NYU film studies curriculum.**

Mitchell graduated from NYU with what he understood to be a complete doctrine on storytelling theory in his arsenal. Yet he felt his screenplays lacked the potency he desired. Something was still missing in his understanding of the way stories operated. There was something he needed to discover to elevate his stories into the stratosphere, to join the ranks of the professional-level elite storytellers.

Mitchell spent the next ten years studying every available book and "expert" on storytelling, but he found they mostly taught the same regurgitated information presented with each instructor's unique twist, but none provided a complete solution or Clarity about how to craft a great story.

It was then in 2002, after endlessly studying the movie *Liar Liar*, that Mitchell found the key—the core concepts upon which Your Storytelling Potential Method is based.

These insights have been praised by industry professionals. Many of whom have paid top dollar for Mitchell's consulting services. They formed the basis of the first instructional course he compiled for screenwriters— the Mega Course. These are the principles around which the enormously successful Plot Control screenwriting software is based. And in the nearly two decades since, they have been developed and adapted for software serving novelists (Chapter Control), television writers and producers (Episode Control), college essay writers (Essay Dog), and even applications for business entrepreneurs running webinars and launching new products. Literally, anyone needing to tell a story. All told, tens of thousands of people have benefitted from his courses, software, and project consulting services.

Russell Phillips came to Your Storytelling Potential Method as a satisfied customer.

Russ graduated from the Communications Program (Cinema Sequence) at SMU in Dallas, Texas. While there, he earned a spot in visiting UCLA professor Richard Walter's screenwriting seminar.

He has written more than a dozen screenplays, is an experienced stand-up comic, and has acted in a few short films. His scripts opened some doors and helped him forge some valuable industry contacts, but none of the projects quite came together. In the pursuit of stronger script writing skills, he acquired a robust library of how-to books and continued to register for available advanced learning courses. But life took him further and further from his creative ambitions.

Russ was an early Plot Control user and Mega Course student. After many years away from creative writing, he revisited the Mega Course as part of his journey of rediscovery during the early days of the 2020 worldwide pandemic. The second time through the course, Russ found the message of Thematic Relevance powerfully resonant. He recognized that what Mitchell German's method offered was not merely a fresh explanation of all the same ideas on storytelling but a very different paradigm for how a story should be constructed.

The worldwide pandemic was also a time when many shut-ins were rediscovering the classic Public Television painting instructor, Bob Ross. Russ saw a parallel with the painter's method of filling in a painting from back to front—starting with the sky and distant mountains and working toward the foreground, finishing with the sharpest detailed featured subject of the picture. This seemed to be the thinking behind Mitchell's teaching. So Russ emailed Mitchell to thank him for the insights in the Mega Course.

Russ enthusiastically joins Mitchell to help bring this method in its new form, the Your Storytelling Potential Method, to top professional and novice Author-Storytellers the world over.

ADDITIONAL RESOURCES

Your Storytelling Potential: The Online Course and Workshop
The Your Storytelling Potential Method is a structured approach to developing a story that ensures an Author-Storyteller will produce well-thought-out and Layered stories with relevant three-dimensional characters and deep and meaningful interwoven themes. A story written using the Your Storytelling Potential approach has a substantially greater chance of standing out and getting recognized, no matter your chosen form of expression—movies, novels, television, plays, comics & graphic novels, short stories, oral presentations, etc.
Visit: https://www.yourstorytellingpotential.com

Your Storytelling Potential: Worksheets
These worksheets accompany Your Storytelling Potential. They guide any writer helping them construct amazing and Layered stories, with three-dimensional characters, proper structure, and rich & relevant themes. Download them for FREE.
Download your worksheets: https://www.yourstorytellingpotential. com/worksheets

Your Storytelling Potential: Action Guides
These action guides were developed as part of the Your Storytelling Potential Method. They were designed for the kinesthetic learner—those who prefer to master by doing. With that in mind, these guides are the most streamlined immersion into the Your Storytelling Potential Method.

Expect a minimum of explanation, almost no analytical examples from published works, and an emphasis on instruction for diving into putting this system into action.

Visit: https://www.yourstorytellingpotential.com/action-guides

Plot Control 4.0: Screenwriting and Story Development Software

The most powerful screenwriting tool ever created combined with the most powerful story building methodology. With Plot Control you can build three dimensional characters, Layer your plots, integrate themes and subplots, develop your Core Elements & A/B Parallel Structure, write your scripts, and format your screenplays.

Visit: https://www.plotcontrol.com

Chapter Control 4.0: Novel Writing and Story Development Software

The most powerful novel writing tool ever created combined with the most powerful story building methodology. With Chapter Control you can build three dimensional characters, Layer your plots, integrate themes and subplots, develop your Core Elements & A/B Parallel Structure, structure & order your chapters, and write your drafts.

Visit: https://www.chaptercontrol.com

Episode Control 1.0: TV Show Development Software

For writers, producers, directors, and anyone interested in developing episodic material, whether for TV, streaming, YouTube, or the written word. Episode Control provides the framework and structure upon which all great TV shows, movie franchises, and novel series are based. With Episode Control you can build characters, develop seasons, create episodes, write scripts, and more.

Visit: https://www.episodecontrol.com

Screenplay and Manuscript Reviews Services

Your Storytelling Potential offers the most potent and informative review services for screenwriters and novelists. Because of the unique approach to storytelling, Mitchell German and Your Storytelling Potential can provide accurate analysis and actionable feedback for writers, filmmakers, and any storyteller.

Visit: https://www.yourstorytellingpotential.com

GLOSSARY

3 Branches: At the highest level of conceptualizing a story, there are *three* components that converge to create a well-told story. In the Your Storytelling Potential Method, we refer to these as "branches." They are Character, the A-Story, and the B-Story.

A/B Parallel Structure: In the Your Storytelling Potential Method, a brainstorming step for constructing a story reliant on the two-story model that underpins the system. In this exercise, the Author-Storyteller defines the major beats of action that push the A-Story forward independent from a second track charting the development of the B-Story.

A-Story: A new Problem or Opportunity that enters the ongoing story of the Main Character. The A-Story collides and merges with the Main Character's B-Story for the duration of the Revealed Story as told by the Author-Storyteller. The A-Story defines the starting point and ending point of the Revealed Story. It provides the catalyst for the Main Character's Transformation. Although the A-Story affects the Main Character, the A-Story truly belongs to another Character, which we call the Proximate Cause Character. The A-Story is one of the 3 Branches of a story.

A-Story Dialog: All speech between Characters that advances the A-Story. A-Story dialog tends to be more functional than B-Story dialog.

Act I: In a standard Three-Act Structure, Act I represents roughly the first 25% of the story. It includes the Introduction, which establishes the Main Character's Ordinary World and Characterization as well as the Setting for the A-Story. Act I presents the Primary Situation and its Convergence with the Main Character's life. It initiates the Main Character's

Logical Solution to the Primary Situation. Act I concludes as the Main Character encounters the Primary Obstacle to their Logical Solution.

Act I Layer: Of the Core Elements, the B-Story's Underlying Cause, The Main Character's Logical Solution, and the A-Story's Primary Situation. These three Elements are the main focus of the business of Act I.

Act II: In a standard Three-Act Structure, Act II represents roughly the middle 50% of the story. Act II begins with the introduction of the Primary Obstacle, which stands in the way of the success of the Main Character's Logical Solution. Act II has two distinct parts. The Main Character remains committed to their initial Logical Solution to the Primary Situation up to the Midpoint. The Midpoint of Act II may be either the success or Failure of the Logical Solution, but regardless, the Logical Solution always fails to resolve the Primary Situation. The second part of Act II tends to be a more thematic-oriented exploration of the Primary Situation as the Main Character has to abandon their initial Logic and search for a better solution. This involves a period of Despair that leads to one or more significant discoveries. This is where the Main Character completes their Transformation. Act II ends with the Main Character achieving a Clarity that formulates the Resolution Goal.

Act II-a, b, c, d, etc.: Repetitive middle acts in a story with four or more acts or the middle episodes/books in a TV Show or book series.

Act II Layer: Of the Core Elements, the B-Story's Resolution Goal, the Character's Discovery, and the A-Story's Primary Obstacle. These three Elements are the major focuses of the business of Act II.

Act II-Part 1: The first half of Act II from the end of Act I through to the Midpoint. Act II-Part 1 is primarily the exercise of the Main Character's attempts to circumvent the Primary Obstacle using their Logical Solution. It tends to lean more toward the A-Story.

Act II-Part 2: The second half of Act II from the Midpoint through to the beginning of Act III. Act II-Part 2 deals with the aftermath of the Midpoint Failure. A period of Despair that leads to the search for a new solution to the Primary Situation. The action of Act II-Part 2 tends to lean toward an exploration of the Theme as the Main Character moves toward Transformation and makes the discoveries that bring them to Clarity.

Act III: In a standard Three-Act Structure, Act III represents roughly the final 25% of the story. Act III begins with the Main Character's Clarity in forming a Resolution Goal. Armed with the Resolution Goal, The Main Character engages the Primary Situation in a new way, which leads to the Climax of the A-Story. After the Climax resolves the Primary Situation, there is generally some material devoted to the Resolution, which demonstrates the Main Character's Commitment to their Transformation. We call this cementing of the Transformation the Revealed Potential. The Resolution also gives a glimpse of the Unknown Future, the new life the Main Character will lead after the Revealed Story's conclusion.

Anointed Character: A type of Main Character who enters the Revealed Story uniquely qualified to engage the A-Story's Primary Situation for some transcendent reason. All Main Characters should be "Uniquely Extraordinary" because they are exactly right for their story, but this class of Main Character *must* be the Main Character in their story because of reasons beyond their innate characteristics and personality. Most often, they are Anointed Characters by birthright. Often these characters have special powers. Examples would be Luke Skywalker, Harry Potter, Wonder Woman, or King Arthur.

Antagonist: If present, the most significant character whose interests oppose those of the Main Character. The Antagonist, one of the Antagonist's agents, and/or the Antagonist's plans in action are often the Primary Obstacle for the Main Character. The Antagonist is the most common type of Proximate Cause Character. Not every story contains an Antagonist. Some stories with an Antagonist have another character who is the Proximate Cause Character.

Archetype: In the study of literature, Archetypes are the generalized model definition of characters and the functions they serve. Many systems of narrative analysis categorize every story's characters according to these broad general definitions. In the Your Storytelling Potential Method, we do not rely upon Archetypes in the construction of characters. Instead, we see the more fertile path lies in considering characters as the cause of the problems, opportunities, and Obstacles that move a story forward. Archetypes place unnecessary limitations on the crafting of characters, who should be seen as individuals, not function categories.

Author-Storyteller: In this system and book, we refer to the reader and prospective student of this method as the "Author-Storyteller" to best encompass the broad spectrum of creative people who might benefit from this information and these insights. This system is not form-specific, meaning these principles apply equally to screenwriting, novel writing, short story writing, comics, and graphic novel writing, oral presentations, and any other story construction application possible.

B-Story: The ongoing story of the Main Character. The B-Story is much larger than the A-Story from the Main Character's point of view. In essence, it is their ongoing life. It has a Hidden Past and extends beyond the end of the Revealed Story into the Unknown Future. The B-Story in well-told narratives also presents the Main Character with a Problem or Opportunity, and often the collision of the Primary Situation with this B-Story Problem or Opportunity can be the Primary Obstacle. This B-Story Problem or Opportunity is called the Underlying Cause. B-Story is one of the 3 Branches of a story.

B-Story Dialog: All speech between characters that deals with the Underlying Cause and Thematic concerns in a story. B-Story dialog tends to be deeper than the pure function-driven quality of A-Story dialog.

Beginning: A term we ask students of the Your Storytelling Potential Method to drop in reference to the starting point of the Revealed Story. In this system, we emphasize the persistence of time from before the Now of the A-Story and beyond its end. Therefore, the term "Introduction" is preferable. "Beginning" has a tabula rasa connotation—a story springing from nowhere into the life of a character. We believe a story needs to be constructed to account for the Hidden Past of both the Main Character's ongoing B-Story and that of the Proximate Cause in the A-Story.

Branch: Any of the three main conceptual elements that make up a story. They are Character, the A-Story, and the B-Story.

Character: Broadly, any person or sentient entity referenced as part of a story. Specifically, Character is one of the three Branches of a story. In this usage, "Character" refers to the totality of the Main Character which includes their Characterization—insights into the Character's mindset and thought processes framing their Logical Solution and Personal Goal.

Character Arc: A popular term in traditional narratology we ask you to drop in reference to the transformative Journey of the Main Character. "Character Arc" may be understood and defended by proponents of traditional schools as something other than a true, smooth "arc" of transition between two points, but we believe the idea of a "Character Wave" to be a superior concept. The "arc" describes a beginning point and an endpoint but does not suggest the pathway of the Journey in-between. The Your Storytelling Potential Method describes the Character Wave Journey in seven Structural Connection Points and describes the push-and-pull dynamic of forces acting on the Main Character from the Thematic Conflict.

Character Wave: In the Your Storytelling Potential Method, Character Wave describes the Main Character's Journey toward Transformation through the progression of the story. Analogous to the term "character arc" in many traditional systems. The wave refers to the push and pull dynamic of Thematic Conflict between the story's Theme and Opposing Idea exerted upon the Main Character. The Your Storytelling Potential Method describes the Character Wave Journey in seven Structural Connection Points. Also referred to as the "Complete Character Wave."

Characterization: The relevant and specific information about the Main Character that defines who they are and why they are "Uniquely Extraordinary." One of the Twelve Core Elements of the Your Storytelling Potential Method. Characterization is the Introduction-Layer Core Element associated with the Character Branch.

Clarity: The last of the three Transitional Doorways between the four major Movements in story progression that frame the Character Wave Journey. In Act II-Part 2, the Main Character leaves the Midpoint Failure with a sense of Despair. Act II-Part 2 becomes a process of Transformation fueled by Thematic Conflict and Discovery. The Main Character reaches Clarity, a new perspective on how to deal with the Primary Situation. With this Clarity, a Resolution Goal is formed, and the story enters into Act III.

Climax: The outcome of the A-Story and, simultaneously, the outcome of most of the A-Story subplots. The Climax represents the end of the A-Story.

Commitment: The last of the four major Movements of the B-Story side of the Character Wave Journey. Once the Main Character has completed the Transformation process in Act II, they enter Act III with Clarity about their Resolution Goal for dealing with the Primary Situation. The Commitment Movement of Act III represents a cementing of the shift in perspective provided by Transformation. The Transformation is not merely a transitory shift in perspective for dealing with a temporary Problem in the Now but will carry on as part of the Character's outlook in life into the Unknown Future.

Complete Character Wave: See "Character Wave."

Complication: One of the two main types of Primary Obstacles that prevent the Main Character from easily resolving the Primary Situation by implementing their initial Logical Solution.

Convergence: The "First Takeaway" principle of the Your Storytelling Potential Method for story construction. It is the idea that stories achieve a richness, depth, and natural balance when Author-Storytellers construct them with an understanding that every element is born of two or more forces encountering one another. Examples: the A-Story converges with the B-Story, creating the Revealed Story. The Theme opposes the Opposing Idea, creating the Thematic Conflict. In Act II, the Main Character's Despair-fueled search for a new perspective on the Primary Situation converges with new information in the form of Discoveries, which leads to Clarity. The end goal of Convergence is to achieve maximal Relevance of all aspects of the story.

Core Elements: The twelve essential building blocks of a story in the Your Storytelling Potential Method. There are four elements per story

Branch, which correspond to four "Layers" of the Revealed Story: Introduction, Act I, Act II, and Thematic. The Core Elements are designed to allow the Author-Storyteller to think dynamically about the various events in their story as opposed to traditional methods that teach a linear approach.

Desire: The fifth of the seven Structural Connection Points of the Character Wave Journey. Past the Midpoint Failure, the third Movement of the story (Act II-Part 2) of Discovery on the A-Story side and Transformation on the B-Story side create a Desire born of their new Clarity. The Main Character now truly wants the opposite of what they wanted at the outset. The exception would be within stories featuring a Steadfast Main Character, in which case the close Relationship Character who experiences the Transformation in the story reaches Clarity and Desire.

Despair: The middle of the three Transitional Doorways between the four major Movements in story progression that frame the Character Wave Journey. During the first half of Act II, the Main Character attempts to deal with the Primary Situation by implementing their initial Logical Solution, only to be repeatedly thwarted by the Primary Obstacle. This process continues until the Main Character hits the Midpoint Failure, where it now becomes clear the Logical Solution will not resolve the Primary Situation. With Logic out the window, the Main Character falls into a Despair mode that fuels their search for a new solution and moves them further toward a needed Transformation.

Discovery: The third of the four major Movements of the A-Story side of the Character Wave Journey. In the second half of Act II, the Main Character suffers Despair over the Midpoint Failure of their Logical Solution's response to the Primary Situation. The Main Character is now moving toward inner Transformation on the B-Story side. On the A-Story side, they inevitably make one or more important Discoveries that supply them with new information (sometimes empirical facts, sometimes inner reflections, or some combination) that shed new light on how the Primary Situation should be resolved. It is also considered the Act II Layer Core Element of the Character Branch.

Elements: See "Core Elements."

Failure: The fourth of the seven Structural Connection Points of the Character Wave Journey. In general, any missed attempt at reaching any goal can be considered a "failure." But the major Failure, as we see it in this method, comes at the Midpoint of the story with the ultimate Failure of the Logical Solution to resolve the Primary Situation. This type of Failure leads to Despair and seeds the ground for Transformation.

Hidden Past: The understanding that the events unfolding in the Now of the Revealed Story were preceded by relevant events in history leading up to this point. Both the A-Story and the B-Story come into the Now with Momentum supplied by relevant past events.

Inner World: Relative to the Three Branches, the "Inner World" describes the details told in the Revealed Story. As opposed to the "Outer World" of details not used in the Revealed Story but only hinted at or assumed to exist. Only necessary and relevant details should make it into the Revealed Story's Inner World.

Intellectual Property: For the purposes of the discussions in this book, the entirety of a story's extended world, characters, and events across all forms of media and expression in which they appear or are referenced. A major example would be *Star Wars*, which not only includes numerous direct film sequels but several spin-off movies, live-action television shows, animated shows, comic books, novels, video games, theme park attractions, and more.

Introduction: The Your Storytelling Potential Method preferred term for the starting point of any Revealed Story. As opposed to terms such as "Beginning" or "Set-up," which have a greater connotation of starting from a tabula rasa ground zero. This method emphasizes the importance of understanding the relevant Hidden Past supplying Momentum into the opening of the Revealed Story. In that sense, we believe the intended audience of every well-told narrative is "introduced" to a tale already in-progress in many important ways. "Introduction" is also the first of the seven Structural Connection Points of the Character Wave Journey.

Introduction Layer: Of the Core Elements, the B-Story's Ordinary World, the Character's Characterization, and the A-Story's Setting, which encompasses the Proximate Cause. These three Elements should be established as early as possible to set the stage and affect all of the action throughout the story.

IP: Short for "Intellectual Property." See definition above.

Journey: Broadly, the movement of the Main Character through the unfolding events of the Revealed Story. Specifically, one of the two main types of Primary Obstacles that prevent the Main Character from easily resolving the Primary Situation by implementing their initial Logical Solution.

Layer: The conceptual grouping of Core Elements that operate simultaneously and in conjunction with one another across all three Branches. The Twelve Core Elements can be broken into four distinct "Layers." The Layers are: The Introduction Layer, the Act I Layer, the Act II Layer, and the Thematic Layer.

Logic: In storytelling, the initial mindset of the Main Character in response to the Primary Situation. This initial Logic ends at the Midpoint Failure and gives way to Despair. It also stands as the first of the three Transitional Doorways between story Movements. It is also the name of the second of the seven Structural Connection Points of the Character Wave Journey.

Logical Solution: The plan of action that the Main Character pursues in response to the Primary Situation through the first half of the story up to the Midpoint Failure. It is the Act I Layer Core Element of the Character Branch.

Main Character: The Your Storytelling Potential Method preferred term for the primary subject of a story. Also known as the "Protagonist" in most narrative frameworks. In our view, "Protagonist" carries a confusing connotation of a character whose actions drive a story, which is not accurate.

Midpoint Failure: The crisis point that falls roughly halfway through the Revealed Story and separates the two parts of Act II. This is the point where the Main Character has exhausted their attempts to implement their Logical Solution to the Primary Situation. They may be successful in reaching their Logical Solution goal or they may fail to reach it. In either case, the Logical Solution does not resolve the Primary Situation as they expected. The Midpoint Failure leads to Despair.

Momentum: In storytelling, the building of tension caused by the unfolding of events, particularly at the outset of the Revealed Story. Relative to the Main Character, this is especially important on the B-Story side. The Hidden Past should supply a rich basis for the events taking place in the Now once the A-Story gets rolling. We also talk about this dynamic in terms of a powder keg for which the A-Story provides the match to light the fuse.

Movement: Name for the phases that occur during the three Acts (Act I, Act II-Part 1, Act II-Part 2, Act III). There are eight total Movements, four on the A-Story side (Situation, Solutions, Discovery, and Climax) and four on the B-Story side (Reasons, Motivation, Transformation, and Commitment). The overlaps between Movement phases are called the Transitional Doorways (Logic, Despair, and Clarity). The Movements describe the Main Character's Journey of mind, which comprises the Complete Character Wave.

Motivation: The second of the four major Movements of the B-Story side of the Character Wave Journey. In Act I the Reasons Movement presents the Reasons why the Main Character is Uniquely Extraordinary for this story, and introduces a Primary Situation that the Main Character tries to resolve with their Logical Solution. In the first half of Act II, the Motivation Movement presents the Main Character taking action to implement their Logical Solution. The Motivation movement is often in-synch with the Solutions Movement on the A-Story side, which is to say the Logical Solution the Main Character employs makes sense for them both to address the Primary Situation and the Underlying Cause. For example, in the movie *Die Hard*, Detective John McClane's Logical Solution to the hostage crisis in the office building is to "alert the authorities." On the A-Story side (Solutions) this makes sense because "alert the authorities" is a way to thwart the terrorists. On the B-Story side (Motivation) this also makes sense because "alert the authorities" is a more measured way to respond to the Situation while his wife is one of the hostages, as opposed to going in shooting and putting her life at risk.

Negative Value: The undesirable idea or outcome of the Thematic Conflict between the Theme and its Opposing Idea, as assigned by the Author-Storyteller. In most stories where the Main Character makes a Transformation for the better, this is their starting point.

The Now: The duration in time of the Revealed Story. Significant conceptually in the broader context of understanding that a story has a Hidden Past and is moving toward a Revealed Potential that will affect an Unknown Future.

Obstacles: Broadly, any story element that prevents a character from easily reaching a goal. Specifically, in the Your Storytelling Potential Method, it is the third of the seven Structural Connection Points in the Character Wave Journey. "Obstacles" is the next point following "Logic," and it describes the point of the Journey where the success of the Logical Solution is repeatedly frustrated by Obstacles standing in the way.

Opportunity: One of the two main types of Primary Situations or Underlying Causes. The Main Character may be presented with a Situation that provides them a desirable goal they wish to pursue, either in terms of the emergent A-Story or from something stemming from their ongoing B-Story life.

Opposing Idea: At the Thematic Layer of a story, the side of the Thematic Conflict that originates in the B-Story. The Opposing Idea represents the Main Character's outlook at the beginning of the Revealed Story and finds expression in their Personal Goal. The Opposing Idea stands in opposition to the Theme, which comes from the new A-Story Situation. It is the Thematic Layer Core Element of the B-Story Branch.

Ordinary World: In the Your Storytelling Potential Method, the Ordinary World describes the present life of the Main Character at the outset of the Revealed Story. The Ordinary World is the world of the B-Story. It frames the setup, the Personal Goal, and the B-Story subplots.

It includes relevant details from the Hidden Past. This concept of Ordinary World should not be confused with Joseph Campbell's notion of "the world of common day" in his description of the hero's journey. This is a very important distinction. In our view, the Main Character never leaves their Ordinary World. The Ordinary World is bound to the Character. They continue living their life and incorporate the lessons learned in confronting the Problem or Opportunity presented by the A-Story. As the Character is Transformed by the events in the Revealed Story, so too does their Ordinary World change fundamentally. In this sense, the Main Character *never* goes back to their Ordinary World, and in many stories they never literally go back to the physical space they start from either. The Ordinary World is the Introduction Layer Core Element under the B-Story Branch.

Outer World: Relative to the Three Branches, the "Outer World" describes the unrevealed details left out of the Revealed Story as told by the Author-Storyteller. These are the details of the Main Character's life and characterization as well as the background of the Proximate Cause Character and events unfolding on the A-Story side that are less pertinent or completely irrelevant to the Revealed Story but are assumed to exist and are sometimes hinted at.

Personal Goal: In the context of the Revealed Story, the Main Character's thematically-based fundamental Desire. It is the expression of the B-Story Opposing Idea in the Thematic Conflict between Theme and Opposing Idea. Personal Goal is the Thematic Layer Core Element of the Character Branch.

Philosophical Idea: The true nature of Themes and their Opposing Ideas at the heart of the Thematic Conflict. Author-Storytellers do well to keep in mind that effective Themes and Opposing Ideas are broad Philosophical Ideas that can have nuanced exploration through the various subplots. This is fundamentally different from thinking about Themes as detailed political platforms, soapbox messages for the audience, grand transcendental truths, etc.

Plot: The storyline or the linear unfolding of events in the story.

Plotline: The traditional conceptual view of plot structure in which everything that happens is thought to revolve around a single main storyline unfolding in a logical, linear, sequential manner. The Your Storytelling Potential Method uses the two-story model and Simple Story Timeline to plot the events of a story.

Plotline Graph: A visual conceptual model of a Plotline used in literary analysis, such as Freytag's Pyramid. The emphasis of Plotline Graphs is on a single main story and generally depicts some "rising action" (the line moving upward at an angle), a "peak" (according to said system's concept of the story's Climax), and "falling action" (the line sloping downward) toward a "resolution" or "denouement."

Positive Value: The desirable idea or outcome of the Thematic Conflict between the Theme and its Opposing Idea, as assigned by the Author-Storyteller. In most stories where the Main Character makes a Transformation for the better, this is their endpoint.

Premise: The foundational idea of the story. In well-told stories, great Premises are rooted in the B-Story side, particularly in the relevant Hidden Past.

Primary Obstacle: The Complication or Journey that occurs at the end of Act I and launches Act II. It is the major focus of Act II-Part 1. The Primary Obstacle is mainly responsible for the Failure of the Logical Solution and creating the Midpoint Failure. It is the Act II Layer Core Element of the A-Story Branch.

Primary Situation: The new Problem or Opportunity at the heart of the A-Story. It is what the Main Character must deal with in the Now of the Revealed Story. The Primary Situation is linked to the Proximate Cause and the Proximate Cause Character. It links the Main Character to the Proximate Cause. It is considered the Act I Layer Core Element of the A-Story Branch. "Primary Situation" can also be seen as encompassing all A-Story concerns to such a degree that it is not inaccurate to use the term as a synonym for "A-Story."

Problem: One of the two main types of Primary Situations or Underlying Causes. The Main Character may be presented with a Situation that they must face and overcome if they are to achieve their goals, either in terms of the emergent A-Story or from something stemming from their ongoing B-Story life.

Protagonist: In the Your Storytelling Potential system, we prefer the term "Main Character" to "Protagonist" to designate the central figure or primary subject of a story. The issue with "Protagonist" is the possible connotation that this character's actions are the primary driving force of the story. We observe that Main Characters are reactive rather than proactive, thus "Main Character" is more apropos.

Proximate Cause: A term unique to the Your Storytelling Potential Method. The "Cause to the Cause" of the A-Story. It is the fuel that motivates the Proximate Cause Character and is the underlying reason the A-Story is happening. Most often it frames the Proximate Cause Character's major goal. The Proximate Cause almost always originates in the Hidden Past of the A-Story and explains why things are unfolding as they are in the Now. Proximate Cause is the major factor determining the Setting of the A-Story. The term "Proximate Cause" originates in the fields of law and insurance. It's the idea that an event [an injury to body or property requiring compensation, in insurance litigation] would not have happened "but for" the actions of another.

Proximate Cause Character: A term unique to the Your Storytelling Potential Method. The character who is most invested in the outcome of the A-Story. The Proximate Cause Character is responsible for causing the collision between the A-Story and the Main Character's B-Story. The most common type of Proximate Cause Character is the Antagonist, though not all stories have Antagonists, and not all Antagonists are Proximate Cause Characters. If the B-Story is the Main Character's story, it is accurate to say the A-Story is the Proximate Cause Character's story. The Main Character is never the Proximate Cause Character.

Reasons: The first of the four major Movements of the B-Story side of the Character Wave Journey. This Act I opening Movement is about how the Author-Storyteller details the Characterization Core Element information so the audience understands why this Main Character is Uniquely Extraordinary for this story.

Relevance: The key operating principle of the Your Storytelling Potential Method. Every facet of this system is predicated on building maximal Relevance for every element contributing to the construction of a story. The selection of Theme, the Characterization of every character, every line of dialog, and every event that unfolds, all must be guided by the principle of Relevance. Anything that is not relevant to the story does not belong in it. The Core Elements are designed to allow the Author-Storyteller to see their story from a high-level conceptual view to allow the perspective needed to design the story with maximal Relevance.

Resolution: The last of the seven Structural Connection Points of the Complete Character Wave. The Resolution Structural Connection Point resolves the B-Storylines. Once the Character has finally solved the Primary Situation, the Resolution demonstrates the Commitment to the Transformation is cemented. The lesson is learned. Change carries over to the Character's personal life relationships—B-Story. There is a glimpse of the Revealed Potential into the Unknown Future.

Resolution Goal: The new goal the Main Character formulates as a result of the Clarity stemming from Discovery and Transformation in Act II-Part 2. The Character enters Act III knowing how to confront the Primary Situation with this new perspective. It is considered the Act II Layer Core Element of the B-Story Branch.

Revealed Potential: The personal growth of the Main Character after the shift in perspective from their original Personal Goal to the Clarity they gain during the Revealed Story. The lesson they learn and/or hidden strengths discovered by way of this Transformative Journey that sticks with them into their Unknown Future beyond the end of the story. (Also known as the "Unrealized Potential" depending on the point in time within the story.)

Revealed Present: Otherwise known as "the Now" of the Revealed Story. The relevant details of the events unfolding in the Revealed Story as the audience experiences them.

Revealed Story: Also known as the "Inner World," the Revealed Story is the story the Author-Storyteller tells. All of the relevant details. As opposed to the Hidden Story (or "Outer World"), which includes details, events, and characters connected to the A-Story, the B-Story, and the Character Branches but are not considered relevant to the telling of the Revealed Story and are therefore omitted.

Reversals: The sixth of the seven Structural Connection Points of the Complete Character Wave. For the Main Character, as they move from the Transformation and Clarity that brings them to their Resolution Goal, the process of reversing direction from their initial value system that formed their Personal Goal to the new Value system that frames their Resolution Goal requires Reversals. The Character genuinely wants the opposite of what they started off wanting.

Setting: The Now "world" in which the story takes place. Setting is determined by the Proximate Cause. Proximate Cause will define the time, domain, and/or arena of the A-Story. Setting is never the same thing as the Ordinary World, even if it includes the same physical space. Problems and Opportunities modify the "world" for the Main Character. It is considered the Introduction Layer Core Element of the A-Story Branch.

Set-Up: A term we ask students of the Your Storytelling Potential Method not to use to describe the starting point of the Revealed Story. In this system, we emphasize the persistence of time from before the Now of the story and beyond its end. Therefore, the term "Introduction" is preferable. "Set-Up" has a tabula rasa connotation—a story springing from nowhere into the life of a character. We believe a story needs to be constructed to account for the Hidden Past of both the Main Character's ongoing B-Story and that of the Proximate Cause in the A-Story.

Side Plots: The subplots (Journeys of significant relationship characters) from the A-Story side of the Revealed Story. Some of these Plotlines are dedicated to moving the A-Story forward. But A-Story subplots just as often work to express Theme.

Simple Story Timeline: The overview master two-track (A & B stories) parallel structural graph of a well-told story in the Your Storytelling

Potential Method. The Simple Story Timeline breaks down each of the three Acts into four essential objective-based structural beats apiece. Preferable to a Plotline Graph.

Situation: Broadly, a "Situation" is every Problem or Opportunity the Main Character encounters throughout a story. Specifically, "Situation" is the first of the four major Movements of the A-Story side of the Complete Character Wave. This Act I opening Movement is about how the Author-Storyteller details the introduction of the A-Story's Primary Situation.

Solutions: The second of the four major Movements of the A-Story side of the Complete Character Wave. This Movement, which appears in the first half of Act II, follows from the introduction of the Primary Situation and the Main Character's Logical Solution to it in Act I. The Solution Movement is nearly always in alignment with the Motivation Movement on the B-Story side, meaning the Main Character sees their Logical Solution as both the right move for addressing the Primary Situation and for addressing the Problem or Opportunity stemming from their Underlying Cause. The Solutions Movement ends at the Midpoint Failure and the story moves through Despair to Discovery on the A-Story side.

Steadfast Character: A type of Main Character whose Personal Goal is affirmed by the story's Journey rather than transformed by it. Often these are traditional heroic figures portrayed as having clear, strong Values. A person of decisive action surrounded by a world of indecisive supporting characters or people whose judgment has been clouded by circumstances. In such stories, another character undergoes a transformative Journey and comes around to the Main Character's way of thinking. Prime examples are recurring heroes like James Bond or Sherlock Holmes.

Structural Connection Points: The seven steps along the route of the Complete Character Wave Journey. They are: 1. Introduction, 2. Logic, 3. Obstacles, 4. Failure, 5. Desire, 6. Reversals, and 7. Resolution.

Story Structure: The conceptual timeline that shows the relationship of the Core Elements and Thematic movements to one another as the story progresses. The proportional beats of the movements of story elements in relation to one another. The Your Storytelling Potential Method favors a concept of structure that emphasizes conceptual goals and Thematic Relevance over adherence to preset page numbers and rigid timelines. Proper structure will flow naturally from a well-constructed story. Within limits, structure should be flexible depending on the considerations of genre and the individual story. Structure should be one of the last stages of preplanning before writing, following from building out the Core Elements and ensuring all aspects of the narrative are connected through Theme. A great structure can be achieved by employing the Your Storytelling Potential Simple Story Timeline.

Subplot: The relationship of every meaningful character to the Main Character. In the Your Storytelling Potential view, all of the revealed B-Story and most of the revealed A-Story are told by means of subplots. A "Plotline" is mainly an illusion of all of the constituent comingling subplot threads running parallel and wrapping around one another. Subplots come in two varieties: A-Story subplots (called "Side Plots") and B-Story subplots (called "Theme Plots"). Theme is primarily expressed through subplots.

Thematic Conflict: The conceptual or philosophical struggle between the Theme and its Opposing Idea. The push-and-pull dynamic of these forces acting on the Main Character is responsible for the "wave" motion of the Complete Character Wave.

Thematic Connection: The understanding that what prevents the Main Character from reaching their Personal Goal is the same reason that they now face the Problem or Opportunity coming from their B-Story Underlying Cause and the A-Story Primary Situation. This reason determines the Theme. For example, in *Liar Liar*, the Main Character Fletcher's *lying* is both the reason he has a poor relationship with his family, causing his son to make a wish that he cannot lie for a day, and the reason he is chosen by his law firm to win the difficult divorce case. His Personal Goal is to have a good relationship with his family, particularly with his son, but his *lying* nature prevents that goal. Unifying this reason for all three Thematic Layer Core Elements creates the Thematic Relevance that the Author-Storyteller needs.

Thematic Elements: The *five* Core Elements that are most closely, *most directly* related to the Theme. In addition to the three Thematic Layer Elements (Theme, Opposing Idea, and Personal Goal), the Ordinary World and the Characterization should also be largely shaped by the Theme. The Thematic Layer Elements are primarily concepts. The Ordinary World and the Characterization are more concrete, outward expressions of the Theme in a well-told story, as opposed to a random character living a randomly assembled life in a random environment—no matter how "interesting" those random attributes might seem.

Thematic Layer: Of the Core Elements, the B-Story's Opposing Idea, the Character's Personal Goal, and the A-Story's Theme. These three Elements define the Thematic Conflict at the heart of the story.

Thematic Relevance: The primary objective of story construction. Certain elements must be "functionally relevant," meaning character actions, motivations, and dialog that move the A-Story forward and provide the framework for the plot. But the deeper work of a well-told story is ensuring everything included has Thematic Relevance, meaning it all contributes to the Thematic Conflict of the philosophical argument between the Theme versus the Opposing Idea. Various subplots may explore the Theme from different angles and nuances, but anything that does not move the A-Story forward nor contribute to the Thematic aspect of a story does not belong. Ideally, the elements included should accomplish both at the same time.

Theme: At the Thematic Layer of a story, the side of the Thematic Conflict that originates in the A-Story. It is a Philosophical Idea that challenges the Main Character's outlook and Personal Goal. Theme stands in opposition to the Opposing Idea, which comes from the B-Story's Underlying Cause. It is the Thematic Layer Core Element of the A-Story Branch. Broadly, Theme is the glue that binds the A and B stories. This is the core of a truly great story!

Theme Plots: The subplots (Journeys of significant relationship characters) from the B-Story side of the Revealed Story. Part of the function of A-Story subplots (aka "Side Plots") is to move the A-Story forward. B-Story subplots are best thought of as "Theme Plots" because they are primarily focused on forwarding the Thematic Conflict, driving the Character Wave Journey.

Three-Act Structure: The recommended basic structure for students of the Your Storytelling Potential Method. The vast majority of stories require only three acts. This method teaches the precise movements and objectives of each act. In the very rare stories requiring more than three acts, what we generally observe between Acts I and III is a repeat of the movements of Act II as outlined in this system. This is especially true for episodic television or book series. Therefore such stories run Act I, Act II-a, Act II-b... (and so on), and then Act III.

Transformation: Broadly, Transformation or a Transformative Event is the point of a story. Revealed Stories are about how a new Problem or Opportunity brings change in a Main Character's life. Specifically, Transformation is the third of the four major Movements of the B-Story side of the Complete Character Wave. Following the Midpoint Failure, the Main Character's mindset moves from Motivation, through Despair, into a period of Transformation. Transformation on the B-Story side of the Complete Character Wave is facilitated by the Discovery Movement on the A-Story side.

Transformative Event: The point of a story is to chronicle a Transformative Event in the life of the Main Character. It is the point of the A-Story that frames the Revealed Story.

Transition: The movement of mind of the Main Character (or close relationship character, if the Main Character is steadfast) over the course of the Revealed Story. The Now of the Revealed Story should be seen as a period of Transition.

Underlying Cause: The Problem or Opportunity at the heart of the B-Story. It is what the Main Character must deal with in the context of their personal life, often mirroring the Primary Situation on the A-Story side. The Underlying Cause is linked to the Underlying Cause Character, who may also be the Main Character if the major Underlying Cause is a form of internal struggle. More often, there is a separate Underlying Cause Character in the Main Character's life. It is considered the Act I Layer Core Element of the B-Story Branch. "Underlying Cause" can also be seen as encompassing all B-Story concerns to such a degree that it is not inaccurate to use the term as a synonym for "B-Story."

Underlying Cause Character: A character who causes the Problem or Opportunity within the B-Story. This character causes the Theme to express itself in both the A and B stories. The character that makes the "Theme" happen. There can be multiple Underlying Cause Characters, each expressing the Theme and causing a unique Problem or Opportunity within the B-Story. The Main Character may be an Underlying Cause Character, though more commonly it is another character within the B-Story.

Uniquely Extraordinary: The idea that all Main Characters should be designed in such a way that they—and only they—could be the Main Character of this story. This is not to be confused with "Anointed Characters," who are a special brand of Main Character with a birthright or special powers. Even the most grounded, "average" Main Character should have traits and a mindset that makes them a perfect fit for the exact transformative Journey this A-Story Primary Situation is about to give them. It has to be *this* Main Character, and *no one else.*

Unknown Future: The Main Character's B-Story life after the conclusion of the Revealed Story. The Resolution after the A-Story Climax usually gives the audience some glimpse of what the future holds in store for the Main Character, post-Transformation. If the story ends tragically with the Main Character's death, then the Resolution would hint at the ongoing lives of those B-Story characters affected by the events.

Unrealized Potential: The personal growth of the Main Character before the shift in perspective from their original Personal Goal to the Clarity they gain over the course of the Revealed Story. The lesson they learn and/or hidden strengths discovered by way of this Transformative

Journey that sticks with them into their Unknown Future beyond the end of the story. (Also known as the "Revealed Potential" depending on the point in time within the story.)

Value: Relative to the Thematic Conflict, the Author-Storyteller's assignment of which side of the Theme-versus-Opposing Idea dynamic is "positive" for the Main Character and which side is "negative" for the Main Character. This is not necessarily a moral dilemma and/or judgment. "Value" may align with the Author-Storyteller's views, or they may consciously wish to explore a story and character that upholds views contrary to theirs. "Value" is *not* determined by society, moral-philosophical systems, or any other outside agency.

A free ebook edition is available with the purchase of this book.

To claim your free ebook edition:

1. Visit MorganJamesBOGO.com
2. Sign your name CLEARLY in the space
3. Complete the form and submit a photo of the entire copyright page
4. You or your friend can download the ebook to your preferred device

Morgan James
BOGO™

A **FREE** ebook edition is available for you or a friend with the purchase of this print book.

CLEARLY SIGN YOUR NAME ABOVE

Instructions to claim your free ebook edition:
1. Visit MorganJamesBOGO.com
2. Sign your name CLEARLY in the space above
3. Complete the form and submit a photo of this entire page
4. You or your friend can download the ebook to your preferred device

Print & Digital Together Forever.

Snap a photo

Free ebook

Read anywhere

CPSIA information can be obtained
at www.ICGtesting.com
Printed in the USA
JSHW021705310323
39757JS00001B/1